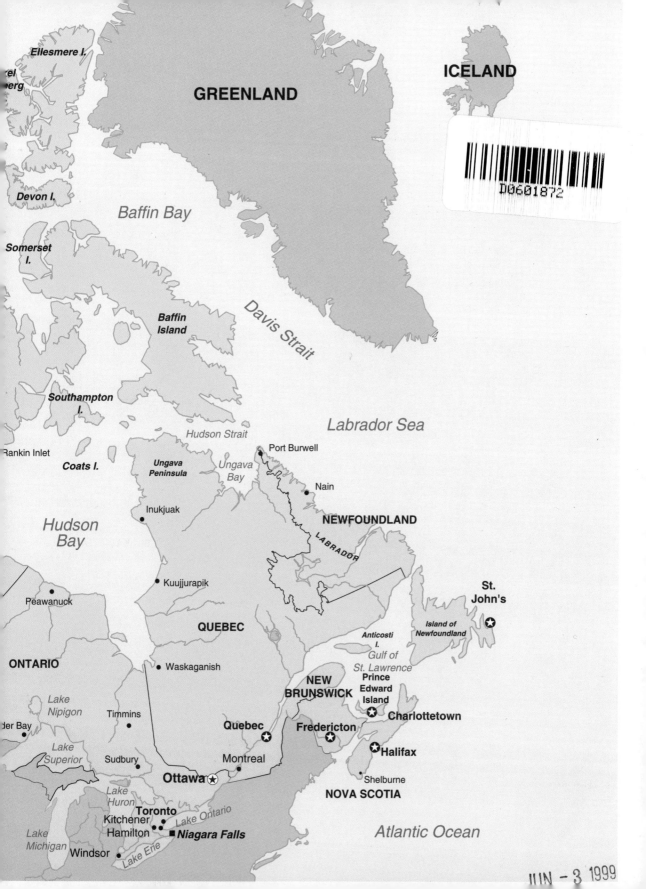

Ellesmere I.

erg

GREENLAND

ICELAND

Devon I.

Baffin Bay

Somerset
I.

Baffin
Island

Davis Strait

Southampton
I.

Labrador Sea

Hudson Strait

Rankin Inlet

Coats I.

Ungava
Peninsula

Ungava
Bay

Port Burwell

Nain

Inukjuak

NEWFOUNDLAND

LABRADOR

Hudson
Bay

Kuujjurapik

Peawanuck

St.
John's

Island of
Newfoundland

QUEBEC

Anticosti
I.

ONTARIO

Waskaganish

Gulf of
St. Lawrence

NEW
BRUNSWICK

Prince
Edward
Island

Lake
Nipigon

Timmins

Charlottetown

der Bay

Lake
Superior

Sudbury

Quebec

Fredericton

Montreal

Halifax

Ottawa

Shelburne

Lake
Huron

Toronto

NOVA SCOTIA

Kitchener
Hamilton

Lake Ontario

Niagara Falls

Lake
Michigan

Windsor

Lake Erie

Atlantic Ocean

Junior Worldmark Encyclopedia of the Canadian Provinces

Junior Worldmark Encyclopedia of the Canadian Provinces

U·X·L

AN IMPRINT OF GALE

Detroit   New York   Toronto   London

JUNIOR WORLDMARK ENCYCLOPEDIA OF THE CANADIAN PROVINCES

Timothy L. Gall and Susan Bevan Gall, *Editors*

Dave Salamie, InfoWorks Development Group, *Editor*

U•X•L Staff

Jane Hoehner, *U•X•L Developmental Editor*
Carol DeKane Nagel, *U•X•L Managing Editor*
Thomas L. Romig, *U•X•L Publisher*
Mary Beth Trimper, *Production Director*
Evi Seoud, *Assistant Production Manager*
Shanna Heilveil, *Production Associate*
Cynthia Baldwin, *Product Design Manager*
Barbara J. Yarrow, *Graphic Services Supervisor*
Mary Krzewinski, *Cover Designer*

Copyright © 1997
U•X•L
An Imprint of Gale Research
All rights reserved including the right of reproduction in whole or in part in any form.

ISBN 0-7876-1490-4

Library of Congress Cataloging-in-Publication Data
Junior Worldmark encyclopedia of the canadian provinces / edited by Timothy Gall
and Susan Bevan Gall
    p. cm.
Includes bibliographical references and index.
ISBN 0-7876-1490-4 (alkaline paper)
1. Canada—Encyclopedias. I. Gall, Timothy II. Gall, Susan Bevan
F1008.J86 1996
971'.003—dc20   96-34240
                                                   CIP

10 9 8 7 6 5 4 3 2

CONTENTS

READER'S GUIDE

Junior Worldmark Encyclopedia of the Canadian Provinces presents profiles of the 10 Canadian provinces and two territories, arranged alphabetically in one volume. Also included is an article on Canada itself. The *Worldmark* design organizes facts and data about every province in a common structure. Every profile contains a map, showing the state and its location in the nation.

Sources

Due to the broad scope of this encyclopedia many sources were consulted in compiling the information and statistics presented in this volume. However, special recognition is due to the many tourist bureaus, convention centers, press offices, and provincial agencies that contributed data and information, including the photographs that illustrate this encyclopedia.

Profile Features

The *Junior Worldmark* structure—40 numbered headings—allows students to compare two or more provinces in a variety of ways.

Each province profile begins by listing the origin of the provincial name, its nickname, the capital, the date it entered the union, the provincial motto, and a description of the coat of arms. The profile also presents a picture and textual description of the provincial flag. Next, a listing of the official provincial animal, bird, fish, flower, tree, gem, etc. is given. The introductory information ends with the standard time given by time zone in relation to Greenwich mean time (GMT). The world is divided into 24 time zones, each one hour apart. The Greenwich meridian, which is 0 degrees, passes through Greenwich, England, a suburb of London. Greenwich is at the center of the initial time zone, known as Greenwich mean time. All times given are converted from noon in this zone. The time reported for the state is the official time zone.

Organization

The body of each profile is arranged in 40 numbered headings as follows:

[1] **LOCATION AND SIZE.** Statistics are given on area and boundary length.

[2] **TOPOGRAPHY.** Dominant geographic features including terrain and major rivers and lakes are described.

[3] **CLIMATE.** Temperature and rainfall are given for the various regions of the province in both English and metric units.

[4] **PLANTS AND ANIMALS.** Described here are the plants and animals native to the province.

[5] **ENVIRONMENTAL PROTECTION.** Destruction of natural resources—forests, water supply, air—is described here. Statistics on solid waste production, hazard-

ous waste sites, and endangered and extinct species are also included.

[6] **POPULATION.** Census statistics, population estimates are provided. Population density and major urban populations are summarized.

[7] **ETHNIC GROUPS.** The major ethnic groups are described. Where appropriate, some description of the influence or history of ethnicity is provided.

[8] **LANGUAGES.** The regional dialects of the province are summarized as well as the number of people speaking languages other than English at home.

[9] **RELIGIONS.** The population is broken down according to religion and/or denominations.

[10] **TRANSPORTATION.** Statistics on roads, railways, waterways, and air traffic, along with a listing of key ports for trade and travel, are provided.

[11] **HISTORY.** Includes a concise summary of the province's history from ancient times (where appropriate) to the present.

[12] **PROVINCIAL GOVERNMENT.** The form of government is described, and the process of governing is summarized.

[13] **POLITICAL PARTIES.** Describes the significant political parties through history, where appropriate, and the influential parties in the mid-1990s.

[14] **LOCAL GOVERNMENT.** The system of local government structure is summarized.

[15] **JUDICIAL SYSTEM.** Structure of the court system and the jurisdiction of courts in each category is provided. Crime rates are also included.

[16] **MIGRATION.** Population shifts since the end of World War II are summarized.

[17] **ECONOMY.** This section presents the key elements of the economy. Major industries and employment figures are also summarized.

[18] **INCOME.** Wages and income are summarized.

[19] **INDUSTRY.** Key industries are listed, and important aspects of industrial development are described.

[20] **LABOR.** Statistics are given on the civilian labor force, including numbers of workers, leading areas of employment, and unemployment figures.

[21] **AGRICULTURE.** Statistics on key agricultural crops, market share, and total farm income are provided.

[22] **DOMESTICATED ANIMALS.** Statistics on livestock—cattle, hogs, sheep, etc.—and the land area devoted to raising them are given.

[23] **FISHING.** The relative significance of fishing to the province is provided, with statistics on fish and seafood products.

[24] **FORESTRY.** Land area classified as forest is given, along with a listing of key forest products and a description of government policy toward forest land.

[25] **MINING.** Description of mineral deposits and statistics on related mining activity and export are provided.

[26] **ENERGY AND POWER.** Description of the province's power resources, including electricity produced and oil reserves and production, are provided.

[27] **COMMERCE.** A summary of trade within Canada and with the rest of the world.

[28] **PUBLIC FINANCE.** Revenues and expenditures are provided.

[29] **TAXATION.** The tax system is explained.

[30] **HEALTH.** Statistics on and description of such public health factors as disease and suicide rates, principal causes of death, numbers of hospitals and medical facilities appear here.

[31] **HOUSING.** Housing shortages and government programs to build housing are described. Statistics on numbers of dwellings and median home values are provided.

[32] **EDUCATION.** Statistical data on educational achievement and primary and secondary schools is given. Major universities are listed, and government programs to foster education are described.

[33] **ARTS.** A summary of the major cultural institutions is provided.

[34] **LIBRARIES AND MUSEUMS.** The number of libraries, their holdings, and their yearly circulation is provided. Major museums are listed.

[35] **COMMUNICATIONS.** The state of telecommunications (television, radio, and telephone) is summarized.

[36] **PRESS.** Major daily and Sunday newspapers are listed together with data on their circulations.

[37] **TOURISM, TRAVEL, AND RECREATION.** Under this heading, the student will find a summary of the importance of tourism to the province and factors affecting the tourism industry. Key tourist attractions are listed.

[38] **SPORTS.** The major sports teams in the province, both professional and collegiate, are summarized.

[39] **FAMOUS PEOPLE.** In this section, some of the best-known citizens of the province are listed. When a person is noted in a province that is not the province of his of her birth, the birthplace is given.

[40] **BIBLIOGRAPHY.** The bibliographic listings at the end of each profile are provided as a guide for further reading.

Because many terms used in this encyclopedia will be new to students, the volume includes a glossary and a list of abbreviations and acronyms. A keyword index completes the volume.

Comments and Suggestions

We welcome your comments on the *Junior Worldmark Encyclopedia of the Canadian Provinces* as well as your suggestions for features to be included in future editions. Please write: Editors, *Junior Worldmark Encyclopedia of the Canadian Provinces*, U•X•L, 835 Penobscot Building, Detroit, Michigan 48226-4094; or call toll-free: 1-800-877-4253.

Guide to Articles

All information contained within an article is uniformly keyed by means of a boxed number to the left of the subject headings. A heading such as "Population," for example, carries the same key numeral (6) in every article. Therefore, to find information about the population of Alberta, consult the table of contents for the page number where the Alberta article begins and look for section 6.

Introductory matter for each province includes: Origin of state name
Nickname
Capital
Date and order of statehood
Motto
Flag
Coat of arms
Symbols (animal, tree, flower, etc.)
Time zone.

Sections listed numerically

1 Location and Size
2 Topography
3 Climate
4 Plants and Animals
5 Environmental Protection
6 Population
7 Ethnic Groups
8 Languages
9 Religions
10 Transportation
11 History
12 Provincial Government
13 Political Parties
14 Local Government
15 Judicial System
16 Migration
17 Economy
18 Income
19 Industry
20 Labor
21 Agriculture
22 Domesticated Animals
23 Fishing
24 Forestry
25 Mining
26 Energy and Power
27 Commerce
28 Public Finance
29 Taxation
30 Health
31 Housing
32 Education
33 Arts
34 Libraries and Museums
35 Communications
36 Press
37 Tourism, Travel, and
    Recreation
38 Sports
39 Famous Persons
40 Bibliography

Alphabetical listing of sections

Agriculture   21
Arts   33
Bibliography   40
Climate   3
Commerce   27
Communications   35
Domesticated Animals   22
Economy   17
Education   32
Energy and Power   26
Environmental Protection 5
Ethnic Groups   7
Famous Persons   39
Fishing   23
Forestry   24
Health   30
History   11
Housing   31
Income   18
Industry   19
Judicial System   15

Labor   20
Languages   8
Libraries and Museums   34
Local Government   14
Location and Size   1
Migration   16
Mining   25
Plants and Animals   4
Political Parties   13
Population   6
Press   36
Provincial Government   12
Public Finance   28
Religions   9
Sports   38
Taxation   29
Topography   2
Tourism, Travel, and
    Recreation   37
Transportation   10

Explanation of symbols

A fiscal split year is indicated by a stroke (e.g. 1994/95).
Note that 1 billion = 1,000 million = 10^9.
The use of a small dash (e.g., 1990–94) normally signifies the
    full period of calendar years covered (including the end year indicated).

ALBERTA

ORIGIN OF PROVINCE NAME: Named after Princess Louise Caroline Alberta, fourth daughter of Queen Victoria.

NICKNAME: Princess Province, Energy Province, or Sunshine Province.

CAPITAL: Edmonton.

ENTERED CONFEDERATION: 1 September 1905.

MOTTO: *Fortis et liber* (Strong and free).

COAT OF ARMS: In the center, the provincial shield of arms displays the red Cross of St. George at the top on a white background (representing the province's bond with the United Kingdom), foothills and mountains in the center (symbolizing the Canadian Rockies), and a wheat field at the bottom (representing the province's chief agricultural crop). Above the shield is a crest with a beaver carrying a royal crown on its back. Supporting the shield are a lion to the left and pronghorn antelope to the right. Beneath the shield the provincial motto appears, with a grassy mount and wild roses.

FLAG: The flag bears the provincial shield of arms centered on a royal ultramarine blue background.

FLORAL EMBLEM: Wild rose (also known as prickly rose).

TARTAN: Alberta Tartan (green, gold, blue, pink, and black).

MAMMAL: Rocky Mountain bighorn sheep.

PROVINCIAL BIRD: Great horned owl.

TREE: Lodgepole pine.

STONE: Petrified wood.

TIME: 5 AM MST = noon GMT.

1 LOCATION AND SIZE

The westernmost of Canada's three prairie provinces, Alberta is bordered on the north by the Northwest Territories, on the east by Saskatchewan, on the south by the US state of Montana, and on the west by British Columbia. Alberta lies between the 49th and 60th parallels, at virtually the same latitude as the United Kingdom. Alberta is 756 miles (1,217 kilometers) from north to south and between 182 to 404 miles (293 and 650 kilometers) in width from west to east. Nearly equal in size to the state of Texas and covering an area of some 255,284 square miles (661,185 square kilometers), the province is Canada's fourth largest.

2 TOPOGRAPHY

Roughly half of the southwestern section of the province is dominated by mountains and foothills—striking reminders of the glaciers that, over millions of years, formed, moved, and receded in the area. Peaks of the Rocky Mountains located in Alberta range from 6,989 to 12,294 feet (2,130 to 3,747 meters) in elevation.

The foothills, which form a gentle link between mountain and prairie landscapes, feature heavily forested areas and grasslands used for grazing cattle. Beneath their surface, the foothills contain some of the province's richest deposits of coal and sour gas (natural gas containing hydrogen sulfide which needs refining before being used in household furnaces and for other common uses).

The remainder of the province—approximately 90% of the land area—forms part of the interior plain of North America. The plains include the forested areas that dominate the northern part of the province and the vast stretches of northern muskeg (bog) that overlie much of Alberta's oil and gas deposits and oil sands (sand mixed with petroleum).

3 CLIMATE

Alberta has what is known as a continental climate. It is characterized by vivid seasonal contrasts in which long, cold winters are balanced by mild to hot summers. The climate also features an unusually high number of sunny days, no matter what the season. In fact, Alberta has more sunny days than any other province and is therefore sometimes called the "Sunshine Province." Although the whole province is covered in cold air in winter, in the southwest a mild wind, the "Chinook," frequently funnels through the mountains from the Pacific Ocean.

The average daily temperature for Calgary ranges from 10°F (-12°C) in January to 73°F (23°C) in July. Normal daily temperatures for Edmonton are 5°F (-15°C) in January and 63°F (17°C) in July. The

Alberta Population Profile

Estimated 1994 population:	2,716,000
Population change, 1981–91:	13.8%
Leading ancestry group:	British
Second leading group:	German
Foreign born population:	15%
Population by ethnic group:	
Multiple backgrounds:	42%
British:	20%
German:	7%
Ukrainian:	4%
French:	3%
Aboriginal Peoples:	3%
Dutch:	2%
Scandinavian:	2%
Polish:	1%
Italian:	1%
Other single origins:	15%
Aboriginal peoples:	68,000
Métis:	40,000

Population by Age Group

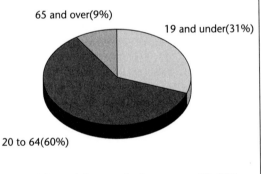

65 and over(9%)

19 and under(31%)

20 to 64(60%)

Top Cities with Populations over 10,000

City	Population	Natl. Rank
Edmonton (metro area)	839,924	5
Calgary (metro area)	754,033	18
Lethbridge	60,974	45
Red Deer	58,134	49
Medicine Hat	52,681	52
Fort McMurray	49,204	55
Grande Prairie	28,271	86
Grand Centre	24,265	92
Lloydminster	17,283	107
(part in Alberta)	10,042	
Camrose	13,420	123

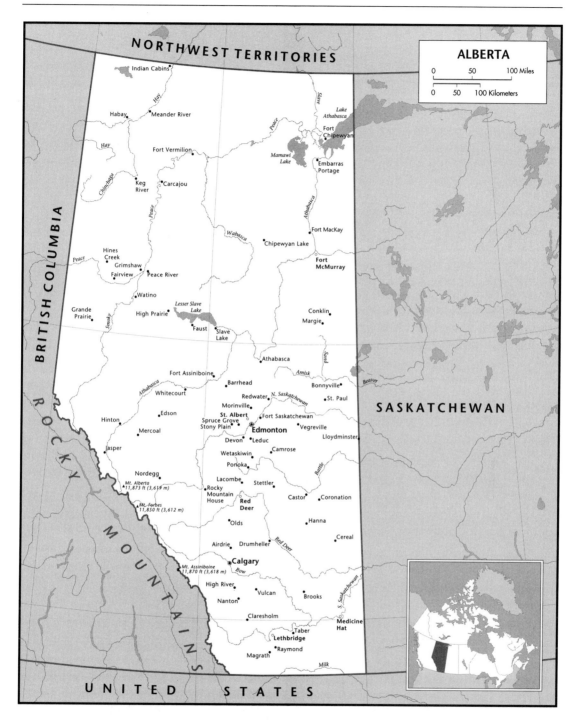

NORTHWEST TERRITORIES

Indian Cabins

Habay • Meander River

Hay

Fort Vermilion

Hay

Keg River • Carcajou

Chinchaga

Peace

Wabasca

Chipewyan Lake

Peace

Hines Creek

Grimshaw

Fairview • Peace River

Watino

Grande Prairie

Smoky

High Prairie

Lesser Slave Lake

Faust • Slave Lake

Conklin

Margie

Peace

Lake Athabasca

Fort Chipewyan

Mamawi Lake

Embarras Portage

Athabasca

Fort MacKay

Fort McMurray

Slave

BRITISH COLUMBIA

ROCKY

Hinton

Jasper

Edson

Mercoal

Nordegg

Mt. Alberta
11,873 ft (3,619 m)

Mt. Forbes
11,850 ft (3,612 m)

Athabasca

Whitecourt

Fort Assiniboine

Barrhead

Redwater • N. Saskatchewan

Morinville

St. Albert
Spruce Grove
Stony Plain

Edmonton

Fort Saskatchewan

Vegreville

Devon • Leduc

Wetaskiwin

Ponoka

Lacombe

Rocky Mountain House

Red Deer

Olds

Airdrie • Drumheller

Mt. Assiniboine
11,870 ft (3,618 m)

Calgary

Bow

High River

Nanton

Claresholm

Vulcan

Magrath

Taber

Lethbridge

Raymond

Milk

Stettler

Castor • Coronation

Hanna

Cereal

Red Deer

Brooks

S. Saskatchewan

Medicine Hat

Camrose

Lloydminster

Battle

Bonnyville

St. Paul

Beaver

Amisk

Spirit

SASKATCHEWAN

Athabasca

MOUNTAINS

UNITED STATES

ALBERTA

0   50   100 Miles

0   50   100 Kilometers

warmest recorded temperature in Alberta was 110°F (43.3°C) on 21 July 1931 at Bassano Dam; the coldest was -78°F (-61.1°C) on 11 January 1931 at Fort Vermilion.

4 PLANTS AND ANIMALS

Alberta has 1,767 known species of vascular plants (ferns and all plants that reproduce through seeds), of which 87 are rare in Canada and 59 rare in North America. Nonvascular species (such as mosses and lichens) number 1,180, of which 30–50% are rare in North America. The slender mouse-ear-cress plant is endangered.

Alberta animal species include 90 mammals, 270 breeding birds, 50 fish, 18 reptiles and amphibians, and 20,000 insects. Endangered mammals include the swift fox, wood bison, and woodland caribou; endangered birds include the burrowing owl, ferruginous hawk, mountain plover, peregrine falcon, piping plover, trumpeter's swan, and whooping crane. Threatened animals include the blackfooted ferret, the yellow-cheeked vole, Baird's sparrow, the greater prairie chicken, the loggerhead shrike, the longbilled curlew, the upland sandpiper, the short-horned lizard, the western hognose snake, the great plains toad, the long-toed salamander, and the northern leopard frog.

5 ENVIRONMENTAL PROTECTION

Since the 1950s, Alberta's development policy for using forests and other renewable resources has viewed land, water, vegetation, and wildlife management as one ecosystem (an ecological unit consisting of the organisms and the environment within a given area). The use of these resources is based strictly on keeping the ecosystem intact.

Air quality is generally good, and the incidence of smog is much less frequent in Edmonton and Calgary than in other large Canadian cities. The province has the highest rate of carbon dioxide emissions per capita (per person) in Canada, with cars contributing 8% to Alberta's carbon dioxide emissions. Solid waste for landfills in 1992 amounted to 2.23 million tons (2.02 million metric tons), or 1.08 tons (0.98 metric tons) per person. In 1993, Alberta had 338 landfills and 23 large-scale composting programs and facilities.

Water pollution is one of the more notable environmental concerns in Alberta. In certain lakes and rivers mercury levels in some types of fish have forced Health and Welfare Canada to issue fish consumption advisories. Most of the mercury found in fish comes from natural sources in soils and sediment in Alberta. Additional problems, however, come from dioxins and furans, toxins that are generated from the burning of organic materials and also originate in waste water discharges from industrial sites. In Alberta, paper mills are the most common source for dioxin and furan contamination of water resources.

In 1992/93, Alberta Environmental Protection was formed from the merger of the former departments of Forestry, Lands and Wildlife, and Environment, and the Parks Division of the former department

Photo Credit: Alberta Tourism Partnership.

Mountain goats live in the Banff and Jasper National Parks in southwestern Alberta. About half of southwestern Alberta is covered by mountains and foothills.

of Tourism and Recreation. The new agency is responsible for providing and maintaining clean air, water, and soil; protecting wildlife, forests, parks, and other natural resources; and making sure that the development of these resources is truly sustainable. On 1 September 1993 the Alberta Environmental Protection and Enhancement Act (AEPEA) went into effect, aiming to improve the province's environment through a variety of programs.

6 POPULATION

As of 1994, Alberta had an estimated 2,716,000 inhabitants. In 1991, approximately 80% of Albertans lived in urban areas. More than half lived in the two main cities—Edmonton, the province's capital (with a population of 605,538); and Calgary, (with a population 692,885). The greater Edmonton and Calgary metropolitan areas had populations of 839,924 (fifth highest in Canada) and 754,033 (sixth highest), respectively, in 1991. Other urban areas, and their 1991 populations include: Lethbridge, 60,974; Red Deer, 58,134; Medicine Hat, 52,681; Fort McMurray, 49,204; and Grand Prairie, 28,271. With two-thirds of the population under the age of 40, the province has one of the youngest populations in the industrialized world. This is, in part, due to the high level of migration to Alberta since the late 1960s.

7 ETHNIC GROUPS

Roughly 44% of Albertans are of British descent. Other ethnic backgrounds with the largest number of people are German, Ukrainian, French, Scandinavian, and Dutch. In 1991, Alberta had some 68,000 Native People (of Aboriginal descent) and 40,000 Métis (people of mixed European and Aboriginal descent). The largest Aboriginal bands are at Blood and Saddle Lake. Smaller ethnic groups, tracing their heritage to virtually every country in the world, make up the remaining 24% of the population.

8 LANGUAGES

English is the mother tongue of the majority of Albertans (82.2% in 1991) and is the primary language used in the province. French, German, and Ukrainian, however, are the dominant languages spoken in some communities.

9 RELIGIONS

Most Christian faiths are represented in Alberta. In 1991, 48.4% of the population, or about 1,232,000 people, was Protestant, including 425,100 United Church of Canada members, 175,600 Anglicans, 137,500 Lutherans, 63,600 Baptists, 53,500 Pentecostals, and 48,400 Presbyterians. Alberta also had about 674,600 Catholics (646,600 Roman Catholics and 28,000 Ukrainian Catholics), 43,300 people of Eastern Orthodox faith, 30,500 Moslems, 20,400 Buddhists, 12,700 Sikhs, 10,200 Hindus, and 10,200 Jews. Some 509,100 Albertans had no religious affiliation in 1991.

10 TRANSPORTATION

After the Canadian confederation was formed in 1867, the Canadian Pacific Railway was built, linking Alberta with the rest of Canada. Today, VIA Rail Canada provides transcontinental rail service with stops in Edmonton and Jasper.

The Trans-Canada Highway links Saskatchewan with Medicine Hat and Calgary before continuing on to Banff National Park and British Columbia. The Yellowhead Route of the Trans-Canada Highway connects Edmonton with Lloydminster and Saskatchewan in the east and with Jasper National Park and British Columbia in the west. Few highways exist in the northern half of the province. As of 1991, there were 8,478 miles (13,643 kilometers) of primary highways and 9,397 miles (15,123 kilometers) of secondary highways. Alberta had 1,878,709 registered motor vehicles in 1991.

Urban transit in 1991 consisted of 1,436 buses, 3 trolley coaches, 122 light-rail vehicles, and 3 other vehicles. These vehicles together provided more than 97.2 million passenger trips of more than 45.9 million miles (73.9 million kilometers). Greyhound and Red Arrow provide bus service to most of the urban areas.

Edmonton and Calgary each have international airports served by such carriers as Air Canada, American Airlines, Canadian Airlines International, Delta, Horizon Air, KLM, Lufthansa, Northwest, and United. In 1991, Calgary Interna-

Calgary is Alberta's largest city and was the host of the 1988 Winter Olympics.

tional served over 3.7 million passengers, while Edmonton International handled 1.7 million passengers.

11 HISTORY

The Native Peoples, whose ancestors are thought to have crossed the Bering Sea from Asia thousands of years ago, were the first people to live in what is now Alberta. The Blackfoot, Blood, Piegan, Cree, Gros Ventre, Sarcee, Kootenay, Beaver, and Slavey Indians were the sole inhabitants of what was then a vast wilderness territory. They spoke a variety of Athapaskan and Algonkian languages. The early Albertans, particularly the woodland tribes of the central and north-

ern regions, became valuable partners of the European fur traders who arrived in the 18th century.

European Exploration and Settlement

The first European explorer to reach what is now Alberta was Anthony Henday, in 1754. He was an agent of the Hudson's Bay Company, a British fur-trading firm. Peter Pond, from a Scottish firm called the North West Company, established the first fur-trading post in the area in 1778. The Hudson's Bay Company gradually extended its control throughout a huge expanse of northern North America known as Rupert's Land and the North-Western Territories, including the region occupied by present-day Alberta. From that time, the region was fought over by the Hudson's Bay Company and the North West Company, each of which built competing fur-trading posts. The rivalry ended in 1821, when the two companies merged under the Hudson's Bay Company name.

Expeditions led by Henry Youle Hind and John Palliser discovered that parts of the region had exceptionally good land for farming, especially the fertile belt north of the Palliser Triangle (a particularly arid zone). As a result of these findings, the British decided not to renew the license of the Hudson's Bay Company. In 1870, the North-Western Territories was acquired by the Dominion of Canada and administered from the newly formed province of Manitoba.

Beginning with the arrival of the railway in 1883, the population started to grow quickly. Other factors that helped the population grow were the discovery of new strains of wheat particularly suited to the climate of the Canadian prairies, the lack of new farmland in the United States, and the end of an economic depression throughout North America. On 1 September 1905, Alberta—named for Princess Louise Caroline Alberta, fourth daughter of Britain's Queen Victoria—became a province of Canada with Edmonton as its capital city. The province of Alberta was created by joining the District of Alberta with parts of the districts of Athabasca, Assiniboia, and Saskatchewan.

Early Years as a Province

During World War I (1914–18), Canada lost more than 68,000 soldiers. Veterans returning to Alberta faced a bleak future of scarce low-paying jobs, while tariffs on imports kept prices for consumer goods high. Albertan farmers, as in the other prairie provinces, had prospered from high wheat prices during World War I, but with the end of the war global grain markets collapsed and wheat prices fell 50% by 1920. Affected farmers organized the United Farmers Movement in Alberta in 1921 to protest the low farm product prices and high transportation rates, and played an important role in provincial politics of the 1920s.

During the 1920s, grain prices recovered and Canada experienced a period of rapid growth in industry. Transportation improvements—railways and roads—enabled businesses to flourish. Automobiles, telephones, electrical appliances, and other consumer goods became widely available.

Alberta, like the other prairie provinces, was one of the poorest areas of Canada during the Great Depression. In addition to the problems with prices during the early 1920s, droughts and frequent crop failures devastated the economy of the province. Social welfare programs rapidly expanded during the 1930s, with much of the burden placed on the provincial and municipal governments.

1940s–1990s

Following World War II (1939–45), consumer spending and immigration to Canada rapidly increased. Urbanization spread quickly by means of the National Housing Act, which made home ownership more easily available. Unemployment insurance and other social welfare programs were also created following the war. Under the leadership of Prime Minister Louis St. Laurent, old age pensions were increased in 1951 and a national hospital insurance plan was introduced in 1957.

In the 1980s, Alberta objected to federal control over oil pricing. The province also objected to the National Energy Program announced in late 1980 which reduced Alberta's share of oil revenues.

Canada's unity as a confederation has often been widely questioned. Most recently, the popular defeat of both the Meech Lake Accord of 1987 and the Charlottetown Accord of 1992 has failed to solve the issue of Québec's role in Canada. As a result, western Canadian voters, many of whom feel that the federal government treats them as less important than other Canadians, have recently voted to elect representatives who favor increased power for the provinces and decreased power for the federal government.

12 PROVINCIAL GOVERNMENT

The structure of the provincial government reflects that of the federal government. For example, the provincial premier, as the majority party leader of the legislature, functions much like the Canadian prime minister. Provincial legislators, like their federal counterparts in Parliament, are elected to represent a constitutional jurisdiction and pass legislation. They do

so as members of the 83-seat Legislative Assembly. A provincial lieutenant-governor approves laws passed by the legislature, much like the Governor General at the federal level. There is no provincial equivalent, however, to the federal Senate.

13 POLITICAL PARTIES

Political affiliation was not important in Alberta until the 1910s, when differences between the Liberal Party and the Conservative Party became more prominent. A growing nonpartisan (not connected with a party) movement in the late 1910s saw the rise of the United Farmers of Alberta (UFA); the UFA held the majority from 1921 to 1935. The Social Credit Party (Socred), based on the belief that the government should control credit, held the vast majority of legislative seats from the mid-1930s to the early 1970s. During their period in power, the welfare state was expanded.

The most recent general election was held on 15 June 1993. The parties held the following number of seats in Alberta's Legislative Assembly in 1994: Conservatives, 51; Liberals, 31; and Independents, 1.

Premiers of Alberta

Term	Premier	Party
1905–10	Alexander Cameron Rutherford	Liberal
1910–17	Arthur Lewis Sifton	Liberal
1917–21	Charles Stewart	Liberal
1921–25	Herbert Greenfield	United Farmers
1925–34	John Edward Brownlee	United Farmers
1934–35	Richard Gavin Reid	United Farmers
1935–43	William Aberhart	Social Credit
1943–68	Ernest Charles Manning	Social Credit
1968–71	Harry Edwin Strom	Social Credit
1971–86	Peter Lougheed	Conservative
1986–92	Donald Ross Getty	Conservative
1992–	Ralph Klein	Conservative

14 LOCAL GOVERNMENT

Albertan municipal government consists of rural and urban municipal governments. Rural municipal governments (counties and municipal districts whose elected councils are responsible for all services) are large land areas with relatively few people. In these areas, the provincial government provides all services and collects the taxes. Urban municipalities are autonomous (self-governing) political units. These include summer villages (resort areas), villages, towns, new towns (with special borrowing privileges), and cities. In order for an area to be incorporated, a summer village must contain 50 separate buildings that are occupied annually for six months, a village must have 75 such residences occupied annually for six months, a town needs 1,000 inhabitants, and a city must have a population of at least 10,000. Alberta has 16 cities, 109 towns, 29 counties, 21 municipal districts, and numerous villages and summer villages.

15 JUDICIAL SYSTEM

The Canadian Constitution grants provincial jurisdiction over the administration of justice, and allows each province to organize its own court system and police forces. The federal government has exclusive domain over cases involving trade and commerce, banking, bankruptcy, and criminal law. The Federal Court of Canada has both trial and appellate (having the power to review the judgment of another court) divisions for federal cases. The 9-judge Supreme Court of Canada is an appellate court that determines the con-stitutionality of both federal and provincial statutes. The Tax Court of Canada hears appeals of taxpayers against assessments by Revenue Canada.

The provincial court system in Alberta has a total of six primary divisions (Magistrate, Surrogate, Family, Juvenile, Division, and Queen's Bench) and one intermediate appellate court. The Magistrate court deals with less serious cases, has no jury, and rarely deals with private laws. The Division court is a small-claims court hearing cases involving less than c$2,000. The Court of Queen's Bench has unlimited jurisdiction in civil and criminal matters.

In 1990, there were 74 homicides in Alberta, for a rate of 3 per 100,000 persons. Breaking and entering offenses in 1989 numbered 435 per 100,000 people for businesses and 695 per 100,000 people for residences.

16 MIGRATION

Tracing the roots of Alberta's 2.5 million people begins with the province's Native, or Aboriginal, Peoples and leads to virtually every corner of the globe. During the last ice age, portions of Alberta served as an ice-free corridor through which Aboriginal Peoples made the trek from Asia. The province's native people formed the bulk of the area's population until the 1880s, when they were outnumbered by growing populations of Europeans. In 1881, there were barely more than 1,000 non-native people in the area that was to become the province of Alberta. Ten years later, 17,500 non-native people occupied the territory.

Between the 1890s and the 1920s, immigrants from many countries came in response to the Canadian government's aggressive efforts to promote immigration and encourage agricultural development. After World War I, most of the immigrants came from Europe or the United States. By the end of the immigration push in 1921, there were 584,454 Albertans. After World War II, the pattern changed. Beginning in the 1960s, immigrants came from all over the world, including the Pacific Rim, Asia, and the Caribbean.

In 1991, Alberta gained 7,264 residents from migration between provinces (70,696 people entered the province and 63,432 left for other provinces). Most of this migration (in both directions) was with British Columbia.

17 ECONOMY

Alberta's economy is based on agriculture, energy, and other resource-based industries. Since the 1970s, Alberta has experienced rapid economic growth in such industries as petrochemicals, forest products, electronics, and communications. Other growth areas are tourism and business services, including computer software, engineering, and scientific and technical services.

Alberta avoided the worst of the North American recession of 1990–92. Energy exports (especially natural gas) are increasing because of the lower value of the Canadian dollar and increased demand in the United States.

18 INCOME

The average Albertan had an annual income of c$23,414 in 1989. Average family income in the province was c$48,975. In 1992, average weekly wages in the manufacturing sector amounted to c$619.24, second highest in western Canada (after British Columbia). As of December 1992, average weekly earnings in the province amounted to c$552.09.

19 INDUSTRY

Food and beverage processing remains the largest manufacturing industry in Alberta in terms of both sales and employment. In 1992, the value of processed food shipments amounted to c$4.3 billion, while the beverage industry accounted for c$442 million. Petrochemicals and plastics, forest products, metals and machinery, and refineries have all become increasingly important parts of Alberta's economy. A wider variety of industrial products—including aerospace and transportation equipment, and industrial and specialty chemicals—is also being manufactured in Alberta.

Alberta's manufacturing shipments increased in value from c$15.1 billion in 1986 to c$19.41 billion in 1992. The largest contributors to the 1992 total were: food and beverages, c$4.96 billion; refined petroleum, c$3.19 billion; chemical products, c$3.1 billion; forest products, c$2.07 billion; fabricated metals, c$943 million; primary metals, c$891 million; printing and publishing, c$741 million; electronics, c$708 million; machinery (non-electrical), c$646 million; construction materials, c$619 million; and plastics, c$277 million.

20 LABOR

In 1993, Alberta had a labor force of 1,926,000. That year, 69.7% of all Albertans 15 years and older were in the labor force, the highest participation rate in Canada.

As of December 1994, about 1,302,600 persons were employed, with 101,800 unemployed, for an overall unemployment rate of 7.2%. The sectors with the largest number of employed persons were: retail trade, 169,800; health and social services, 119,400; manufacturing, 109,200; other services, 103,200; education, 89,700; accommodation, food, and beverages, 89,300; agriculture, 85,800; construction, 85,600; business services, 83,300; public administration, 67,900; transportation and storage, 59,300; wholesale trade, 55,800; communications and utilities, 42,500; finance and insurance, 41,400; and real estate and insurance agents, 25,300. Unemployment by sector was highest in logging and forestry (16.9%), construction (15.4%), and accommodation, food, and beverages (13.1%).

Alberta has the lowest proportion of unionized workers in Canada. As of December 1994, some 273,100 workers were members of unions, or about 21% of all employed labor. Unionization rates were highest in public administration (73.9%), education (64%), and health care (50.6%). They were lowest in services (2.6%).

21 AGRICULTURE

Alberta has one of the world's most productive agricultural economies, producing about 20% of the value of Canada's annual output. Some 13 million hectares (32 million acres) of land are under cultivation. While wheat remains the primary crop, the production of new crops continues to expand. Of Canada's total crop production, Alberta typically produces 24% of the wheat, 40% of the canola, 45% of the oats, and 49% of the barley. Production figures in 1993 were: wheat, 86,374,76 tons (7,838,000 metric tons); barley, 7,198,264 tons (6,532,000 metric tons); canola, 2,274,528 tons (2,064,000 metric tons); and oats, 1,614,430 tons (1,465,000 metric tons). Crop receipts totaled about c$2.1 billion in 1993.

According to the 1991 federal census, Alberta had 57,245 farms on 20,891,000 hectares (51,425,000 acres), about half of which is used for crops. Living on a ranch or farm is a valued way of life. Average income for a farm operator was c$30,150 in 1992, of which c$17,800 was off-farm income.

22 DOMESTICATED ANIMALS

Cattle and their keepers arrived in Alberta in the 1870s, about 20 years before the farmers. Eventually the ranchers and farmers learned to live together in peace; farmers cultivated land in southeastern and central Alberta, while livestock production predominated in the western foothills of the Canadian Rocky Mountains. Approximately 22 million hectares (54 million acres) of cultivated and uncultivated land are used as pasture and forage

Photo Credit: Alberta Tourism Partnership.

Alberta is the westernmost of Canada's three prairie provinces. Wheat, barley, and oats are important grain crops.

for livestock. Alberta maintains the largest livestock population in Canada, accounting for 42% of the country's beef cattle, 15% of the hogs, and 24% of the sheep and lambs. The livestock population in 1993 included 5 million head of cattle, 1.85 million pigs, and 323,000 sheep. Total farm cash receipts from livestock in 1993 came to c$2.9 billion. Farm cash receipts for cattle production amounted to c$2.1 billion in 1993, and hog production generated sales of c$322 million.

Alberta also has more horses than anywhere else in Canada. Apiculture (beekeeping) produced 11,870 tons (10,771 metric tons) of honey in 1993 and generated c$15 million in sales.

23 FISHING

Sport fishing in Alberta's numerous lakes and streams is an important part of the tourism industry. Prominent species sought include brown trout, eastern brook trout, northern pike, rainbow trout, walleye, and yellow perch.

Alberta is divided into eight fish management districts; each is responsible for the maintenance of local stocks. In 1993, the Fish Culture Branch of the Alberta Fish and Wildlife Service stocked 3.76 million trout (including 3.13 million rainbow trout), 16.35 million walleye fry, and 0.52 million walleye fingerlings.

24 FORESTRY

Over one half of the province of Alberta, or approximately 135,100 square miles (350,000 square kilometers), is covered by forests. Of the total forest area, 83,400 square miles (216,000 square kilometers) are classified as commercially productive forest land and contain both hardwood and softwood species. Lumber and pulp are the most important forestry products in terms of value of shipments. Becoming more important, however, are higher value-added products such as newsprint, panelboard products, particleboard, laminated veneer and beams, cabinetry, and home and office furniture.

25 MINING

Besides oil, natural gas, and coal, Alberta mines small quantities of sulfur, sand, gravel, limestone, salt, and gold. In 1992, production of salt amounted to 1,371,990 tons (1,245,000 metric tons), and of gold, 77 pounds (35 kilograms). The value of production in 1992 for minerals was c\$239 million; for nonmetals, c\$147.7 million; and for metals, c\$464,000.

26 ENERGY AND POWER

Long known as Canada's "energy province," Alberta has more than 80% of the country's reserves of conventional crude oil, over 90% of its natural gas, and all of its bitumen and oil-sands reserves. The oil and natural gas sector responded to the challenges of unstable energy prices in the 1980s by significantly reducing production and operating costs. In 1991, crude oil and equivalent production totaled 2,824,928,571 cubic feet (79,098,000 cubic meters), or 82% of the nation's total, valued at c\$9.6 billion.

Alberta's refineries, which serve most of western Canada, constitute about 20% of Canada's total refining capacity. Five refineries have a combined capacity of just under 375,000 barrels per day. Transportation fuels (including gasoline, diesel fuel, and aviation fuel) make up 80% of all production. Other products include heating oil, asphalt, petrochemical feedstock, kerosene, ethylene derivative products, and lubricants. The Interprovincial Pipe Line (IPL), which originates in Edmonton and passes through Saskatchewan, transports crude oil from both Alberta and Saskatchewan to markets in eastern Canada and the United States.

In 1991, electricity generated totaled 44.5 billion kilowatt hours and consumption within the province amounted to 41.1 billion kilowatt hours.

27 COMMERCE

In 1992, retail sales amounted to more than c\$19 billion, and per capita (per person) spending was the highest in Canada. The service sector accounts for more than 60% of Alberta's economic output. More than two-thirds of Alberta's employment is found in such industries as business and financial services, transportation, retail trade, health and education services, and tourism. Calgary has Canada's third-largest concentration of corporate offices.

28 PUBLIC FINANCE

The fiscal year runs from 1 April to 31 March. For fiscal year 1992/93, total revenues were c$13.97 billion; expenditures were c$16.8 billion. Major expenditure areas were health, education, social services, agriculture and economic development, interest on debt, regional planning and development, and protection of persons and property.

29 TAXATION

Albertans have the lowest overall tax burden in Canada. Alberta is the only province that has no provincial retail sales tax, and it has the lowest gasoline tax (c$.09/liter) in Canada. Alberta's basic personal income tax rate of 45% is the lowest in Canada. In 1993, a typical two-income Albertan household earning c$55,000 paid c$2,815 in provincial and $5,703 in federal income taxes. Other taxes include a cigarette tax of c$1.75 per pack, and a health care tax of c$27 (individual) or c$54 (family) per month.

The provincial corporate income tax rate is 15.5% for large corporations, 14.5% for large manufacturers and processors, and 6% for small businesses, all among the lowest in Canada.

30 HEALTH

In 1992 there were 42,039 live births in Alberta, for a rate of 16 per 1,000 residents. The death rate in 1992 was 5.6 per 1,000 residents, with 14,679 deaths occurring that year. Therapeutic abortions in Alberta numbered 6,621 in 1990, for a rate of 10.8 per 1,000 females aged 15–44 and a ratio of 15.4 per 100 live births. Reported cases of selected diseases in 1990 included chicken pox, 14,314; pertussis, 4,851; gonococcal infections, 1,255;

Photo Credit: Alberta Tourism Partnership.

The legislative building in Edmonton, Alberta's capital. Provincial legislators are elected to represent a constitutional jurisdiction and pass legislation.

campylobacteriosis, 842; and salmonellosis, 791. There were 83 new AIDS cases reported in 1990; in 1991, the total number of cases was 354.

As of 1993, Alberta had 177 hospitals and health centers. In the late 1980s, there were 117 general hospitals with 13,355 beds, and 29 pediatric, psychiatric, rehabilitation, and extended health care hospitals with 4,821 beds.

31 HOUSING

In 1990, the average resale value of a home was c$128,484 in Calgary, and c$101,040 for Edmonton. The average monthly rent for a two-bedroom apartment in Calgary in 1990 was c$595, while the metropolitan area apartment vacancy rate was 2%. The average monthly rent for Edmonton was c$515, with a vacancy rate of 1.8%.

32 EDUCATION

The first schools in Alberta were founded by Catholic and Protestant missionaries in the mid-1800s. When Alberta entered the Canadian confederation in 1905, there was one provincial education system which allowed separate schools for the dissenting religious minority. The 1930s saw the introduction of social studies, junior high schools, rural school administration, adult education, and increased benefits for teachers.

Public education in Alberta is a shared responsibility of the provincial government and local school boards. In areas such as curriculum and teacher certification, Alberta Education (the provincial education department) has overall authority. Local school boards employ teachers and operate schools at the elementary (grades 1–6), junior high (grades 7–9), and high school (grades 10–12) levels.

In 1993/94, Alberta had 483,594 students enrolled in grades 1–12, with about 1% registered in home education. An additional 40,930 children attended Early Childhood Services (ECS), an optional pre-grade 1 program offered jointly by the provincial government and local school boards or community operators. In 1993/94, 188 private schools (primarily religious or language-based) enrolled 17,103 students; these schools receive about 70% of the provincial funding provided to public schools.

In 1990/91, full-time university students numbered 48,614 (43,186 undergraduate, 5,428 graduate), while part-time enrollment was 17,657 (15,383 undergraduate, 2,274 graduate). The University of Alberta in Edmonton is Canada's second-largest English-language university. In 1990/91 it enrolled 24,678 full-time students. Enrollment in postsecondary community colleges in 1990/91 was 25,168, of which 20,826 were enrolled in career programs and 4,342 were in university transfer programs.

33 ARTS

Cultural activities in Edmonton include the Edmonton Symphony Orchestra, the Alberta Ballet, the Edmonton Opera Company, and more professional live theater companies per person than any other city in Canada. Every year, Edmonton hosts an international jazz festival and a large alternative theater celebration. Calgary's Centre for the Performing Arts is the permanent home of the Calgary Philharmonic Orchestra and has three theaters. In 1990/91, Alberta's 46 performing arts companies gave 4,763 performances before a total attendance of 1,358,209.

34 LIBRARIES AND MUSEUMS

Alberta's history is the focus of many museums and historical sites, including the Royal Tyrrell Museum of Paleontology, Frank's Slide, Head-Smashed-In Buffalo Jump, the Reynolds-Alberta Museum, and the Remington Alberta Carriage Centre.

Photo Credit: Alberta Tourism Partnership.

Rodeos are popular summer sporting events. The Calgary Stampede, held annually in early July, is the largest rodeo in the world.

35 COMMUNICATIONS

As of 1994, Alberta had 37 AM and 14 FM radio stations, and 12 television stations. Calgary has 7 AM and 8 FM radio stations and 3 television stations, while Edmonton has 9 AM and 8 FM radio stations and 4 television stations.

36 PRESS

Daily newspapers in the two largest metropolitan areas are the *Calgary Herald* and *The Calgary Sun*, and the *Edmonton Journal* and *The Edmonton Sun*. Other daily newspapers are published in Fort McMurray, Grande Prairie, Lethbridge, Medicine Hat, and Red Deer.

37 TOURISM, TRAVEL, AND RECREATION

The province offers a multitude of attractions to visitors, and prides itself on the magnificent Rocky Mountains, especially the celebrated Jasper and Banff national parks.

Since 1985, the number of overseas visitors has almost doubled, to 451,200 visitors in 1992. Many of Alberta's tourists come from the England, Japan, Germany, and Australia.

The West Edmonton Mall is the world's largest combined shopping/entertainment center.

[38] SPORTS

Rodeos, many of which are part of the North American Rodeo Circuit, are popular sporting events during the summer months throughout Alberta. The Calgary Stampede, held annually during the first ten days of July, is the largest rodeo in the world.

Alberta has two National Hockey League (NHL) teams: the Calgary Flames and the Edmonton Oilers, both in the Pacific Division of the Western Conference. The Flames won the Stanley Cup in 1989, while the Oilers took the championship in 1984, 1985, 1987, 1988, and 1990. The Oilers' success in the 1980s was partially due to Wayne Gretzky, who received the NHL's most valuable player award every year between 1980 and 1987 while at Edmonton. The Calgary Stampeders and Edmonton Eskimos play in the Canadian Football League (CFL); the Stampeders won the Grey Cup in 1971 and 1992, and the Eskimos took the CFL championship in 1954–56, 1975, 1978–82, 1987, and 1993. Other professional teams include the Triple A level teams for Major League Baseball's Florida Marlins (the Edmonton Trappers) and Seattle Mariners (the Calgary Canons). Calgary gained international attention as the host of the Olympic Winter Games in 1988.

[39] FAMOUS ALBERTANS

Progressive Conservative Charles Joseph "Joe" Clark (b.1939), originally from High River, served as Canada's prime minister from June 1979 to March 1980.

Famous Albertans in entertainment include actors Fay Wray (b.1907), Conrad Bain (b.1923), and Michael J. Fox (b.1961). Joni Mitchell (b.1943) and k. d. lang (b.1961) are prominent Albertan singers.

Notable literary persons include poet and novelist Earle Birney (b.1904), communications theorist Marshall McLuhan (1911–80), novelist Robert Kroetsch (b.1927), novelist and short story writer W. P. Kinsella (b.1935), and novelist Katherine Govier (b.1948).

Hockey star Lanny McDonald (b.1953) is a native of Hanna, while three-time World Figure Skating champion Kurt Browning (b.1966) was born in Caroline.

[40] BIBLIOGRAPHY

Bakken, Edna. *Discover Canada: Alberta*. Toronto: Grolier, 1991.
Bumsted, J. M. *The Peoples of Canada*. New York: Oxford University Press, 1992.
LeVert, Suzanne. *Let's Discover Canada: Alberta*. New York: Chelsea House, 1991.
Sorensen, Lynda. *Canada: Provinces and Territories*. Vero Beach, Fla.: Rourke Book Co., 1995.
Wansborough, M. B. *Great Canadian Lives*. New York: Doubleday, 1986.
Weihs, Jean. *Facts about Canada, Its Provinces and Territories*. New York: H. W. Wilson, 1995.
Yates, Sarah. *Alberta*. Minneapolis: Lerner Publications, 1996.

BRITISH COLUMBIA

ORIGIN OF PROVINCE NAME: The name signified the British territorial domain over its Crown colony. Columbia Lake, the Columbia River, and the province were named in honor of Christopher Columbus.

CAPITAL: Victoria.

NICKNAME: The Pacific Province.

ENTERED CONFEDERATION: 20 July 1871.

MOTTO: *Splendor sine occasu* (Splendor without diminishment).

COAT OF ARMS: In the center, the provincial shield of arms displays the Union Jack (the flag of the United Kingdom) in the upper half with an antique gold crown in the center; the lower half of the shield has a golden sun setting over alternating blue and white wavy lines (see "Flag" below for symbolism). Above the shield, standing on a royal crown, is a lion with Pacific dogwood garlanded around its neck. Supporting the shield are an elk on the left and a bighorn sheep on the right. Beneath the shield the provincial motto appears on a scroll entwined with Pacific dogwood flowers.

FLAG: The Union Jack is in the upper third of the flag, symbolizing the province's origins as a British colony. An antique gold crown in the center of the Union Jack represents the sovereign power that links the nations of the British Commonwealth. In the lower two-thirds is a golden sun setting over alternating blue and white waves representing the Pacific Ocean.

FLORAL EMBLEM: Pacific dogwood.

TARTAN: Blue, green, white, and gold on a red background.

PROVINCIAL BIRD: Steller's jay.

TREE: Western red cedar.

MINERAL: Jade.

TIME: 5 AM MST = noon GMT; 4 AM PST = noon GMT.

1 LOCATION AND SIZE

British Columbia, Canada's westernmost province, is bordered on the north by the Yukon Territory and the Northwest Territories; on the east by Alberta; on the south by the US states of Montana, Idaho, and Washington; and on the west by the Pacific Ocean and the US state of Alaska. Its area of 367,669 square miles (952,263 square kilometers) makes British Columbia Canada's third-largest province (occupying almost 10% of the total national land surface). The province is nearly four times the size of Great Britain, two and one-half times larger than Japan, larger than every US state except Alaska, and bigger than all but 30 nations in the world.

Given its location, British Columbia is a gateway to the Pacific and Asia. Often categorized as part of Canada's "West," the province is actually a distinct region both geographically and culturally.

2 TOPOGRAPHY

British Columbia is one of North America's most mountainous regions, offering remarkable topographical contrasts. Where the Pacific Ocean reaches the continent, there are a chain of islands, large and small, running from north to south. Some of these islands are nestled in fjords (narrow water passages with steep shores on either side) carved in the majestic Coastal Mountains, which rise more than 6,500 feet (2,000 meters) above sea level.

To the east of the Coastal Mountains lies a rolling upland of forests, natural grasslands, and lakes. Further east, the Rocky Mountains—with peaks more than 13,000 feet (4,000 meters) high—separate British Columbia from neighboring Alberta. In the northeast, a small corner of the province is an area of plains.

3 CLIMATE

The province's climate is as diverse as its topography. For example, the mild coastal region receives abundant precipitation—from 51 to 150 inches (130 to 380 centimeters) of rain a year—while the interior has a continental climate featuring long, cold winters and mild to hot summers. Other parts of the province are almost desert-like, with very hot summers followed by very cold winters. The highest temperature recorded in British Columbia was 112°F (44.4°C) on 16 July 1941 at Lillooet; the lowest was -74°F (-58.9°C) on 31 January 1947 at Smith River. Overall, Victoria is ranked as having the mildest cli-

British Columbia Population Profile

Estimated 1996 population:	3,822,700
Population change, 1981–91:	20.9%
Population by ethnic origin:	
Multiple origins:	40.5%
British origins:	24.8%
Chinese:	5.5%
German:	4.8%
East Indian:	2.7%
Aboriginal:	2.3%
French:	2.1%
Dutch:	2.0%
Ukrainian:	1.6%
Italian:	1.5%
Filipino:	0.9%
Polish:	0.8%
Norwegian:	0.6%
Japanese:	0.6%
Other single origins:	9.3%

Population by Age Group

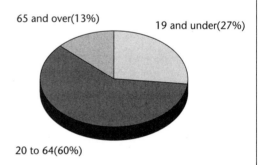

65 and over(13%)

19 and under(27%)

20 to 64(60%)

Top Cities with Populations over 10,000

City	Population	% Change 1986–91
Vancouver	471,844	9.4
Surrey	245,173	35.1
Burnaby	158,858	9.4
Richmond	126,624	16.7
Saanich	95,577	15.2
Delta	88,978	11.8
Coquitlam	84,021	21.3
Kelowna	75,950	24.1
North Vancouver	75,157	10.1
Victoria	71,228	7.4

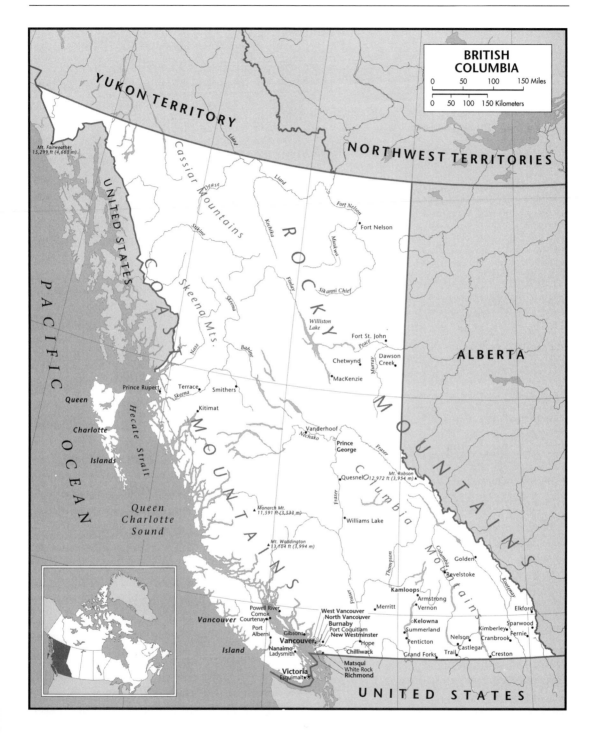

mate of any Canadian city, with an average daily temperature of 37°F (3°C) in January and 61°F (16°C) in July.

4 PLANTS AND ANIMALS

British Columbia.is home to 280 mammal species, 500 bird species, 453 fish, 21 amphibians, and 17 reptile species. Invertebrate species are estimated at between 50,000 and 70,000, including 35,000 species of insects. There are an estimated 2,580 species of vascular plants (ferns and all plants that reproduce through seeds), 1,000 types of mosses and liverworts, 1,000 lichens, 522 species of attached algae, and more than 10,000 fungi species.

Some of the more distinguishable mammal species are: shrew, mole, bat, rabbit, pika, beaver, vole, lemming, mouse, porcupine, gopher, squirrel, chipmunk, coyote, wolf, fox, cougar, lynx, bobcat, otter, sea lion, wolverine, marten, fisher, skunk, ermine, weasel, raccoon, black bear, grizzly bear, mountain goat, bighorn sheep, moose, deer, elk, and caribou.

5 ENVIRONMENTAL PROTECTION

The Environmental Protection Division of the British Columbia Ministry of Environment, Lands and Parks (BCE) is responsible for protecting the environment by regulating waste discharges and controlling the impact of polluting substances. The division consists of four branches within the BCE: the Air Resources Branch; Evaluation, Economics and Lab Services; the Industrial Waste and Hazardous Contaminants Branch; and the Municipal Waste Branch.

Aside from concerns over global greenhouse gas emissions and ozone depletion, local air quality problems include: smog in the Lower Fraser Valley (which includes the Vancouver metro area); acid deposits in soils from acid rain, mainly in southwest British Columbia; industrial pollution; and smoke from forestry activities, open burning, and domestic wood stoves. In 1991/92, Canada's first vehicle emission testing program, AirCare, began in the Lower Fraser Valley.

Pulp mills and mining activities, which discharge chemical waste, are contributors to soil pollution in the province, which has the strictest regulations in Canada on the discharge of chlorinated organic compounds. By the year 2000, British Columbia wants to reduce the amount of municipal and solid wastes requiring disposal by 50%. Local recycling programs play an important role in this goal—besides traditional residential waste recycling programs, British Columbia also has regulations or programs to recycle used lubricating oil, waste gypsum wallboard, and used tires and lead acid batteries.

Water management policy issues include water export and the impact of industry on rivers and streams. Recent concerns over nitrate and pesticide contamination of aquifers (naturally occurring underground reservoirs of water) from agricultural activities have resulted in several experimental projects aimed at sustaining water quality without hurting the agricultural industry.

Photo Credit: The Province of British Columbia.

Rafting is popular on the Fraser River in central British Columbia.

6 POPULATION

For 1996, the population of British Columbia is estimated at 3,822,700 residents. In 1991, 50.6% of the population was female and 49.4% male. Persons under 24 years of age constitute 34% of the population, with youths under 14 accounting for 20%.

Nearly 60% of all British Columbians live in the Victoria and Vancouver areas. The Vancouver area is home to more than 1.6 million people, making it the third-largest Canadian metropolitan area; metropolitan Victoria has nearly 288,000 inhabitants and ranks 14th nationwide.

7 ETHNIC GROUPS

The majority of British Columbia's inhabitants are of British origin, but the population is enriched by immigrants and descendants of immigrants of all nationalities. More than 100,000 British Columbians are descendants of the thousands of Chinese who took part in the construction of the Canadian Pacific Railway in the late 19th century. The Japanese began to arrive in the 1890s, becoming merchants and fishermen. Today, Vancouver has North America's second-largest Chinese community. More than 60,000 British Columbia residents are from India, and 16,000 are from

Japan. British Columbians of Asian heritage have contributed tremendously to the province's economic and cultural vitality.

The Aboriginal population (Native Peoples) of British Columbia, which began to decline with the arrival of the first European settlers, is enjoying new strength. The Aboriginal Peoples had grown in numbers to more than 165,000 by 1991, and have developed strong organizations. This new energy coincides with a rebirth in Aboriginal cultural and artistic expression.

8 LANGUAGES

English was the native tongue of 80.2% of British Columbia residents in 1991. French speakers made up 1.6% of the population while 18.2% of the people had some other first language, chiefly Chinese and Punjabi.

9 RELIGIONS

In 1991, 44.5% of British Columbia's population, or about 1,460,500 people, was Protestant, including 426,650 United Church of Canada members, 331,500 Anglicans, 108,300 Lutherans, 85,300 Baptists, 72,200 Pentecostals, and 65,600 Presbyterians. British Columbia also had about 610,500 Catholics (600,600 Roman Catholics and 9,900 Ukrainian Catholics), 23,000 people of Eastern Orthodox faith, 75,500 Sikhs, 36,100 Buddhists, 26,250 Moslems, 19,700 Hindus, and 16,400 Jews. About 1,017,400 British Columbians had no religious affiliation in 1991.

10 TRANSPORTATION

British Columbia has some 4,225 miles (6,800 kilometers) of mainland railway track operated by BC Rail, Canadian National (CN) Rail, Canadian Pacific (CP) Rail, and other railways. CP Rail provides railcar barge service to Vancouver Island, and CN Rail operates the Aquatrain service from Prince Rupert to Alaska.

Highways in British Columbia provide all-weather service to most of the province. In 1993, there were 13,785 miles (22,185 kilometers) of paved road, 12,181 miles (19,602 kilometers) of unpaved road, 2,589 bridges, and 136 tunnels and snowsheds (shelters against snowslides). In 1991, British Columbia had some 1,470,000 licensed passenger cars and 513,000 commercial vehicles; there also are more than 58,000 motorcycles and mopeds registered in the province.

Vancouver has the largest dry cargo port on the Pacific Coast of North America. In 1991, shipments through the Vancouver port totaled 77.9 million tons (70.7 million metric tons) from 9,614 arriving vessels. Other year-round deepwater ports are located at Prince Rupert, New Westminster, Nanaimo, Port Alberni, Campbell River, and Powell River.

Ferry service is extensive, with the British Columbia Ferry Corporation using 40 vessels on 24 routes between the lower mainland, Vancouver Island, and other coastal points. In 1991, provincial ferries carried 20 million passengers and 7.8 million vehicles.

Urban transit in 1991 consisted of 1,040 buses, 114 light-rail vehicles, and 2 other vehicles. These vehicles together provided more than 141.8 million passenger trips of more than 52.3 million miles (84.2 million kilometers).

Air service is provided through a network of airports, floatplane (planes that take off from and land on water) facilities, and heliports. In 1991, Vancouver International Airport served over 7.1 million passengers, including more than 3.1 million international passengers. The airport plans to have a c$350 million expansion complete by mid-1996 and a third runway by 1997, allowing it to become the primary international hub on the West Coast.

11 HISTORY

The Aboriginal Peoples of British Columbia developed one of the richest and most complex cultures north of Mexico. Because of the diversity of the Pacific Coast—mild to cold climate, seashore to mountains—the tribes that settled in this area developed completely different cultures and languages. The coastal inhabitants were experts at wood sculpture, as their totem polls attest even today. They were also famous for their skill and courage in whaling. As for their social system, it was marked by occasions such as the potlatch—a ceremony in which important gifts were given to guests—and by theatrical displays.

European Exploration and Settlement

In 1774, the first Europeans (under the flag of Spain) visited what is now British Columbia. In contrast with eastern Canada, where the English and French were the two nationalities fighting over territory, Spain and Russia were the first countries to claim ownership of parts of British Columbia. In the 18th century, the Spanish claimed the West Coast from Mexico to Vancouver Island. At the same time, the Russians were making an overlapping claim for control of the Pacific Coast from Alaska to San Francisco.

In 1778, Captain James Cook of Great Britain became the first person to chart the region. The first permanent colony, in present-day Victoria, was established by the British in 1843.

When gold was discovered in the Lower Fraser Valley in 1857, thousands of people came in search of instant wealth. To help maintain law and order, the British government established the colony of British Columbia the following year. In 1866, when the frenzy of the gold rush was over, the colony of Vancouver Island joined British Columbia. The colony was cut off from the rest of British North America by thousands of miles and a mountain range. The promise of a rail link between the Pacific Coast and the rest of Canada convinced British Columbia to join the Canadian confederation in 1871.

Early 20th Century

Canada lost more than 68,000 soldiers in World War I (1914–18). Veterans returning to British Columbia faced a bleak future of scarce low-paying jobs, while tariffs on imports kept prices for consumer goods high. During the 1920s, Canada experienced a period of rapid growth in industry. Forestry and mining became prominent industries in British Columbia. Transportation improvements—railways and roads—enabled businesses to flourish. Automobiles, telephones, electrical appliances, and other consumer goods became widely available.

Just as in the United States, all of Canada suffered during the Great Depression. In addition to the problems with prices during the early 1920s, droughts and frequent crop failures devastated the national economy, which still relied heavily on agriculture. Social welfare programs rapidly expanded during the 1930s, with much of the burden placed on the provincial and municipal governments.

1940s–1990s

Following World War II (1939–45), consumer spending and immigration to Canada rapidly increased. Urbanization spread quickly by means of the National Housing Act, which made home ownership more easily available. Unemployment insurance and other social welfare programs were also created following the war. Under the leadership of Prime Minister Louis St. Laurent, old age pensions were increased in 1951 and a national hospital insurance plan was introduced in 1957.

Canada's unity as a confederation has often been widely questioned. Most recently, the popular defeat of both the Meech Lake Accord of 1987 and the Charlottetown Accord of 1992 has failed to solve the issue of Québec's role in Canada. As a result, western Canadian voters, many of whom feel that the federal government treats them as less important than other Canadians, have recently voted to elect representatives who favor increased power for the provinces and decreased power for the federal government.

12 PROVINCIAL GOVERNMENT

The structure of the provincial government reflects that of the federal government. For example, the provincial premier, as the majority party leader of the legislature, functions much like the Canadian prime minister.

The premier and cabinet ministers make up the Executive Council, which acts as the main governing body. Provincial legislators, like their federal counterparts in Parliament, are elected to represent a constitutional jurisdiction and pass legislation. They do so as members of the 75-member Legislative Assembly. A provincial lieutenant-governor approves laws passed by the legislature, much like the Governor General at the federal level. There is no provincial equivalent, however, to the federal Senate.

The province of British Columbia originally existed as two separate British Crown colonies—the island colony of Vancouver Island with its capital at Victoria and the mainland colony of British Columbia with its capital on the Fraser River at New Westminster. In 1866, the two colonies were officially united.

13 POLITICAL PARTIES

Political parties did not directly control the provincial legislature from the 1870s

Photo Credit: The Province of British Columbia.

Legislative buildings in Victoria, British Columbia's capital. Located on Vancouver Island, historic Victoria has many English-style gardens.

to the early 1900s. Instead, informal personal relationships between individual legislators were used to form issue-specific coalitions. During this era, provincial legislators often were wealthy merchants, lawyers, industrialists, and landowners who conspired with the government to create dynastic business empires. After five years of instability, this system fell out of favor in 1903, and the Conservative Party held the majority until 1916.

Liberals and Conservatives alternated as majority and minority in the Legislative Assembly until 1933, when socialists (from several different parties) became a sizable minority. The Co-operative Commonwealth Federation (CCF) arose during the 1940s as an alternative to the Liberal and Conservative parties. During the 1950s, the Social Credit Party became prominent, particularly in rural regions. The New Democratic Party (NDP) became popular with organized labor in the 1960s, and aligned itself with the CCF.

The most recent general election was held on 17 October 1991. The parties held the following number of seats in British Columbia's Legislative Assembly in 1994: New Democratic Party, 53; Liberals, 14; Social Credit Party, 6; and Independents, 2.

Premiers of British Columbia

Term	Premier	Party
1871–72	John Foster McCreight	
1872–74	Amor de Cosmos	
1874–76	George Anthony Walkem	
1876–78	Andrew Charles Elliott	
1878–82	George Anthony Walkem	
1882–83	Robert Beaven	
1883–87	William Smithe	
1887–89	Alexander Edmund Batson Davie	Conservative
1889–92	John Robson	Liberal
1892–95	Theodore Davie	
1895–98	John Herbert Turner	
1898–1900	Charles Augustus Semlin	Conservative
1900	Joseph Martin	Liberal
1900–02	James Dunsmuir	Conservative
1902–03	Edward Gawler Prior	Conservative
1903–15	Richard McBride	Conservative
1915–16	William John Bowser	Conservative
1916–18	Harlan Carey Brewster	Liberal
1918–27	John Oliver	Liberal
1927–28	John Duncan MacLean	Liberal
1928–33	Simon Fraser Tolmie	Conservative
1933–41	Thomas Dufferin Pattullo	Liberal
1941–47	John Hart	Coalition Government
1947–52	Byron Johnson	Coalition Government
1952–72	William Andrew Cecil Bennett	Social Credit
1972–75	David Barrett	New Democratic
1975–86	William Richards Bennett	Social Credit
1986–91	Wilhelmus Nicholaas Theodore Vander Zalm	Social Credit
1991	Rita Margaret Johnston	Social Credit
1991–	Michael Franklin Harcourt	New Democratic

14 LOCAL GOVERNMENT

There are several types of local or municipal government (depending on the needs of the community), ranging from improvement districts, which provide single services such as fire protection or garbage collection, to villages, towns, cities, and district municipalities. As of May 1991, British Columbia had 39 cities, 15 towns, 44 villages, 50 districts, and 1 Indian government district. Revenue for municipal services comes mainly from property taxation and grants from the provincial government, with some additional revenue from license fees, business taxes, and public utility projects.

15 JUDICIAL SYSTEM

The Canadian Constitution grants provincial jurisdiction over the administration of justice, and allows each province to organize its own court system and police forces. The federal government has exclusive domain over cases involving trade and commerce, banking, bankruptcy, and criminal law. The Federal Court of Canada has both trial and appellate divisions for federal cases. The 9-judge Supreme Court of Canada is an appellate court that determines the constitutionality of both federal and provincial statutes. The Tax Court of Canada hears appeals of taxpayers against assessments by Revenue Canada.

The provincial judiciary in British Columbia is composed of the Court of Appeal, the Supreme Court of British Columbia, County Courts, and provincial courts consisting of criminal, family, and small claims.

In 1990, there were 108 homicides in the province, for a rate of 3.5 per 100,000 persons. Breaking and entering offenses in 1989 numbered 536 per 100,000 people for businesses and 1,013 per 100,000 people for residences.

16 MIGRATION

British Columbia continues to attract Canadians and foreigners alike: 40,000 persons settle in the province each year, and its population now exceeds 3.8 million.

In 1991, British Columbia gained a net 33,447 residents from migration within Canada (80,302 entered British Columbia and 46,855 left), making the province the fastest-growing province in terms of internal migration. Most new British Columbians who came from other parts of Canada in 1991 came from Alberta (38%) and Ontario (29%).

17 ECONOMY

Agriculture and fishing, especially salmon fishing, are two key sectors of the economy of British Columbia. Other important areas of the economy include: forestry and logging, mining, manufacturing, construction, utilities, transportation and storage, communications, services to business, education, health, accommodation and food, public administration and defense, and finance, insurance, and real estate.

18 INCOME

Individual income in 1990 averaged c$24,881. The average individual income for females was c$18,357, or 59% of average income for males. Average family income in the province was c$48,011 in 1989. Average weekly earnings for all sectors in 1991 amounted to c$535.

19 INDUSTRY

Manufacturing in British Columbia is still largely resource-based, but is being gradually diversified by high-tech and computer-based industries related to telecommunications and the aerospace and subsea industries. British Columbia has the most balanced export market of all of Canada's provinces, with the United States, Japan, the European Union, and the Pacific Rim countries as its customers. In 1990, the value of manufactured shipments was c$25.36 billion. The largest contributors were: wood products, c$6.16 billion; food products, c$3.17 billion; refined petroleum and coal products, c$1.71 billion; fabricated metal products, c$1.35 billion; printing and publishing, c$986.6 million; and paper and allied products, c$912.1 million.

20 LABOR

The British Columbian labor force in 1991 came to 1,652,000, with an overall participation rate of 66.4%. Employment that year amounted to 1,489,000 (56% male, 44% female), with 163,000 unemployed, for an unemployment rate of 9.9%. The sectors with the largest number of employed persons in 1991 were: services, 565,800; trade, 269,500; manufacturing, 171,200; transportation, communication, and utilities, 129,500; construction, 102,700; finance, insurance, and real estate, 89,300; public administration, 83,400; agriculture, 32,800; forestry, 22,300; mining, 14,900; and fishing and trapping, 7,500.

More than 37% of all employees are unionized. In 1991, the largest unions were the B.C. Government Employees' Union, with 42,534 members; the Canadian Union of Public Employees, 38,843; the International Woodworkers of America-Canada, 35,082; and the B.C. Teachers' Federation, 33,875.

21 AGRICULTURE

British Columbia had 19,225 farms in 1991 on a total of over 5.9 million acres (14.6 million hectares). These farms employed 61,135 people. The most valuable commodities grown are floricultural and nursery items (including potted plants, cut flowers, bedding plants, and foliage plants), followed by vegetables, berries (strawberries, cranberries, and raspberries), grapes, tree fruit, and grains and oilseeds. The Mainland-Southwest region is the most agriculturally active, followed by the Thompson-Okanagan region and Vancouver Island. The valleys of the southern interior, principally the Okanagan Valley, are famous for cultivation of tree fruits and grapes and for their wine industry. The cooler, wetter climate of the Lower Fraser Valley produces rich crops of berries and vegetables, while the Peace River region accounts for 85% of the province's grain production. Field crop production in 1992 included 62,373 tons (56,600 metric tons) of barley, 57,745 tons (52,400 metric tons) of oats, 54,660 tons (49,600 metric tons) of wheat, and 1,653 tons (1,500 metric tons) of rye. In 1993, farm cash receipts were estimated at c$1.5 billion.

Greenhouses in British Columbia cover 163 acres (66 hectares) and produce cucumbers, lettuce, tomatoes, and peppers. Floriculture is carried out on 227 acres (92 hectares) and annually generates c$80 million in sales. The province also produces the greatest amount of fresh mushrooms in western North America, annually marketing some 33 million pounds (15 million kilograms). The largest ginseng farm in the world is in British Columbia, covering more than 1,458 acres (590 hectares) and with an estimated 1994 production valued at c$33 million.

22 DOMESTICATED ANIMALS

The Fraser Valley accounts for most dairy, poultry, and hog farming. The central interior of British Columbia is the primary site of the cattle industry. As of 1 July 1993, the livestock population included 591,000 cattle, 74,000 dairy cows, and 201,100 hogs. The province's dairy cows are among Canada's most productive, with an annual milk production of 135 million gallons (510 million liters). Egg production amounted to about 50 million dozen in 1993. In 1992, cash receipts for dairy products amounted to c$260 million; cattle, c$246 million; poultry and eggs, c$217 million; and hogs, c$40 million. Meat and poultry processing annually generate about c$850 million in British Columbia. More than 135 farms throughout the province raise reindeer, fallow deer, and plains bison for specialty markets.

23 FISHING

Over 40 species of finfish and shellfish native to the waters off British Columbia are harvested and marketed by the province's fishing and related industries, which are largely based on Vancouver Island. In 1993, the total catch was 308,764 tons (280,185 metric tons), valued at c$422.6 million. In 1992, British Columbia had some 16,000 commercial anglers, operating from about 6,000 fishing boats. Salmon is generally the most important species, followed by roe herring, groundfish varieties, and shellfish. In addition, the province also had 560 fish farms in 1992. The farmed salmon production of 22,040 tons (20,000 metric tons) in 1992

English Bay at Vancouver. The Vancouver area is Canada's third-largest metropolitan area.

ranked fifth in the world. Oyster production, almost entirely farmed, has more than doubled since the early 1980s.

24 FORESTRY

The British Columbian economy is based on the province's great natural resources, primarily its vast forests, which cover 56% of its total area. The provincial government owns about 90% of the forest land in British Columbia. Available productive forest land covers 112 million acres (45.3 million hectares) or 47% of the province, with about 96% of that area covered with conifers. The principal species harvested are lodgepole pine, spruce, hemlock, balsam, Douglas fir, and cedar. Coastal forests consist primarily of hem-

lock, while lodgepole pine and spruce are the main interior species. Conifers are converted into lumber, newsprint, pulp and paper products, shingles and shakes, poles, and piling—about half the total softwood inventory of Canada.

In 1993, the timber harvest was 2.8 billion cubic feet (78.8 million cubic meters), with coastal forests accounting for only one-third. In 1991, output of forest-based products included lumber, 1.1 billion cubic feet (31.4 million cubic meters); plywood, 50 million cubic feet (1.4 million cubic meters); pulp, 7,385,604 tons (6,702,000 metric tons); paper and paperboard, 1,288,238 tons (1,169,000 metric tons); and newsprint, 1,669,530 tons

(1,515,000 metric tons). The softwood timber harvest annually accounts for about 6% of the world total (and about half the Canadian total). British Columbia's exports of softwood lumber account for about 35% of the world export total. In 1993, the province's forest industry had factory shipments of c$13.8 billion, or 50% of the value of all shipments from manufacturers in the province. The industry directly employed some 94,000 people.

By law, all public lands that are harvested must be reforested. From 1930 to 1993, the British Columbia Forestry Service planted 3 billion seedlings. Each year more than 200 million seedlings from 19 species are planted to replace trees that have been harvested, destroyed by fire, or damaged by pests. The seedlings have a survival rate of 87%.

25 MINING

Mining in British Columbia dates back to the mid-1800s, when coal was mined on Vancouver Island, and has expanded to now include base and precious metals. The abundance of minerals and easy access to markets has made mining an important economic sector. Copper, gold, and zinc are the leading metals extracted; sulfur and asbestos are the leading industrial minerals. The value of British Columbia's solid mineral production accounts for about 15% of the national total. As of 1995, there were 21 mines operating in British Columbia.

26 ENERGY AND POWER

The most valuable mineral resources in British Columbia are coal, petroleum, and natural gas. Improved prices for natural gas and increased demand from the US market have recently caused fuel mineral activity to surge. In 1991, crude oil and equivalent production totaled 80,821,429 cubic feet (2,263,000 cubic meters), valued at c$292 million. In 1993/94, known reserves of natural gas increased from 854 trillion cubic feet (239 billion cubic meters) to 875 trillion cubic feet (245 billion cubic meters). Known reserves of crude oil rose from 554 billion cubic feet (15.5 billion cubic meters) to 643 billion cubic feet (18 billion cubic meters), with production of 71 billion cubic feet (2 billion cubic meters) in 1993/94. Two new projects, the Alkolkolex Plant Hydro Project (a hydroelectric plant) and an expansion of the Aitken Creek Gas Processing Plant northeast of Fort St. John, were approved in 1993/94.

British Columbia's abundant fresh water supply has led to the extensive development of hydroelectric energy. In 1991, total electricity generation exceeded 62.9 billion kilowatt hours, of which nearly 96% was provided by hydroelectric power and the remaining 4% by conventional thermal generation. Consumption of electricity within the province totaled 2.7 billion kilowatt hours in 1991. Most electric power is supplied by the British Columbia Hydro and Power Authority, a provincial Crown corporation.

27 COMMERCE

Retail trade in British Columbia totaled c$23.5 billion in 1991, down from c$24.2 billion in 1990. Provincial retail sales were c$7,300 per capita (per person) in 1991, higher than the national average of c$6,700. The metropolitan Vancouver area is the primary commercial area in British Columbia, accounting for over 50% of total provincial sales. Other large markets exist in metropolitan Victoria, Kelowna, and Kamloops. Leading retail areas by sales in 1991 included supermarkets and grocery stores, c$5.5 billion; motor and recreational vehicle dealers, c$5.2 billion; general merchandise stores, c$2.7 billion; gasoline service stations, c$2 billion; automotive parts, accessories, and service, c$1.2 billion; drugstores and pharmacies, c$1.1 billion; clothing stores, c$1 billion; and household furniture and appliance stores, c$1 billion.

28 PUBLIC FINANCE

The fiscal year extends from 1 April to 31 March. For fiscal year 1992/93, total revenues were c$18.6 billion; expenditures were c$20.6 billion. Major expenditure areas were health, education, social services, natural resources and economic development, transportation, protection of persons and property, and interest on debt.

29 TAXATION

The basic personal income tax rate in 1993 was 52.5%, with high income surtaxes of 30–50%. The retail sales tax was 7%. Major consumption taxes in 1993 included gasoline and tobacco. In 1991, the average family in British Columbia had a cash income of c$50,500 and paid c$23,645 in taxes.

Corporate income tax rates in 1993 were as follows: small business rate, 10%; general business rate, 16.5%; and capital tax rate, 0.3–3%.

30 HEALTH

In 1992 there were 46,156 live births in British Columbia, for a rate of 13.4 per 1,000 residents. The death rate in 1992 was 7.1 per 1,000 residents, with 24,615 deaths occurring that year. Therapeutic abortions in British Columbia numbered 11,518 in 1990, for a rate of 15.8 per 1,000 females aged 15–44 and a ratio of 25.2 per 100 live births. Reported cases of selected diseases in 1990 included giardiasis, 2,235; campylobacteriosis, 1,916; chicken pox, 1,702; gonococcal infections, 1,500; and salmonellosis, 991. There were 176 new AIDS cases reported in 1990; in 1991, the total number of cases was 977.

As of March 1992, health care institutions in British Columbia consisted of 96 acute care hospitals, 17 diagnostic and treatment centers, 20 extended care hospitals, 5 rehabilitation hospitals, 1 federal hospital, and 6 Red Cross outposts. In the late 1980s, there were 92 general hospitals with 17,234 beds, and 23 pediatric, psychiatric, rehabilitation, and extended health care hospitals with 4,119 beds.

31 HOUSING

In 1990, the average resale value of a home was c$226,385 in Vancouver, and c$160,743 for Victoria. The average monthly rent for a two-bedroom apartment in Vancouver in 1990 was c$751, while the metropolitan area apartment vacancy rate was 0.9%. The average rent for Victoria was c$615 per month, with a vacancy rate of 0.3%.

32 EDUCATION

In 1992, British Columbia had 1,599 public schools and approximately 527,000 pupils; independent schools numbered 246 and had a total enrollment of 37,000. The Ministry of Education provides overall management of the school system by setting a framework to ensure basic equality in school programs across the province. Direct administration is provided by locally elected school boards of trustees in 75 school districts.

British Columbia has four publicly funded universities: the University of British Columbia in Vancouver, with a 1991 total enrollment of 36,034; Simon Fraser University in Burnaby, with 17,335 students; the University of Victoria, with 14,791 students; and the University of Northern British Columbia in Prince George, which was just opened for enrollment in 1992. In 1990/91, full-time university students numbered 42,096 (35,043 undergraduate, 7,053 graduate), while part-time enrollment was 19,433 (17,834 undergraduate, 1,599 graduate).

British Columbia also has an extensive non-university, postsecondary education system providing academic, technical, vocational, career, and adult basic education programs. These programs are administered from four university colleges, nine community colleges, and five technical institutes. Enrollment in postsecondary community colleges in 1990/91 was 27,427, of which 13,041 were enrolled in career programs and 14,386 were in university transfer programs.

33 ARTS

Vancouver is the center for cultural arts in British Columbia. In 1990/91, British Columbia's 51 performing arts companies gave 5,750 performances before a total attendance of 1,721,017.

34 LIBRARIES AND MUSEUMS

British Columbia has 18 municipal public library systems. The most prominent academic library system is the University of British Columbia Libraries in Vancouver. Vancouver has the University of British Columbia's Museum of Anthropology (which includes totem poles and many ceremonial objects of Northwest Native art), the Vancouver Museum, the Vancouver Maritime Museum, and the Vancouver Art Gallery. The Royal British Columbia Museum in Victoria, founded in 1886, focuses on the natural and human history of the province.

35 COMMUNICATIONS

In 1991, telephone service in British Columbia used 1,990,000 service lines and served over 98% of the province's homes. There were 72 radio stations (49 AM, 23 FM) in 1994, and 10 television stations, which used 259 rebroadcasting stations. Cable service was provided to 82% of all homes in 1991 by 145 systems.

36 PRESS

British Columbia has 17 daily newspapers; major metropolitan newspapers include

Long Beach, on southwestern Vancouver Island, is a part of Pacific Rim National Park.

The Vancouver Sun, the *Victoria Star*, and the *Times-Colonist* (Victoria). *The Sing Tao Chinese Daily* and the *World Journal* are Chinese-language daily papers published in greater Vancouver. Other Vancouver periodicals feature editions in Punjabi, French, and several other languages.

37 TOURISM, TRAVEL, AND RECREATION

Tourism is an important economic sector. Each year, about 15 million people visit British Columbia. With over 15.8 million acres (6.4 million hectares) of parkland, the Rocky Mountains remain the biggest attraction. British Columbians make about 45 million recreational visits to provincial forests per year, annually spending about c$2 billion in recreational activities in those areas.

Also very popular is coastal British Columbia, with its beaches, hiking trails, artist colonies, wildlife reserves, whale-sighting locales, and other attractions.

Of increasing attraction to visitors are the Queen Charlotte Islands, large parts of which have recently been set aside as parkland. The area contains untouched wilderness and unique plant species. The abandoned Haida village of Ninstints on Anthony Island in the Queen Charlotte Islands is of such historical and cultural importance that it has been designated a world heritage site by the United Nations Educational, Scientific, and Cultural Organization (UNESCO).

38 SPORTS

The Vancouver Canucks of the National Hockey League (NHL) play in the Pacific Division of the Western Conference. The B.C. Lions of the Canadian Football League also play in Vancouver and won the Grey Cup in 1964 and 1985.

39 FAMOUS BRITISH COLUMBIANS

Sir James Douglas (b.Guyana, 1803–77), considered the "Father of British Columbia," founded Fort Victoria in 1843 and became Vancouver Island's first colonial governor. Kim Campbell (b.1947), who was Canada's first female prime minister, is from British Columbia.

Famous actors have included John Ireland (b.1914), Raymond Burr (1917–93), James Doohan (b.1920), Alexis Smith (b.1921), Yvonne De Carlo (b.1924), Barbara Parkins (b.1942), and Rae Dawn Chong (b.1962). Musicians David Foster and Bryan Adams (b.1959) are also prominent entertainers.

Prominent British Columbian authors include poet and fiction writer George Bowering (b.1935) and novelists Sheila Watson (b.1909), Jack Hodgins (b.1938), and Brian Fawcett (b.1944). The scientist, educator, and author David Suzuki (b.1936) was born in Vancouver.

Hockey stars include Juha Widing (1948–85) and Brian Spencer (1949–88).

40 BIBLIOGRAPHY

Bowers, Vivien. *British Columbia*. Minneapolis: Lerner Publications, 1995.

Bumsted, J. M. *The Peoples of Canada*. New York: Oxford University Press, 1992.

LeVert, Suzanne. *Let's Discover Canada: British Columbia*. New York: Chelsea House, 1991.

Nanton, Isabel. *Discover Canada: British Columbia*. Toronto: Grolier, 1994.

Sorensen, Lynda. *Canada: Provinces and Territories*. Vero Beach, Fla.: Rourke Book Co., 1995.

Wansborough, M. B. *Great Canadian Lives*. New York: Doubleday, 1986.

Weihs, Jean. *Facts about Canada, Its Provinces and Territories*. New York: H. W. Wilson, 1995.

MANITOBA

ORIGIN OF PROVINCE NAME: Likely comes from either the Cree Indian *manitowapow* or the Ojibway Indian *Manitou bou* (both of which mean "the narrows of the Great Spirit"). The words referred to Lake Manitoba, which narrows to less than 5/8 of a mile (1 kilometer) at its center. The waves hitting the loose surface rocks of its north shore produce curious bell-like and wailing sounds, which the first Aboriginal Peoples believed came from a huge drum beaten by the spirit Manitou.

NICKNAME: Keystone Province.

CAPITAL: Winnipeg.

ENTERED CONFEDERATION: 15 July 1870.

MOTTO: *Gloriosus et liber* (Glorious and free).

COAT OF ARMS: In the center, the provincial shield of arms displays in the lower two-thirds a buffalo standing on rock on a green background, symbolizing Manitoba's prairie nature and the historically important Red River buffalo hunt. The red Cross of St. George appears in the upper third and represents the province's bond to the United Kingdom. Above the shield is a crest with a red-and-silver-mantled gold helmet and a beaver holding a pasqueflower and carrying a royal crown on its back. Supporting the shield on the left is a unicorn with a green and silver collar from which hangs a Red River cart wheel. A white horse supports the right side and wears a bead and bone collar from which hangs an Indian symbol. Beneath the shield are displayed grain, pasqueflowers, white spruce trees, and symbols for water. The provincial motto appears on a scroll at the base.

FLAG: On a field of red, the Union Jack (the flag of the United Kingdom) occupies the upper quarter on the staff side. The provincial coat of arms is centered in the half farthest from the staff.

FLORAL EMBLEM: Pasqueflower, known locally as prairie crocus.

TARTAN: Manitoba Tartan (maroon and green, with yellow, dark green, and azure blue).

PROVINCIAL BIRD: Great gray owl.

TREE: White spruce.

TIME: 6 AM CST = noon GMT.

1 LOCATION AND SIZE

Manitoba is bordered by the Northwest Territories to the north, Hudson Bay to the northeast, Ontario to the east, the US states of Minnesota and North Dakota to the south, and Saskatchewan to the west. Manitoba, along with Alberta and Saskatchewan, is one of the three prairie provinces and is located in the center of Canada. Manitoba's total area is 261,000 square miles (676,000 square kilometers), with a total land area of 212,000 square miles (548,000 square kilometers).

2 TOPOGRAPHY

Elevations rise slowly from sea level at Hudson Bay to the higher areas of the south and west. Most of Manitoba lies between 500 and 1,000 feet (150 and 300 meters) above sea level. But in the Turtle, Riding, Duck, and Baldy Mountains, heights rise to 2,300 feet (700 meters) or higher. The highest point in Manitoba is Baldy Mountain, in Duck Mountain Provincial Park, at 2,726 feet (831 meters).

Manitoba is known as the land of 100,000 lakes, a legacy of enormous Lake Agassiz which covered much of the province after the glaciers retreated. Lake Winnipeg, Lake Winnipegosis, and Lake Manitoba dominate the southern topography; Lake Winnipeg is the fifth largest freshwater lake in North America. The north shows enormous changes from the glaciers' movements and is covered in forest.

3 CLIMATE

Manitoba is one of the sunniest provinces in Canada. It has what is known as a continental climate, which features great temperature extremes. Summer temperatures in Manitoba range from an average of 62–75°F (17–24°C) in June to 45–65°F (8–18°C) in September. Winter temperatures average 8 to 30°F (-13 to 0°C). Typical of southern Manitoba, the normal daily January temperature in Winnipeg is about -4°F (-20°C), while the normal daily July temperature is about 66°F (19°C). In Thompson, in the center of northern Manitoba, the normal daily temperature ranges from about -17°F (-27°C) in January to 59°F (15°C) in July. The warmest recorded

Manitoba Population Profile

Estimated 1994 population:		1,131,000
Population change, 1981–91:		6.4%
Leading ancestry group:		British
Second leading group:		German
Population by ethnic group:		
Aboriginal peoples:		72,000
Métis:		33,000
Urban/rural populations:		
Urban:	787,175	72.1%
Rural:	304,767	27.9%

Population density: 4.33 persons per square mile
(1.67 per square kilometer)

Population by Age Group

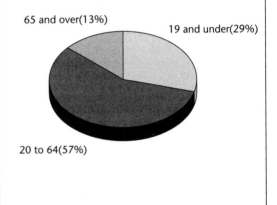

65 and over(13%)

19 and under(29%)

20 to 64(57%)

Top Cities with Populations over 10,000

City	Population	Natl. Rank
Winnipeg (metro area)	652,354	7
Brandon	38,567	70
Thompson	15,046	115
Portage la Prairie	13,186	124

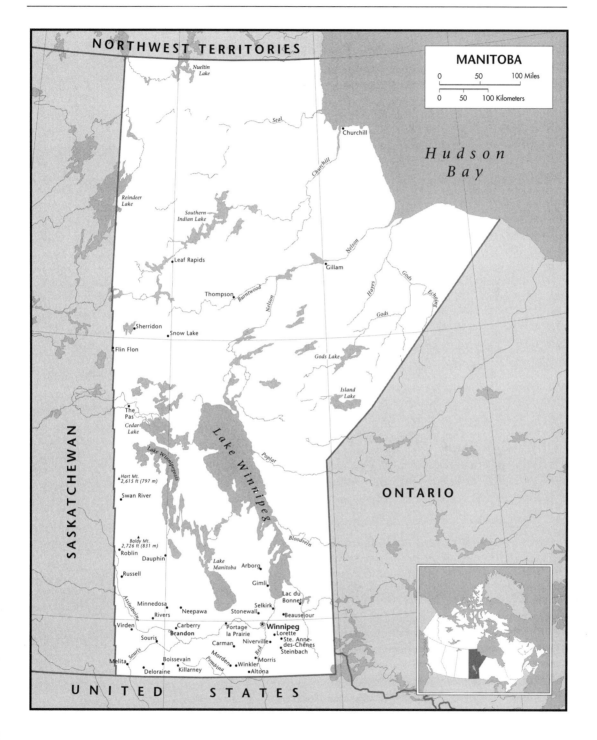

NORTHWEST TERRITORIES

Nueltin Lake

Seal

Churchill

Hudson Bay

Churchill

Reindeer Lake

Southern Indian Lake

Nelson

Leaf Rapids

Gillam

Gods

Echoing

Thompson

Burntwood

Nelson

Hayes

Gods

Sherridon

Snow Lake

Gods

Flin Flon

Gods Lake

Island Lake

The Pas

Cedar Lake

Lake Winnipegosis

Lake Winnipeg

Poplar

ONTARIO

Hart Mt.
2,615 ft (797 m)

Swan River

SASKATCHEWAN

Bloodvein

Baldy Mt.
2,726 ft (831 m)

Roblin

Dauphin

Lake Manitoba

Arborg

Russell

Gimli

Lac du Bonnet

Minnedosa

Selkirk

Assiniboine

Rivers

Neepawa

Stonewall

Beausejour

Virden

Carberry

Portage la Prairie

Winnipeg

Lorette

Souris

Brandon

Carman

Niverville

Ste. Anne-des-Chênes

Melita

Souris

Boissevain

Morden

Winkler

Morris

Steinbach

Deloraine

Killarney

Pembina

Altona

Red

UNITED   STATES

Over half of Manitoba's population lives in the Winnipeg metropolitan area.

temperature in Manitoba was 112°F (44.4°C) on 11 July 1936 at St. Albans, while the coldest was -63°F (-52.8°C) on 9 January 1899 at Norway House.

4 PLANTS AND ANIMALS

there are remnants of the native prairie grasses in protected areas of the central plains. Basswoods, cottonwoods, and oaks are common tree species there. Pelicans, beavers, raccoons, red foxes, and white-tailed deer are commonly found near Lake Manitoba; bison were once numerous there too but now exist only in small herds in protected areas. Some 27 species of waterfowl nest in southern Manitoba through the summer, and fall migrations bring thousands of ducks and geese. Polar

bears and beluga whales are native to the Churchill area.

5 ENVIRONMENTAL PROTECTION

Manitoba annually releases about 642,466 tons (583,000 metric tons) of nitrogen dioxide and carbon monoxide (gases that cause smog), 610,508 tons (554,000 metric tons) of sulfur dioxide and nitrogen oxide compounds, and the equivalent of 3,763,330 tons (3,415,000 metric tons) of carbon dioxide. Manitoba generates about 0.8% of Canada's annual hazardous waste, and creates about 1,102,000 tons (1,000,000 metric tons) of solid waste (0.894 tons, or 0.811 metric tons, per resident) each year. Manitoba has 440 landfills, 17 licensed hazardous waste sites, and no municipal incinerators. Daily water usage is about 8.536 cubic feet (0.239 cubic meters) per person; 47.2% of water withdrawals are for residential households.

6 POPULATION

About 58% of Manitoba's 1,131,000 people live in metropolitan Winnipeg, the provincial capital; the Winnipeg metropolitan area is the seventh-largest in Canada. The second-largest city is Brandon, in southwestern Manitoba, with 38,567 people. The only other cities in the province are Thompson, Portage la Prairie, and Flin Flon.

7 ETHNIC GROUPS

Although Manitoba is one of the smaller provinces in population, it is an important center for a number of ethnic groups. It is one of the most important centers of Ukrainian culture outside Ukraine. It also has one of the largest populations of Mennonites in the world. More than 115,000 people trace their ancestry to Aboriginal Peoples or Métis (people of mixed Aboriginal and European ancestry). Winnipeg has the largest French community outside of Québec. Gimli has the largest Icelandic community anywhere outside of Iceland.

8 LANGUAGES

In 1991, 74.5% of all residents reported English as their mother tongue, while 4.7% claimed French. Other first languages—including Ukrainian, Icelandic, and various indigenous languages—were reported by 20.8% of Manitobans.

9 RELIGIONS

In 1991, 51% of all Manitobans—556,890 people—were Protestant. The leading Protestant denominations were United Church of Canada, 203,100; Anglican, 95,000; Lutheran, 55,700; Pentecostal, 21,850; Baptist, 20,750; and Presbyterian, 16,400. The province had about 331,950 Catholics—30.4% of the popuation—with 297,000 Roman Catholics and 34,950 Ukrainian Catholics. About 20,750 Manitobans were of Eastern Orthodox faith and approximately 14,200 were Jewish. Buddhists, Moslems, Sikhs, and Hindus were also present, each with less than 5,500 followers. About 152,900 Manitobans—14%—had no religious affiliation in 1991.

10 TRANSPORTATION

The Trans-Canada Highway connects Winnipeg with Kenora, Ontario, to the east and with Portage la Prairie and Brandon to the west before continuing on to Saskatchewan. In 1990, Manitoba had 779,069 registered motor vehicles, consisting of 543,095 passenger cars; 224,273 trucks, tractor trucks, and buses; 11,680 motorcycles and mopeds; and 21 other vehicles.

Urban transit in 1991 consisted of 578 motor buses which provided over 52.1 million passenger trips covering more than 16.7 million miles (26.9 million kilometers).

In 1991, Winnipeg International Airport served more than 1.7 million passengers. Winnipeg is also a major hub for the two major railroad networks in Canada,

Canadian Pacific Rail and Canadian National Rail.

11 HISTORY

The Assiniboine Indians were the first inhabitants of Manitoba. Other tribes included the nomadic Cree, who followed the herds of bison and caribou on their seasonal migrations.

European Exploration and Settlement

In their search for the rich Orient through the Northwest Passage (a fabled sea passage to Asia), Europeans reached Manitoba through Hudson Bay. Unlike most of the rest of Canada, the northern parts of the province were settled before the south. In 1612, English explorer Captain Thomas Button wintered two ships at the mouth of the Nelson River, on Hudson Bay. Later, a party led by French explorer and fur trader Pierre Gaultierde La Vérendrye explored the Red and Winnipeg Rivers in the years 1733–38 and built several outposts.

Early European interest in Manitoba centered on the fur trade. In 1670, the Hudson's Bay Company was created, and King Charles II of England granted it a large tract of land named Rupert's Land. The company set up fur-trading posts to exploit the country's wealth. During the 18th century, the Montreal-based North West Company and the Hudson's Bay Company developed a fierce rivalry, each wishing to gain greater control over the fur trade.

In 1812, the first European agricultural settlement was established in the area around the junction of the Red and Assiniboine Rivers by Lord Selkirk, a Scottish nobleman. He sent a number of Scottish Highlanders to settle land he had secured from the Hudson's Bay Company. He called the area Assiniboia. The Selkirk colony suffered through floods, problems arising from unfamiliarity with the environment, and rivalries within the fur trade. Nevertheless, the settlement survived.

Transition to Provincehood

In 1836, Assiniboia was transferred to the Hudson's Bay Company by the Selkirk family. In the 1860s, the provinces of Canada, anxious to expand into the great northwest, offered to buy the land from the Hudson's Bay Company. Lengthy negotiations for the transfer of sovereignty of the Hudson's Bay Company lands to Canada followed. But little regard was given to the wishes of the inhabitants, especially the Métis (people of mixed Aboriginal and European blood) who made up 60% of the area's population.

The Métis were upset that they were being left out of the negotiations and were concerned about American and Canadian settlers moving into their territory. The Métis feared that their land rights and culture would be lost. Under the leadership of Louis Riel, the Métis opposed the Canadian proposals in an uprising known as the Red River Rebellion. Riel succeeded in establishing a locally elected, provisional government in December 1869. Delegates

Photo Credit: Canadian Tourism Commission photo.

Historic Fort Prince of Wales, on Hudson Bay near Churchill. Churchill has been called the "polar bear capital of the world," because it is the only human settlement where polar bears can be observed in the wild.

of this provisional government negotiated terms with the new federal government of Canada. Within months, Manitoba became a province of the Dominion of Canada, officially entering the confederation on 15 July 1870.

Early Years as a Province

The new "postage stamp" province (so named because of its square shape and small size) consisted then of only 13,900 square miles (36,000 square kilometers) surrounding the Red River Valley. But the province did not remain that small; its boundaries were stretched in 1881 and again in 1912. Bolstered by its central location as the entry point to western Canada, Manitoba grew quickly during its first 50 years as a province. With the help of the railway, thousands of settlers from eastern Canada and from countries all over the world made Manitoba their home.

In early 1919, workers in the metals and building trades in Winnipeg staged a strike to protest problems of collective bargaining and union recognition by management. Canada's only general strike in its history, the Winnipeg Strike, began on 15 May 1919 when 22,000 sympathetic workers picketed.

During World War I (1914–18), Canada lost more than 68,000 soldiers. Veterans returning to Manitoba faced a bleak future of scarce low-paying jobs, while tariffs on imports kept prices for consumer goods high. Manitoban farmers, like those in the other prairie provinces, had prospered from high wheat prices during World War I, but with the end of the war global grain markets collapsed and wheat prices fell 50% by 1920. Affected farmers organized the United Farmers Movement in Manitoba in 1922 to protest the low farm product prices and high transportation rates, and played an important role in provincial politics of the 1920s.

During the 1920s, grain prices recovered, and Canada experienced a period of rapid growth in industry. Transportation improvements—railways and roads—enabled businesses to flourish. Automobiles, telephones, electrical appliances, and other consumer goods became widely available.

Manitoba, like the other prairie provinces, was one of the poorest areas of Canada during the Great Depression. In addition to the falling grain prices of the 1920s, droughts and frequent crop failures devastated the economy of the province. Social welfare programs rapidly expanded during the 1930s, with much of the burden placed on the provincial and municipal governments.

1940s–1990s

Following World War II (1939–45), consumer spending and immigration to Canada rapidly increased. Urbanization spread quickly by means of the National Housing Act, which made home ownership more easily available. Unemployment insurance and other social welfare programs were also created following the war. Under the leadership of Prime Minister Louis St. Laurent, old age pensions were increased in 1951 and a national hospital insurance plan was introduced in 1957.

Canada's unity as a confederation has often been widely questioned. Most recently, the popular defeat of both the Meech Lake Accord of 1987 and the Charlottetown Accord of 1992 has failed to solve the issue of Québec's role in Canada. Manitoba (along with New Brunswick) failed to ratify the Meech Lake Accord of 1987 because many voters felt Québec would gain preferential status. Along these lines, western Canadian voters in general, many of whom feel that the federal government treats them as less important than other Canadians, have recently voted to elect representatives who favor increased power for provinces and decreased power for the federal government.

12 PROVINCIAL GOVERNMENT

The structure of the provincial government reflects that of the federal government. For example, the provincial premier, as the majority party leader of the legislature, functions much like the Canadian prime minister. Provincial legislators, like their federal counterparts in Parliament, are elected to represent a constitutional jurisdiction and pass legislation. They do so as members of the 57-seat Legislative

Assembly. A provincial lieutenant-governor approves laws passed by the legislature, much like the Governor General at the federal level. There is no provincial equivalent, however, to the federal Senate.

13 POLITICAL PARTIES

After Manitoba joined the confederation, the Conservatives held power until the late 1880s. The Liberal provincial government after the 1890s often campaigned for xenophobic (anti-foreigner) policies which targeted non-British immigrants.

The most recent general election was held on 11 September 1990. The parties held the following number of seats in Manitoba's Legislative Assembly: Progressive Conservatives, 29; New Democrats, 19; Liberals, 7; and vacant, 2.

Premiers of Manitoba

Term	Premier	Party
1870–71	Alfred Boyd (Chief Minister)	Conservative
1871–72	Marc-Amable Girard (Ch. Min)	Conservative
1872–74	Henry Joseph Clarke (Ch. Min.)	Conservative
1874	Marc-Amable Girard	Conservative
1874–78	Robert Atkinson Davis	Conservative
1878–87	John Norquay	Conservative
1887–88	David Howard Harrison	Conservative
1888–1900	Thomas Greenway	Liberal
1900	Sir Hugh John Macdonald	Conservative
1900–15	Sir Rodmond Palen Roblin	Conservative
1915–22	Tobias Crawford Norris	Liberal
1922–28	John Bracken	United Farmers
1928–43	John Bracken	Liberal Progressive
1943–48	Stuart Sinclair Garson	Liberal Progressive
1948–58	Douglas Lloyd Campbell	Liberal Progressive
1958–67	Dufferin Roblin	Conservative
1967–69	Walter Cox-Smith Weir	Conservative
1969–77	Edward Richard Schreyer	New Democratic
1977–81	Sterling Rufus Lyon	Conservative
1981–88	Howard Russell Pawley	New Democratic
1988–	Gary Albert Filmon	Conservative

14 LOCAL GOVERNMENT

Manitoba has no counties or regional governments, but is divided into incorporated cities, towns, villages, and rural municipalities. In order for a community to be incorporated into a village, there must be 750 residents and a tax base of c$750,000, while towns must have 1,500 inhabitants and an assessment of c$1.5 million. An incorporated city must have a population of 10,000. Manitoba has 5 cities, 35 towns, 39 villages, and 105 rural municipalities. Municipal elections are held every three years.

15 JUDICIAL SYSTEM

The Canadian Constitution grants provincial jurisdiction over the administration of justice, and allows each province to organize its own court system and police forces. The federal government has exclusive domain over cases involving trade and commerce, banking, bankruptcy, and criminal law. The Federal Court of Canada has both trial and appellate divisions for federal cases. The 9-judge Supreme Court of Canada is an appellate court that determines the constitutionality of both federal and provincial statutes. The Tax Court of Canada hears appeals of taxpayers against assessments by Revenue Canada.

In 1990, there were 38 homicides in Manitoba, for a rate of 3.5 per 100,000 persons. Breaking and entering offenses in 1989 numbered 440 per 100,000 people for businesses and 921 per 100,000 people for residences.

16 MIGRATION

For many years, most Manitobans were of British origin. But changes in migration and immigration patterns have produced a province where no ethnic group is numerically dominant. Manitoba is home to dozens of groups from all over the world, which has enriched the province's economy, culture, and society.

In 1991, Manitoba lost a net 7,663 residents from migration between provinces (18,758 entered Manitoba and 26,421 left). Ontario was the province of origin for 32% of total internal migration to Manitoba in 1991. Meanwhile, 28% of Manitobans moving elsewhere in Canada that year relocated in Ontario.

17 ECONOMY

Manitoba's early economy was based on agriculture, with manufacturing and transportation later becoming vital sectors. Manitoba now has a very diversified economy, but the service sector is the most important. The central location of the province makes Manitoba an attractive base for a wide variety of services, notably in transportation and wholesale distribution.

18 INCOME

As of June 1990, the average weekly earnings for workers in manufacturing were c$426.13, while those in the electrical products industries earned c$426.13 per week. Average family income in the province was c$46,285 in 1989. As of December 1992, average weekly earnings in the province amounted to c$494.71.

19 INDUSTRY

Manufacturing is the largest goods-producing area of the economy. Food and transportation equipment have long been the leading manufacturing industries. Other important industries are primary and fabricated metals, electrical goods, clothing and textiles, and printing and publishing. In 1990, the total value of shipments by manufacturers was c$6.7 billion. The largest contributors were: food products, c$1.5 billion; transportation equipment, c$763.8 million; electrical and electronic products, c$562.8 million; primary metals, c$559.5 million; machinery, c$523.9 million; and printing and publishing, c$482.3 million.

20 LABOR

Manitoba's labor force in 1992 decreased by 6,000 to 535,000, compared with 541,000 in 1991. Employment in the province's service sector was 357,000 in 1992 (down from 364,000 in 1991). Goods-producing industries saw employment decrease 4,000 jobs from 1991 to 1992. The unemployment rate stood at 9.6% for 1992 and was 9.9% in March 1993.

As of 1990, 36% of the paid workers in Manitoba were union members. From 1981–90, union membership increased by 27.5%, from 123,638 to 157,600 union members.

21 AGRICULTURE

Agriculture is the economic basis of rural Manitoba. It also supports thousands of jobs in towns and cities. Wheat is the most important crop, accounting for about a third of crop production value. The province is the leading Canadian producer of flaxseed, sunflower seeds, buckwheat, and field peas.

Of the total land area, 26.7% has some agricultural potential. In 1991 more than 50% of the potential agricultural land was actually used for agriculture. Manitoba had 25,706 farms in 1991, with 98.7% of them family-operated. For 1993, the quantities of the principal field crops produced were: wheat, 4,050,291 tons (3,675,400 metric tons); hay, 3,269,083 tons (2,966,500 metric tons); barley, 1,367,582 tons (1,241,000 metric tons); canola, 974,719 tons (884,500 metric tons); oats, 543,837 tons (493,500 metric tons); flaxseed, 268,778 tons (243,900 metric tons); and sunflower seeds, 52,014 tons (47,200 metric tons). Potatoes and mushrooms are important horticultural crops.

22 DOMESTICATED ANIMALS

Manitoba's livestock population in 1993 included 1,238,000 cattle (9% of the national total); beef cows numbered 458,000 (11% of Canada's total) while dairy cows numbered 54,000 (4%). The hog population that year was 1,440,000 (13% of the Canadian total); sheep and lambs, 36,000 (4%); hens and chickens, 6,226,000 (7%); and turkeys, 701,000 (10%). Other livestock in 1991 included 44,130 horses, 40,000 pheasants, 5,895 goats, 13,276 rabbits, and 1,100 bison. In 1993, the livestock population also included 5,000 wild boars, 600 ostriches, and 225 emus and rheas. In 1992/93, Manitoban fur farms produced 1,062 fox pelts and 37,089 mink pelts, valued at c$743,950.

23 FISHING

Commercial fishing on Lake Winnipeg was common in the late 1800s, and helped Icelandic immigrants to build fishing towns including Hecla and Gimli. More recently, however, sport fishing has become an important part of the tourism industry. Fish hatcheries in Grand Rapids and Whiteshell raise trout, walleye, and other species to replenish stock.

24 FORESTRY

Northern Manitoba's forests are dominated by pine, hemlock, and birch. As of 1991, Manitoba's forested area was 65 million acres (26.3 million hectares), of which 37.6 million acres (15.2 million hectares) was considered productive for timber.

25 MINING

Mining is another major Manitoba industry. Metals account each year for at least three quarters of the total value of mining production in the province. The most important metals are nickel, copper, and zinc (the province is a world leader in the production of nickel). Manitoba also produces a number of industrial minerals. Production in 1992 included 93,960 tons (85,263 metric tons) of zinc, 71,488 tons (64,871 metric tons) of nickel, 66,760 tons (60,581 metric tons) of copper, 1,898 tons (1,722 metric tons) of lead, 96,301 pounds (43,682 kilograms) of silver, and 5,796 pounds (2,629 kilograms) of gold. The total value of mineral production in 1992 was c$1,048,951,000, with metals accounting for 91.2% of the total.

26 ENERGY AND POWER

In 1991, crude oil and equivalent production totaled 25,500,000 cubic feet (714,000 cubic meters), valued at C$90 million.

The major rivers of western Canada flow into the lowland region of Manitoba, giving Manitoba 90% of the hydroelectric potential of the prairie region. In 1991, 22.9 billion kilowatt hours of electricity was generated. Consumption within the province amounted to 15.5 billion kilowatt hours.

27 COMMERCE

Agricultural trade is Manitoba's primary commercial base. In 1993, exports of food and agricultural products totaled C$1.4 billion. The United States accounted for C$563.6 million of this total. The food processing industries in Manitoba rely on the various service sectors in the province, including transportation, construction, finance, insurance, and real estate. About 6% of all transportation expenditures in the province involve the movement of raw or processed agricultural products, and about 6% of all construction projects either are on farms or are for agriculture-related industries. Some 14% of provincial expenditures for financial, insurance, and real estate services are derived from farms. Manitoba farms also annually account for 4.5% of the electricity, 58% of the chemicals, and 29% of the gasoline and fuel oil consumed in the province. In 1993, about half of the food sold in Manitoba's 1,463 grocery and other food stores came from products grown and processed in the province.

28 PUBLIC FINANCE

The fiscal year extends from 1 April to 31 March. For fiscal year 1992/93, total revenues were C$6.3 billion; expenditures were C$7.1 billion. Major expenditure areas were health, education and training, family services, economic and resource development, interest on debt, government services, and assistance to local governments and taxpayers.

29 TAXATION

The basic personal income tax rate in 1993 was 52%, with high income surtaxes of 2% and a flat tax rate on net income of 2%. The retail sales tax was 7%. Major consumption taxes were levied on gasoline and tobacco. In 1991, the average family in Manitoba had a cash income of C$45,500 and paid C$18,074 in taxes.

Corporate income tax rates in 1993 were as follows: small business rate, 10%; general business rate, 17%; and capital tax rate, 0.5–3%.

30 HEALTH

In 1992 there were 16,590 live births in Manitoba (for a rate of 14.9 per 1,000 residents), and 8,980 deaths (8.1 per 1,000 population). Therapeutic abortions in Manitoba numbered 2,529 in 1990, for a rate of 10.1 per 1,000 females aged 15–44 and a ratio of 14.6 per 100 live births. Reported cases of selected diseases in 1990 included gonococcal infections, 1,079; salmonellosis, 310; pertussis, 117; tuberculosis, 95; and hepatitis A, 91. There were 4 new AIDS cases reported in 1990; in 1991, the total number of cases was 63.

As of 1993, Manitoba had 90 hospitals and health centers. In the late 1980s, there were 77 general hospitals with 5,896 beds and 8 pediatric, psychiatric, rehabilitation, and extended health care hospitals with 507 beds.

31 HOUSING

In 1990, the average resale value of a home in Winnipeg was c$81,740. The average rent for a two-bedroom apartment in Winnipeg in 1990 was c$534, while the metropolitan area apartment vacancy rate was 6.4%.

32 EDUCATION

In 1990/91, Manitoba had 219,859 students enrolled in its elementary and secondary schools. Of the total enrollment, 197,586 pupils went to public schools, 10,551 to private schools, 11,589 to federal schools, and 133 to schools for the blind and the deaf.

Enrollment in postsecondary community colleges in 1990/91 was 3,963, of which 3,880 were enrolled in career programs and 83 were in university transfer programs.

Winnipeg is the site of the University of Winnipeg which had 2,566 full-time students in 1990/91. Also located in Winnipeg is the University of Manitoba which was established in 1877 and is western Canada's oldest university. It had 14,909 full-time students in 1990/91. Brandon University offers special Aboriginal education programs. In 1990/91, the total university enrollment for the province was 19,698 full-time students (17,474 under-graduate, 2,224 graduate) and 16,162 part-time students (14,900 undergraduate, 1,262 graduate).

33 ARTS

The Royal Winnipeg Ballet was founded in 1939. Other performing arts in Winnipeg include the Manitoba Opera and several classic and contemporary theaters, including one that features productions in French. In 1990/91, Manitoba's 15 performing arts companies gave 1,556 performances before a total attendance of 798,751.

34 LIBRARIES AND MUSEUMS

The Winnipeg Art Gallery houses the world's largest collection of modern Inuit art, in addition to a collection of contemporary, historical, and decorative art. Also located in Winnipeg are the Western Canada Aviation Museum, the Manitoba Children's Museum, the National Aquatic Hall of Fame and Museum of Canada, and the Wildlife Museum. Manitoba's Marine Museum is located in Selkirk.

35 COMMUNICATIONS

As of 1994, Manitoba had 19 AM and 7 FM radio stations, and 8 television stations. Winnipeg alone has 7 AM and 5 FM radio stations and 4 television stations.

36 PRESS

Daily newspapers in Manitoba include the *Winnipeg Sun*, the *Winnipeg Free Press*, *The Brandon Sun*, and the *Flin Flon Reminder*.

The skating pavilion in Winnipeg is a popular site in the winter.

37 TOURISM, TRAVEL, AND RECREATION

Campgrounds, parks, lakes, rivers, and historic sites are the principal attractions for Manitoba's visitors. Both tourists and Manitobans alike can also take advantage of the province's 118 golf courses, most of which are open to the public.

Tourism additionally relies on dozens of community festivals, a number of which have international reputations. Winnipeg's Folklorama is an elaborate two-week summer multicultural celebration. The Jazz Winnipeg Festival in June is Canada's only thematic jazz festival. Other ethnic events include the Winnipeg Folk Festival, Festival du Voyageur, and Oktoberfest. Canada's National Strawberry Festival is held in Portage la Prairie.

38 SPORTS

Manitoba is the home of the Winnipeg Blue Bombers of the Canadian Football League (CFL) and a Winnipeg hockey team in the International Hockey League. The Winnipeg Jets of the National Hockey League (NHL) will move to Arizona in 1996 to become the Phoenix Coyotes. The Blue Bombers were the CFL champions in 1958, 1959, 1961, 1962, 1984, 1988, and 1990. Another professional team in the province is the Winnipeg Goldeyes, which play Double A baseball in the Northern League.

39 FAMOUS MANITOBANS

Controversial hero/outlaw Louis Riel (1844–85) was the founding father of Manitoba and leader of the Métis rebellions of 1870 and 1885. Nellie McClung (b.Chatsworth, Ontario, 1873–1951), an activist and author from Manitou, was instrumental in women's suffrage being attained in Manitoba in 1916.

Noted Manitobans in entertainment include television host Monty Hall (b.1925), singer Gisele MacKenzie (b.1927), and magician Doug Henning (b.1947). All three were born in Winnipeg.

Celebrated Manitoban authors include historian and journalist George Woodcock (b.1912), novelist Adele Wiseman (b.1928), and historian William L. Morton (1908–80). Margaret Laurence (1926–87) used her hometown of Neepawa as the inspiration for the town of Manawaka in her novels. Gabrielle Roy (1909–83) was a noted francophone (French-language) author. Winnipeg soldier Harry Colebourne bought a mascot for his regiment in World War I, naming it Winnie, after his home town. Colebourne's bear became the inspiration for British author A. A. Milne's *Winnie The Pooh*.

Manitoban hockey stars include Robert Earle "Bobby" Clarke (b.1949), from Flin Flon; Walter "Turk" Brody (1914–72), from Brandon; and Bill Mosienko (b.1921) and Terry Sawchuck (1929–70), both from Winnipeg.

40 BIBLIOGRAPHY

Bumsted, J. M. *The Peoples of Canada*. New York: Oxford University Press, 1992.

Emmond, Ken. *Discover Canada: Manitoba*. Toronto: Grolier, 1991.

LeVert, Suzanne. *Let's Discover Canada: Manitoba*. New York: Chelsea House, 1991.

Sorensen, Lynda. *Canada: Provinces and Territories*. Vero Beach, Fla.: Rourke Book Co., 1995.

Wansborough, M. B. *Great Canadian Lives*. New York: Doubleday, 1986.

Weihs, Jean. *Facts about Canada, Its Provinces and Territories*. New York: H. W. Wilson, 1995.

Yates, Sarah. *Manitoba*. Minneapolis: Lerner Publications, 1996.

NEW BRUNSWICK

ORIGIN OF PROVINCE NAME: Named by King George III of England in honor of his German lands, the Duchy of Brunswick-Lunenberg.

CAPITAL: Fredericton.

NICKNAME: Picture Province.

ENTERED CONFEDERATION: 1 July 1867.

MOTTO: *Spem reduxit* (Hope was restored).

COAT OF ARMS: In the center, the provincial shield of arms displays (in a fashion similar to that of the provincial flag) a golden lion at the top and an ancient oared galley riding waves below. Above the shield is an Atlantic salmon carrying a royal crown on its back, on a coronet with four maple leaves, which rests on a helmet. Supporting the shield are antlered white-tailed deer on both the right and the left, each with a collar of Maliseet wampum; from the collar of the deer on the left hangs a small shield displaying the Union Jack (the flag of Great Britain), while the other deer's shield has three fleur-de-lys on a blue background. Beneath the shield the provincial motto appears on a scroll, with a grassy mound, purple violets, and fiddleheads.

FLAG: The flag is based on the province's coat of arms. The golden lion appears in the top third against a red background; the ancient oared galley is displayed in the lower two-thirds riding waves represented by blue and white wavy lines, all against a golden background.

FLORAL EMBLEM: Purple violet.

TARTAN: Blue, forest green, and meadow green, interwoven with gold on red.

PROVINCIAL BIRD: Black-capped chickadee.

TREE: Balsam Fir.

TIME: 8 AM AST = noon GMT.

1 LOCATION AND SIZE

New Brunswick borders Québec on the north, Nova Scotia at the Chignecto Isthmus on the southeast, and the US state of Maine on the west. It is almost rectangular in shape, extending 200 miles (322 kilometers) north to south and 150 miles (242 kilometers) east to west. It is more or less surrounded by water on three sides (the Baie des Chaleurs to the northeast, the Gulf of St. Lawrence and the Northumberland Strait to the east, and the Bay of Fundy to the south). New Brunswick has a land area of 28,400 square miles (73,500 square kilometers).

2 TOPOGRAPHY

The northern part of the province is quite mountainous, the tallest peak being Mount Carleton, which is 2,690 feet (820 meters) high. The interior consists mainly of a rolling plateau, flatter in the east and more hilly in the southeast.

The main rivers are the Miramichi, Nepisguit, Restigouche, and Saint John. Known as *oa-lus-tuk* or "beautiful river" to the Indians, the Saint John River waters the fertile lands of the western part of the province over a distance of 451 miles (725 kilometers). Downstream, in the Madawaska area, the river traces a natural boundary between the state of Maine and Canada.

Twice a day, with the rising tide of the Atlantic Ocean, 110.2 billion tons (100 billion metric tons) of water stream past a rocky headland in the Bay of Fundy. The tides rushing back to the Saint John River actually force the river to temporarily flow upstream at Reversing Falls. The current created is practically equal to the flow of all the world's rivers over a 24-hour period. The eastern end of the Bay of Fundy has tides of nearly 50 feet (15 meters), the highest in the world, which would be sufficient to completely submerge a four-story building.

3 CLIMATE

The climate is generally drier and warmer inland than in the coastal areas. The highest recorded temperature in New Brunswick was 103°F (39.4°C) on 18 August 1935 at Nepisiguit Falls; the lowest was -53°F (-47.2°C) on 2 February 1955 at Sisson Dam. The beach waters on New Brunswick's Gulf of St. Lawrence coast are the warmest of any along the Atlantic north of Virginia.

4 PLANTS AND ANIMALS

Hundreds of thousands of piping plovers and other shorebirds annually take flight

New Brunswick Population Profile

Estimated 1996 population:		761,400
Population change, 1981–91:		3.9%
Population by ethnic origin:		
British origins:		32.6%
English:		23.2%
Irish:		4.8%
Scottish:		4.6%
French:		32.5%
Multiple origins:		30.4%
Aboriginal:		0.6%
German:		0.6%
Dutch:		0.4%
Italian:		0.2%
Chinese:		0.2%
Black:		0.1%
Danish:		0.1%
East Indian:		0.1%
Other single origins:		2.1%
Urban/Rural populations:		
Urban:	345,214	47.7%
Rural:	378,686	52.3%

Population by Age Group

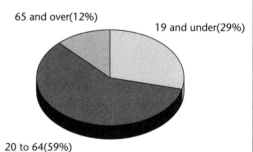

65 and over(12%)

19 and under(29%)

20 to 64(59%)

Top Cities with Populations over 10,000

City	Population	% Change 1986–91
Saint John	74,969	-1.8
Moncton	57,010	2.7
Fredericton	46,466	4.8
Riverview	16,270	4.0
Bathhurst	14,409	-1.9
Edmundston	10,835	-5.8
Dieppe	10,463	16.0

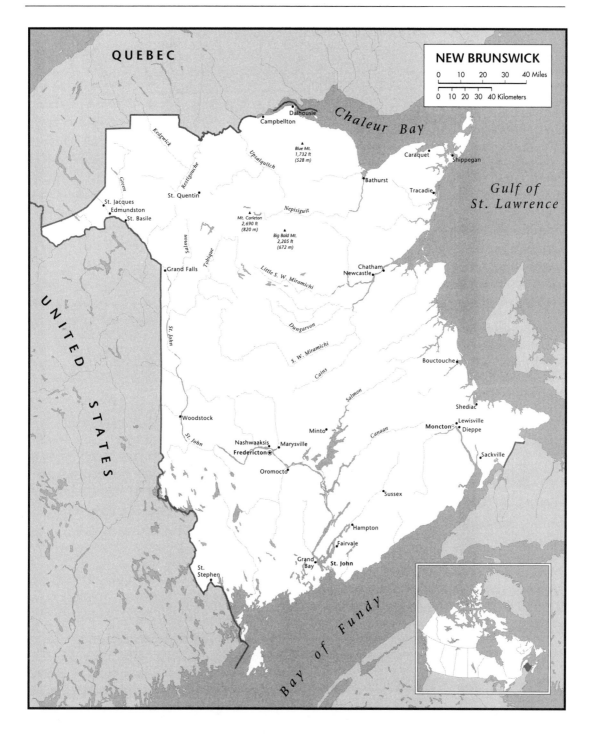

QUEBEC

Chaleur Bay

Dalhousie
Campbellton

Kedgwick

Restigouche

Upsalquitch

Blue Mt.
1,732 ft
(528 m)

Caraquet

Shippegan

Bathurst

Tracadie

Gulf of
St. Lawrence

Green

St. Jacques
Edmundston
St. Basile

St. Quentin

Mt. Carleton
2,690 ft
(820 m)

Nepisiguit

Big Bald Mt.
2,205 ft
(672 m)

Salmon

Tobique

Little S. W. Miramichi

Chatham
Newcastle

Grand Falls

U N I T E D

St. John

Dungarvon

S. W. Miramichi

Cains

Bouctouche

S T A T E S

Salmon

Shediac

Woodstock

Minto

Canaan

Lewisville
Moncton Dieppe

St. John

Nashwaaksis Marysville
Fredericton

Sackville

Oromocto

Sussex

Hampton

Fairvale

St. Stephen

Grand
Bay St. John

Bay of Fundy

from the salt marshes along the coastline at Marys Point, near Riverside-Albert. Every summer, more than 20 different kinds of whales come to the Bay of Fundy to feed in the plankton-rich waters, which also attract large schools of herring and mackerel.

5 ENVIRONMENTAL PROTECTION

The New Brunswick Department of Environment (NBDE) is responsible for preserving, protecting, and enhancing the environment for the benefit of all residents. Major regulatory legislation the NBDE oversees includes the Clean Water Act, the Clean Environment Act, the Pesticides Control Act, the Environmental Trust Fund Act, the Beverage Containers Act, and the Unsightly Premises Act.

New Brunswick has substantially reduced airborne emissions from pulp and paper production facilities, asphalt plants, and other industries since 1973, when the Clean Environment Act was instituted. But prevailing winds carry a great deal of sulfur dioxide and nitrogen dioxide from the highly industrialized areas of central Canada and New England into and across the province. In central New Brunswick, the province itself is the source of only 12% of air pollutants; the other maritime provinces are responsible for 6%; central Canada, 27%; and the US, 55%. As a result, the amount of acid deposited in New Brunswick from acid rain is high. The highest measured ground-level ozone (a main ingredient of smog) in Canada was recorded in the summer of 1993 in Fundy National Park. New Brunswick

contributes about 3% to Canada's total carbon dioxide emissions, seventh among the provinces.

The Watershed Protection Program protects 31 designated watershed areas throughout the province; about 300,000 residents (40% of New Brunswick's population) rely on these areas for fresh water. The program aims to control the quality of water resources by keeping chemical contamination and physical damage to a minimum, and by controlling runoff and erosion from agricultural operations.

Solid waste generation amounts to more than 358,150 tons (325,000 metric tons) per year, equivalent to about 990 pounds (450 kilograms) per person. Most existing dumps in the province are already scheduled for closure, and will be replaced by a system of regional facilities. In order to reduce the solid waste stream, the government has initiated recycling programs and encourages backyard composting.

6 POPULATION

In 1996, the population of New Brunswick was estimated at 761,400, up from 759,300 in 1994 and from 723,900 in 1991. The coasts and river valleys are the areas of heaviest population. Saint John, Canada's oldest incorporated city, is the largest city, followed by Moncton and Fredericton, the provincial capital. The greater Saint John metropolitan area had a population of 124,981 in 1991, for a ranking of 24th in the nation.

The Saint John River waters the fertile lands of western New Brunswick.

7 ETHNIC GROUPS

The heritage of New Brunswick's people is a blended one, combining elements of the French, British, Scottish, and Irish traditions, with later elements of German, Scandinavian, and Asian. The little municipality of New Denmark boasts North America's largest Danish colony. The Aboriginal peoples (Native Peoples) of New Brunswick number more than 12,000, most of them Micmac and Malecite.

8 LANGUAGES

New Brunswick is Canada's only officially bilingual province. In 1991, 65.1% of New Brunswick's residents reported English as their mother tongue and 33.6% declared French as their first language (the highest percentage outside Québec).

9 RELIGIONS

Besides Québec, New Brunswick is the only province where Catholics form the religious majority. In 1991, 54% of the population, or about 390,900 people, was Catholic. There were about 290,300 Protestants (40.1% of the population), including 81,800 Baptists, 76,000 United Church of Canada members, 61,500 Anglicans, 23,200 Pentecostals, 10,100 Presbyterians, and 10,100 Lutherans. New Brunswick also had about 5,800 Buddhists, and less than 750 people each of the following: people of Eastern Orthodox faith, Jews, and Hindus. About 43,400 New Brunswickers had no religious affiliation in 1991.

10 TRANSPORTATION

The TransCanada 2 highway enters New Brunswick from Québec in the northwest and connects Edmundston to Fredericton by following the Saint John River before continuing on to Moncton and Nova Scotia in the southeast. Provincial highways traverse New Brunswick and connect with I-95 and US Highway 1 at the Maine border. As of 31 March 1994, there were 568,013 vehicles (5,527 commercial) and 476,697 licensed drivers in New Brunswick. In 1993/94, c$21.85 million was spent on highway maintenance.

The world's longest covered bridge, spanning the Saint John River, was completed at Hartland in 1899. As of 1994, New Brunswick had some 2,700 bridges, seawalls, causeways, dams, and other water-related structures. In 1993/94, maintenance and repair for these structures amounted to c$8.3 million. Ports in New Brunswick handled 20.7 million tons (18.8 million metric tons) of cargo in 1991; that year, the port of Saint John alone received 1,472 arriving vessels with a combined 20,549,000 gross registered tons and handled 18.7 million tons (17 million metric tons) of cargo.

Urban transit in 1991 consisted of 62 buses which provided over 3.5 million passenger trips of over 1.7 million miles (2.8 million kilometers).

11 HISTORY

The existence of New Brunswick was known to the Europeans as early as the 1400s, when daring Basque fishermen plied their trade off Miscou in the northeast of the province. At that time, the region was inhabited by the Malecite and Micmac Indians.

European Exploration and Settlement

The Micmacs were the first to receive Samuel de Champlain and the French when they landed in New Brunswick in 1604. The Indians established good relations with the French from the outset, helping the French settlers, known as Acadians, to adapt to their new country and taking part in the French attacks on New England.

The British and French feuded over the area for a century. Control passed back and forth until 1713, when all of Acadia was ceded to the British under the Treaty of Utrecht. With time, France lost interest in the Acadians, turning most of its attention to New France and the burgeoning fur trade.

By 1755, England had established its dominance as a colonial power. Fearing that the Acadians were a security threat, the British deported (mainly to the United States) all Acadians who would not swear allegiance to the British Crown. Their exile lasted eight years, after which a significant proportion returned to their homeland. In 1783, the western part of Nova Scotia became the home of thousands of Loyalists who had taken flight in the aftermath of the American Revolution.

These American colonists, wishing to remain faithful to the British Crown, founded communities in the northern part of the province. This mass influx of Loyalists created a rift between Nova Scotia and New Brunswick, and New Brunswick became a separate province in June 1784. In 1867 it joined other provinces to form the Dominion of Canada.

Early 20th Century

During World War I (1914–18), Canada lost more than 68,000 soldiers. Veterans returning to New Brunswick faced a bleak future of scarce low-paying jobs, while tariffs on imports kept prices for consumer goods high. During the 1920s, Canada experienced a period of rapid growth in industry. Transportation improvements—railways and roads—enabled businesses to flourish. Automobiles, telephones, electrical appliances, and other consumer goods became widely available.

As in the US, all of Canada suffered during the Great Depression. In addition to the problems with grain prices during the early 1920s, droughts and frequent crop failures devastated the national economy, which still relied heavily on agriculture. Social welfare programs rapidly expanded during the 1930s, with much of the burden placed on the provincial and municipal governments.

1940s–1990s

Following World War II (1939–45), consumer spending and immigration to Canada rapidly increased. Urbanization spread quickly by means of the National Housing Act, which made home owner-

ship more easily available. Unemployment insurance and other social welfare programs were also created following the war. Under the leadership of Prime Minister Louis St. Laurent, old age pensions were increased in 1951 and a national hospital insurance plan was introduced in 1957.

Canada's unity as a confederation has often been widely questioned. Most recently, the popular defeat of both the Meech Lake Accord of 1987 and the Charlottetown Accord of 1992 has failed to solve the issue of Québec's role in Canada. New Brunswick (along with Manitoba) failed to ratify the Meech Lake Accord of 1987 because many voters felt Québec would gain preferential status. If Québec does eventually secede from Canada, the fate of the traditionally poorer maritime provinces would be uncertain. One or more might explore the possibility of admission to the United States.

12 PROVINCIAL GOVERNMENT

The structure of the provincial government reflects that of the federal government. For example, the provincial premier, as the majority party leader of the legislature, functions much like the Canadian prime minister. Provincial legislators, like their federal counterparts in Parliament, are elected to represent a constitutional jurisdiction and pass legislation. They do so as members of the 58-seat Legislative Assembly. A provincial lieutenant-governor approves laws passed by the legislature, much like the Governor General at the federal level. There is no provincial equivalent, however, to the federal Senate.

13 POLITICAL PARTIES

The Liberal and Progressive Conservative parties control local politics in New Brunswick. The Liberal Party receives much of its support from the ethnic French and Irish Roman Catholic communities, while the Conservative Party is backed largely by ethnic British and Protestant people.

The most recent general election was held on 23 September 1991. The parties held the following number of seats in New Brunswick's Legislative Assembly in 1994: Liberal Party, 46; Confederation of Regions, 8; Progressive Conservative Party, 3; and New Democratic Party, 1.

Premiers of New Brunswick

Term	Premier	Party
1866–67	Peter Mitchell	
1867–70	Andrew Rainsford Wetmore	
1871–72	George Luther Hatheway	
1872–78	George Edwin King	
1878–82	John James Fraser	
1882–83	Daniel Lionel Hanington	
1883–96	Andrew George Blair	Liberal
1896–97	James Mitchell	Liberal
1897–1900	Henry Robert Emmerson	Liberal
1900–07	Lemuel John Tweedie	Liberal
1907	William Pugsley	Liberal
1907–08	Clifford William Robinson	Liberal
1908–11	John Douglas Hazen	Conservative
1911–14	James Kidd Fleming	Conservative
1914–17	George Johnson Clarke	Conservative
1917	John Alexander Murray	Conservative
1917–23	Walter Edward Foster	Liberal
1923–25	Peter John Veniot	Liberal
1925–31	John Macaulay Baxter	Conservative
1931–33	Charles Dow Richards	Conservative
1933–35	Leonard Percy de Wolfe Tilley	Conservative
1935–40	Albert Allison Dysart	Liberal
1940–52	John Babbitt McNair	Liberal
1952–60	Hugh John Flemming	Conservative
1960–70	Louis Joseph Robichaud	Liberal
1970–87	Richard Bennett Hatfield	Conservative
1987–	Frank Joseph McKenna	Liberal

14 LOCAL GOVERNMENT

The provincial government provides all municipal services for rural areas. Cities are required to have 10,000 inhabitants for incorporation; towns, 1,000. Villages need no specific minimum population for incorporation. New Brunswick's municipal governments consist of 6 cities, 27 towns, and 84 villages.

15 JUDICIAL SYSTEM

The Canadian Constitution grants provincial jurisdiction over the administration of justice, and allows each province to organize its own court system and police forces. The federal government has exclusive domain over cases involving trade and commerce, banking, bankruptcy, and criminal law. The Federal Court of Canada has both trial and appellate divisions for federal cases. The 9-judge Supreme Court of Canada is an appellate court that determines the constitutionality of both federal and provincial statutes. The Tax Court of Canada hears appeals of taxpayers against assessments by Revenue Canada.

In 1990, there were 11 homicides in New Brunswick, for a rate of 1.5 per 100,000 persons. Breaking and entering offenses in 1989 numbered 284 per 100,000 people for businesses and 432 per 100,000 people for residences.

16 MIGRATION

Historically, migration in the province has involved the forced deportations of Acadians (the descendants of the original French settlers) and their return during the early to mid-18th century, and an influx of British Loyalists from the American colonies following the American Revolution later in the 18th century.

In 1991, New Brunswick lost 2,377 residents from migration between provinces (14,477 people entered the province and 16,854 left for other provinces). Ontario was the province of origin for 37% of total internal migration into New Brunswick in 1991, and was the province of destination for 34% of residents leaving New Brunswick to live elsewhere in Canada that year. New Brunswick lost 2,120 residents from overall net migration (migration within Canada and with other countries) in 1993. From 1988 to 1993, overall net migration caused the province's population to decrease by 2,648 people.

17 ECONOMY

The most important areas of New Brunswick's economy, in order from largest to smallest, are finance, insurance, and real estate; community and personal services; manufacturing; government; construction; retail trade; utilities; transportation and storage; wholesale trade; logging and forestry; mining; agriculture; and fishing and trapping.

18 INCOME

Personal income in 1993 was estimated at c$18,107 per person, 18% below the national average. In 1992, average weekly earnings amounted to c$494.39, with those employed in the goods-producing sectors averaging c$596.83 per week and service-sector employees averaging c$462.62 per week. Average family income in the province was c$39,245 in 1989.

Photo Credit: Communications NB.

The mix of French Acadian and English culture give Moncton a cosmopolitan quality.

19 INDUSTRY

Leading the manufacturing industries are food and beverages, followed by pulp and paper, sawmills, manufacturers of furniture and other wood-based industries, metal processing, transportation equipment, and processing of nonmetallic ores and primary metals. In 1993, manufacturing shipments amounted to c$5.6 billion, of which paper products accounted for 22.8%; food, 19.6%; wood, 7.9%; fabricated metal products, 3.1%; beverages, 2.5%; printing and publishing, 2%; and other areas, 42.1%.

20 LABOR

In 1993, 563,000 persons in New Brunswick were of legal working age and 332,000 were actively in the labor force, giving an overall participation rate of 59%. Employment amounted to 291,000 in 1993. The sectors with the largest numbers of employed persons were: services, 105,100; trade, 55,300; manufacturing, 36,100; transportation, communication, and utilities, 25,000; public administration, 23,300; construction, 16,000; finance, insurance, and real estate, 13,100; mining, forestry, and fishing, 13,100; and agriculture, 4,100. With some 42,000 residents unemployed in 1993, the unemployment rate stood at 12.6%.

Unionization in New Brunswick stood at 36.9% in 1992. A major confrontation between the provincial government and public service workers occurred in June 1992, when the 20,000 members of the Canadian Union of Public Employees organized a four-day strike that affected every aspect of public service in the province. The strike ended when the government obtained a back-to-work order and the two sides agreed to hold talks with a mediator present to help them reach an agreement.

21 AGRICULTURE

New Brunswick is self-sufficient in the production of forage. Its potatoes are renowned in over 25 countries; strawberries, apples, blueberries, and vegetables are produced for local consumption and for export. In 1991, there were 3,252 farms in the province, with a total area of 923,205 acres (374,222 hectares), of

which 301,079 acres (122,043 hectares) were used for growing crops. Crop receipts in 1993 amounted to c$114.9 million, with potatoes accounting for 58% of the total.

In 1993, the major crops harvested in the province were: 2,650 tons (2,405 metric tons) of rutabagas; 416,000 tons (377,495 metric tons) of hay; 13,260 hundredweight of potatoes; 2,363,000 bushels of barley; 2,047,000 bushels of oats; 175,000 bushels of wheat; 2,475,000 pounds (1,125,000 kilograms) of strawberries; 205,000 bushels of tobacco; 320,000 bushels of apples; 150,000 pints of raspberries; and 3,252,000 kilograms (7,154,000 pounds) of blueberries.

Vegetables are grown on more than 350 farms; some 35 greenhouse vegetable growers produced over 137.9 million pounds (62.7 million kilograms) of tomatoes and 35,000 dozen cucumbers in 1993. Maple syrup production in 1993 amounted to 114,000 gallons (430,700 liters), with a value of more than c$4.2 million.

22 DOMESTICATED ANIMALS

New Brunswick produces enough milk and poultry to satisfy local demand. As of 1 January 1994, New Brunswick had an estimated 22,500 dairy cows, of which 90% were Holsteins. In 1993, the province's 440 dairy farms shipped 30.9 million gallons (116.9 million liters) of milk, 4.1 million pounds (1.9 million kilograms) of butterfat, and 85,329 pounds (38,698 kilograms) of cream.

Photo Credit: Communications NB.

St. John is Canada's oldest city. Twice a day at high tide, the St. John River temporally flows upstream as water surges into the Bay of Fundy.

Poultry production in 1992 amounted to 41.6 million pounds (18.9 million kilograms), 82% chicken, 12% turkey, and 6% other fowl. In 1993, the livestock inventory also included 104,500 cattle, 80,000 hogs, 4,500 sheep, and 1,200 red deer. Total farm receipts from livestock operations in 1993 were c$147.3 million, with dairy accounting for 38%.

Apiculture (beekeeping) in 1993 consisted of 4,900 hives tended by 510 beekeepers, producing 397,000 pounds 180,078 kilograms) of honey and wax. In 1993, the fur industry produced 16,500 mink and 6,900 fox pelts, with a total value of c$539,000.

23 FISHING

More than 50 varieties of fish and shellfish are caught in New Brunswick. As of 1993, there were 8,380 anglers operating from 2,829 boats, with an additional 12,472 persons employed at fish processing plants. Total landings in 1993 amounted to 125,695 metric tons, of which pelagic species (predominantly herring) accounted for 66%; shellfish, 21%; groundfish, 4%; and others, 9%. The value of landings in 1993 exceeded c$194.4 million, with shellfish contributing c$86.7 million. Of the total shellfish value in 1993, lobster accounted for 51%. The town of Shediac is known as the "lobster capital of the world." New Brunswick's fish and shell-fish exports totaled 77,319 tons (70,162 metric tons) valued at c$337.5 million in 1993, of which 70% went to the United States.

In 1993, there were 67 fish farms (up from only 4 in 1983), producing 11,553 tons (10,484 metric tons) of fish (mostly Atlantic salmon and rainbow trout) with a value of c$92.3 million. Mussel farming also grew during the 1980s.

24 FORESTRY

Forests occupy some 15 million acres (6.1 million hectares), or 85% of the land mass. Consequently, wood and wood products are a cornerstone of the economy, with black spruce and fir the leading species. Furniture-making by Acadians became prominent during the 18th and 19th centuries from such plentiful local wood as pine, birch, maple, and butternut. Crown (provincial and federal) lands account for 48% of the province's forests, while industry owns 20% and private woodlot owners account for the remaining 32%. An annual harvest of 254.9 million cubic feet (7.1 million cubic meters) of softwood is required to meet the capacity of the forestry industry. As of 1991, there were 722 logging establishments, with 2,544 employees. In 1993, more than 300 Christmas tree growers produced 440,000 trees (with a value of c$15 million), of which 84% were exported to the United States.

Three nurseries are maintained at King-sclear, Madran, and St. Paul de Kent to produce seedlings for Crown land and some private woodlot reforestation. In 1993, some 14.6 million seedlings were shipped, reforesting about 245,580 acres (6,955 hectares) of Crown lands.

25 MINING

New Brunswickers mine silver, bismuth, cadmium, copper, gold, lead, potash, peat, tungsten, silica, salt, uranium, and zinc. The estimated value of nonfuel mineral production in 1993 was nearly c$747.9 million, with metals accounting for c$492 million of the total. New Brunswick is Canada's leading producer of zinc, bismuth, and lead. Zinc is the leading metal produced by value, representing 77% (c$379.9 million) of the total value of provincial metal production in 1993. New Brunswick ranks second in the nation in production of antimony, peat, and silver. Much of the metals mining occurs in the counties of Restigouche, Northumberland, and Gloucester. Peat moss is mined from the Acadian Peninsula.

Mineral production in 1993 included 680 million pounds (308.6 million kilograms) of zinc, 161 million pounds (73.1 million kilograms) of lead, 23.1 million pounds (10.5 million kilograms) of copper, 491,956.5 pounds (223,150 kilograms) of silver, 344,969 pounds (156,477 kilograms) of bismuth, 257,938 pounds (117,000 kilograms) of cadmium, 7.4 million tons (6.7 million metric tons) of sand and gravel, 3 million tons (2.7 million metric tons) of dimension stone, 302,495 tons (274,496 metric tons) of peat, and 112,552 tons (102,134 metric tons) of sulfur.

26 ENERGY AND POWER

The first coal mined in North America was taken in 1639 from the shores of Grand Lake, and coal is still mined near Minto. Production in 1993 was 429,780 tons (390,000 metric tons), with an estimated value of c$33.8 million. Natural gas, oil, oil shale, and albertite (a rare solid hydrocarbon) are found in southeast New Brunswick near Hillsborough. Crude oil and natural gas production began at Stoney Creek near Moncton in the early 1900s, but production ceased in 1991.

In 1992, the total electricity supply amounted to 20 billion kilowatt hours, of which 80% was produced within New Brunswick. Of the total generation of 16 billion kilowatt hours in 1992, 19% was produced by hydroelectricity and the remainder by thermal plants. The remaining 4 billion kilowatt hours was largely furnished by Québec. Electricity usage in 1992 amounted to 13.9 billion kilowatt hours; industries accounted for 41% of electrical use; residences, 34%; businesses, 17%; and others, 8%. In 1992, New Brunswick delivered 4.3 billion kilowatt hours to other provinces and exported 1.8 billion kilowatt hours to the United States.

27 COMMERCE

In 1992, retail trade in New Brunswick totaled c$4.8 billion (2.6% of the nation's total), or about c$6,358 per person. Leading retail areas by sales in 1992 included supermarkets and grocery stores, c$1.3 billion; motor vehicle and recreational vehicle dealers, c$1.1 billion; general merchandise stores, c$552.9 million; gasoline service stations, c$378.5; and pharmacies and drugstores, c$285.8 million.

28 PUBLIC FINANCE

The fiscal year runs from 1 April to 31 March. For fiscal year 1992/93, total revenues were c$4.2 billion; expenditures totaled c$4.3 billion. The largest expenditure areas were health, education, interest on debt, municipal affairs, income assistance, economic development, central government, and transportation.

29 TAXATION

The basic personal income tax rate in 1994 was 64%, with high income surtaxes of 8%. The retail sales tax was 11%. Major consumption taxes were levied on gasoline and tobacco. In 1991, the average family in New Brunswick had a cash income of c$45,000 and paid c$18,769 in taxes.

Corporate income tax rates in 1993 were as follows: small business rate, 9%; general business rate, 17%; and capital tax rate, 3%.

30 HEALTH

In 1992 there were 9,389 live births in New Brunswick, for a rate of 12.5 per 1,000 residents. The death rate in 1992 was 7.5 per 1,000 residents, with 5,609 deaths occurring that year. Therapeutic abortions in New Brunswick numbered 542 in 1990, for a rate of 3.1 per 1,000 females aged 15–44 and a ratio of 5.5 per 100 live births. Reported cases of selected diseases in 1990 included salmonellosis, 401; campylobacteriosis, 382; chicken pox, 170; giardiasis, 134; and gonococcal infections, 62. There were 10 new AIDS cases reported in 1990; in 1991, the total number of cases was 43.

As of 1993, New Brunswick had 36 hospitals and health centers. In the late 1980s, there were 32 general hospitals with 4,350 beds, and 3 pediatric, psychiatric, rehabilitation, and extended health care hospitals with 818 beds.

31 HOUSING

Housing starts in 1993 totaled 3,693, while completions amounted to 3,631. The value of all residential construction in 1993 amounted to c$655.8 million, up from c$596.1 million in 1991 but down from c$751 million in 1989.

In 1990, the average resale value of a home in Saint John was c$78,041. The average rent for a two-bedroom apartment in Saint John in 1990 was c$414, while the metropolitan area apartment vacancy rate was 3.3%.

32 EDUCATION

Public education classes and services in New Brunswick, Canada's only officially bilingual province, are delivered in both English and French. As of 1993/94, there were 12 anglophone (English-language) school districts (with an enrollment of 92,598 students), and 6 francophone (French-language) districts (with 46,088 students), with a total provincial enrollment of 138,686 students in 407 schools. More than 98% of all students are enrolled in public schools, with the remainder in private or federal schools. In 1992/93, total educational staff numbered 8,665, of which 7,135 were teachers. Total provincial expenditures for public school education exceeded c$4 billion in 1992/93 (c$4,935 per pupil), which was 16.9% of total government expenditures in the province.

The province's universities and their full-time enrollments are as follows: the University of Moncton, 4,834 students; the University of New Brunswick (Fredericton), 8,502; St. Thomas University (Fredericton), 1,358; and Mount Allison University (Sackville), 1,879. In 1990/91, full-time university enrollment was 16,895 (16,031 undergraduate, 864 graduate), while part-time enrollment was 5,500 (4,846 undergraduate, 654 graduate). The New Brunswick College of Craft and Design at Fredericton is the only postsecondary institute of its kind in Canada. Enrollment in career programs in postsecondary community colleges in 1990/91 was 2,664.

33 ARTS

In 1990/91, New Brunswick's five performing arts companies gave 502 performances before a total attendance of 204,103. The Capitol Theatre in Moncton features plays, musicals, and dance troupes.

34 LIBRARIES AND MUSEUMS

Public libraries in New Brunswick include the Albert-Westmoreland-Kent Library Region, the York Regional Library, the Chaleur Library Region, the Saint John Library Region, and the BibliothÈque Regionale du Haut-Saint-Jean. The University of New Brunswick's libraries in

Fredericton are the province's main academic libraries. The Owens Art Gallery in Sackville opened in 1895, making it the oldest university art gallery in Canada. Moncton has the Lutz Mountain Heritage Museum, the Moncton Museum, and the Acadian Museum on the campus of the Université de Moncton.

35 COMMUNICATIONS

As of 1994, New Brunswick had 13 AM and 11 FM radio stations, and 3 television stations. Including relay transmitters, the province has 23 AM (17 English, 6 French) and 31 FM (20 English, 11 French) radio stations.

36 PRESS

Daily newspapers in New Brunswick include the *Telegraph Journal/Evening Times Globe* (Saint John), the *Daily Gleaner* (Fredericton), *The Times-Transcript* (Moncton), and the French-language *L'Acadie Nouvelle* (Caraquet).

37 TOURISM, TRAVEL, AND RECREATION

Tourism is a vital part of the province's economy. In 1991, nearly 1.5 million people visited New Brunswick's tourist attractions, including its two national parks and numerous provincial parks. Fredericton annually hosts the Harvest Jazz and Blues Festival; Canada's Irish Festival is held in Miramichi. The annual Chocolate Festival in Saint Stephen is a tribute to the Ganong candy factory there, where the first chocolate bars were developed in 1910.

38 SPORTS

Professional American Hockey League (AHL) hockey is played in Moncton; local baseball, soccer, and football matches are also popular spectator sports. Sailing, kayaking, canoeing, hiking, cycling, golf, and bird-watching are popular outdoor activities.

39 FAMOUS NEW BRUNSWICKERS

Andrew Bonar-Law (1858–1923), prime minister of Great Britain from 1922–23, was born in Rexton and was the United Kingdom's only prime minister born outside the British Isles. Canadian prime minister Richard Bennett (1870–1947) was born in Hopewell.

Film mogul Louis B. Mayer (b.Russia, 1885–1957) grew up in Saint John. Actors Walter Pidgeon (1897–1984) and Donald Sutherland (b.1935) also came from Saint John.

Noted authors include francophone (French-language) novelist Antonine Maillet (b.1929), and anglophone (English-language) playwright Sharon Pollock (b.1936).

James H. Ganong (1841–88) operated a growing confectionery in Saint Stephen; in 1910, the family business invented the modern chocolate bar.

40 BIBLIOGRAPHY

Bumsted, J. M. *The Peoples of Canada*. New York: Oxford University Press, 1992.

Campbell, Kumari. *New Brunswick*. Minneapolis: Lerner Publications, 1996.

Gann, Marjorie. *Discover Canada: New Brunswick*. Toronto: Grolier, 1995.

LeVert, Suzanne. *Let's Discover Canada: New Brunswick*. New York: Chelsea House, 1992.

Sorensen, Lynda. *Canada: Provinces and Territories*. Vero Beach, Fla.: Rourke Book Co., 1995.

Wansborough, M. B. *Great Canadian Lives*. New York: Doubleday, 1986.

Weihs, Jean. *Facts about Canada, Its Provinces and Territories*. New York: H. W. Wilson, 1995.

NEWFOUNDLAND AND LABRADOR

ORIGIN OF PROVINCE NAME: Italian seafarer Giovanni Caboto (John Cabot) landed on the island portion of the province on 24 June 1497, on the feast of St. John the Baptist. Cabot called the newfound land "St. John's Isle" in honor of the saint, but the contraction of "a newfound land" was quickly coined and became the actual name. The name of the mainland portion is believed to come from Portuguese explorer Gaspar Corte-Real who named the area "Terra del Lavrador," or land of the farmer. Officially called "Newfoundland and Labrador," but commonly known simply as Newfoundland.

NICKNAME: The Rock.

CAPITAL: St. John's.

ENTERED CONFEDERATION: 31 March 1949.

SONG: "Ode to Newfoundland."

MOTTO: *QuÊrite prime regnum Dei* (Seek ye first the Kingdom of God). Coat of Arms: In the center, the provincial shield of arms has a white cross on a red background, with two golden lions representing England and two white unicorns representing Scotland. Above the shield is an elk. Supporting the shield on either side is an Aboriginal Canadian holding a bow. Beneath the shield the provincial motto appears on a scroll, with a grassy mound.

FLAG: The flag, adopted in 1980 and based on Great Britain's Union Jack, has primary colors of red, gold, and blue set against a white background that represents snow and ice. The blue section on the left side stands for Newfoundland's Commonwealth heritage, while the red and gold section on the right side represents the hopes for the future with the arrow pointing the way.

FLORAL EMBLEM: Pitcher plant.

TARTAN: Dark green, gold, white, brown, and red on a medium green background.

PROVINCIAL BIRD: Atlantic puffin.

TREE: Black spruce.

GEMSTONE: Labradorite.

TIME: 8:30 AM NST = noon GMT; 8 AM AST = noon GMT.

1 LOCATION AND SIZE

Nestled into the northeast corner of North America, facing the North Atlantic, is Newfoundland, Canada's most easterly province. Lying between the 46th and 61st parallels, the province consists of two distinct geographical entities: Newfoundland and Labrador.

The island of Newfoundland, which forms the southern and eastern portion of the province, is a large triangular-shaped area of about 43,000 square miles (112,000 square kilometers), while the province's total area is 156,648 square miles (405,720 square kilometers). Located at the mouth of the St. Lawrence River, the island is about halfway between the center of North America and the coast of western Europe. The island of Newfoundland is separated from the Canadian mainland by the Strait of Belle Isle in the north and by the wider Cabot Strait in the south. The mainland, Labrador, is bordered by northeastern Quebec. Approximately two and one-half times as large as the island, it remains a vast, unspoiled wilderness.

2 TOPOGRAPHY

The province's coastline, stretching over more than 10,500 miles (17,000 kilometers), is varied and scenic with its bold headlands, deep fjords (narrow water passages with steep shores on either side), and countless small coves and offshore islands. The interiors of both Labrador and Newfoundland have a rolling, rugged topography, deeply etched by glacial activity and broken by lakes and swift-flowing rivers. Northern Labrador is marked by the spectacular Torngat Mountains, which rise abruptly from the sea to heights of up to 5,420 feet (1,652 meters).

3 CLIMATE

Newfoundland's climate can best be described as moderate and maritime. The island enjoys winters that are surprisingly

Newfoundland & Labrador Population Profile

Estimated 1996 population:		573,300
Population change, 1981–91:		0.001%
Population by ethnic origin:		
British origins:		77.9%
English:		66.6%
Irish:		9.9%
Scottish:		1.6%
Multiple origins:		18.4%
French:		1.7%
Aboriginal:		0.9%
German:		0.2%
Chinese:		0.1%
East Indian:		0.1%
Dutch:		0.1%
Other single origins:		0.6%
Urban/Rural populations:		
Urban:	304,451	53.6%
Rural:	264,023	46.4%

Population by Age Group

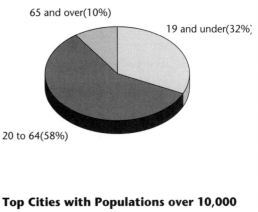

65 and over(10%)

19 and under(32%)

20 to 64(58%)

Top Cities with Populations over 10,000

City	Population	% Change 1986–91
St. John's	95,770	-0.5
Mount Pearl	23,689	16.7
Corner Brook	22,410	-1.4
Conception Bay South	17,590	13.3
Grand Falls-Windsor	14,693	0.2
Gander	10,339	1.3

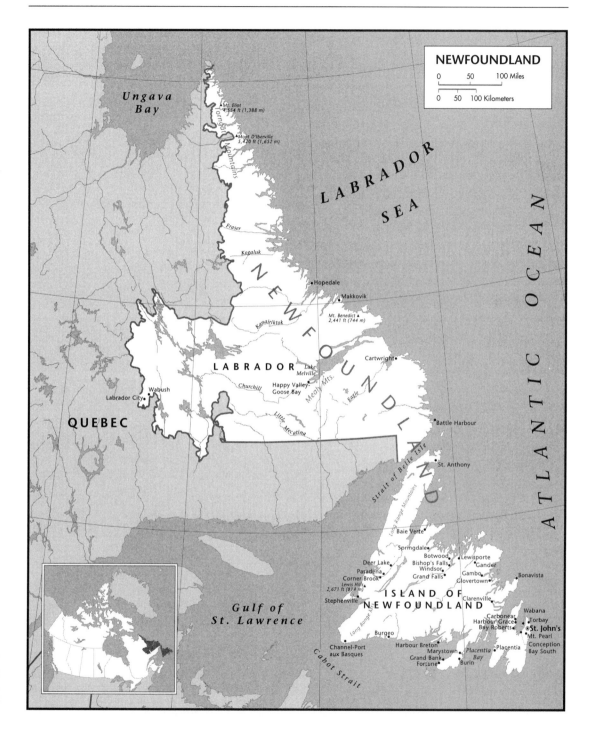

mild by Canadian standards, though with a high rate of precipitation. Labrador, by comparison, has the cold winters and brief summers characteristic of the Canadian mid-North. St. John's is the windiest and foggiest city in Canada, while Churchill Falls receives the most snowfall. Average temperature ranges for St. John's are 19 to 31°F (-7.5 to -0.6°C) in February and 52 to 69°F (11 to 20.5°C) in July, while temperature ranges in Happy Valley-Goose Bay are -8 to 10°F (-22.4 to -12.3) in February and 50 to 70°F (9.8 to 21.1°C) in July. The warmest recorded temperature in Newfoundland was 107°F (41.7°C) on 11 August 1914 at Northwest River, and the coldest was -60°F (-51.1°C) on 17 February 1973 at Esker. The northern lights, or *aurora borealis*, flicker over Labrador.

4 PLANTS AND ANIMALS

Some 22 species of whales, dolphins, and porpoises are found along the coastline—prominent species include humpback, fin, sperm, and minke whales; harbor porpoise; and saddleback dolphin. Labrador has the largest caribou herd in the world.

5 ENVIRONMENTAL PROTECTION

As in the other maritime provinces, drifting air pollution from the industrial areas of central Canada and New England are a local environmental concern. The province itself annually releases about 272,228 tons (269,000 metric tons) of nitrogen dioxide and carbon monoxide (gases that cause smog), 87,058 tons (79,000 metric tons) of sulfur dioxide and nitrogen oxide compounds (gases that produce acid rain), and the equivalent of 2,321,528 tons (2,294,000 metric tons) of carbon dioxide. Newfoundland generates about 0.4% of Canada's annual hazardous waste, and yearly solid waste production amounts to about 0.502 tons (0.496 metric tons) per resident. Newfoundland has 240 landfills, 1 hazardous waste site, and 55 municipal incinerators. Daily water usage is about 16.32 cubic feet (0.457 cubic meters) per capita (per person); 62% of water withdrawals are for residential households.

6 POPULATION

The pattern of settlement in Newfoundland was mainly determined by the fishing industry, and this population distribution has persisted to today. The Avalone Peninsula and northeastern Newfoundland are the traditional bases for the fisheries and continue to be the most heavily populated areas. St. John's, the historic commercial center and capital of the island, is the province's largest city, with a metropolitan area population of 171,859 in 1991 (19th largest in the nation). Other major centers are Grand Falls, Windsor, and Corner Brook. The smaller communities—called outports—remain a major element in Newfoundland society in spite of their size. The twin towns of Labrador City and Wabush, which together form the largest urban community of Labrador, are based on the iron ore mining industries of the area.

7 ETHNIC GROUPS

The province's estimated 1996 population of 573,300 is largely descended from settlers from southwestern England and southern Ireland, who immigrated to

Newfoundland in the late 1700s and early 1800s. In the early 1800s, disease and conflicts with settlers reduced the Beothuk Indians to extinction. There are still a relatively large number of Inuit concentrated in the coastal communities of northern Labrador.

8 LANGUAGES

In 1991, 98.6% of all residents reported English as their native language (the highest such rate among the provinces), with 0.5% claiming French as their mother tongue. The remaining 0.9% consisted largely of the Inuktitut speakers of northern Labrador.

Several distinctly local dialects of English have developed, due in part to the isolation of the province. The mixture of Irish, Dorset, and Devonshire dialects present in Newfoundland has been compared to the speech typical of early 19th century Great Britain. The local dialect of St. John's is particularly noted for its Irish tone.

9 RELIGIONS

In 1991, 61% of the population, or about 346,800 people, was Protestant, including 148,900 Anglicans, 98,300 members of the United Church of Canada, 40,400 Pentecostals, 2,300 Presbyterians, 1,100 Baptists, and less than 600 Lutherans. The province also had about 210,300 Roman Catholics (37% of the population), and less than 600 people each of the following: people of Eastern Orthodox faith, Moslems, and Hindus. About 11,400 people had no religious affiliation in 1991.

10 TRANSPORTATION

A segment of the Trans-Canada Highway runs from Channel-Port aux Basques in the west to St. John's in the east, a distance of 562 miles (905 kilometers). The partially-paved Route 389 connects Labrador City and Wabash to Baie Comeau, Québec. The 327-mile (526-kilometer) Trans-Labrador Highway (Route 500) is a seasonal gravel road linking Labrador City and Happy Valley-Goose Bay. In 1990, Newfoundland had 305,851 registered motor vehicles, consisting of 200,374 passenger cars; 90,394 trucks, truck tractors, and buses; 9,134 motorcycles and mopeds; and 5,949 other vehicles.

In 1991, Newfoundland's ports handled 11.4 million tons (10.3 million metric tons) of cargo; the port at St. John's alone handled 1,043,594 tons (947,000 metric tons) of cargo that year. Ferry service links the Newfoundland cities of Argentia and Port aux Basques to North Sydney, Nova Scotia, and St. Barbe to Blanc Sablon, Québec. Ferries also operate between Newfoundland and Labrador, connecting Lewisporte and St. Anthony to Red Bay, Goose Bay, and Nain.

Urban transit in 1991 consisted of 74 buses which provided over 3.6 million passenger trips of more than 1.6 million miles (2.6 million kilometers). Gander International Airport is a frequent layover for long transcontinental flights. Rail service in the province was discontinued in the late 1980s.

11 HISTORY

The central region of the island of Newfoundland was once the home of the now extinct Beothuk Indians. The first Europeans to visit Newfoundland were Norsemen, who arrived in the late 10th century. (The Norse settlement at l'Anse aux Meadows was the world's first cultural discovery location to receive recognition as a UNESCO [United Nations Educational, Scientific, and Cultural Organization] World Heritage Site.) Other early visitors, the Basques, Portuguese, Spanish, British, and French, staged fishing expeditions in the 16th century and probably even earlier.

European Exploration and Settlement

In 1497, the Italian seafarer Giovanni Caboto (John Cabot) went to investigate what lay in the northern section of the western Atlantic. He landed on the island on 24 June 1497, the feast of St. John the Baptist. Cabot called the new land "St. John's Isle" in honor of the saint, and claimed it for King Henry VII of England, his patron and employer.

Anglo-French colonial warfare shaped the history of Newfoundland during the 1600s and 1700s. France, already well-established on the mainland of eastern Canada, began to make claims to parts of Newfoundland. In 1662, France established a fort and colony at Placentia, despite protests from British merchants and fishermen. The Treaty of Utrecht in 1713 ended a long period of raids and skirmishes by both nations, and reconfirmed British sovereignty over Newfoundland and the fishing banks.

The people of Newfoundland were granted the right to vote for an elected assembly in 1832 and, after much debate, Newfoundland postponed the decision on whether to join the Dominion of Canada.

Early 20th Century

During World War I (1914–18), Canada lost more than 68,000 soldiers. Veterans returning to Newfoundland faced a bleak future of scarce low-paying jobs, while tariffs on imports kept prices for consumer goods high. During the 1920s, however, grain prices recovered and Canada experienced a period of rapid growth in industry. Transportation improvements—railways and roads—enabled businesses to flourish. Automobiles, telephones, electrical appliances, and other consumer goods became widely available.

As in the United States, all of Canada suffered during the Great Depression. In addition to the problems with grain prices during the early 1920s, droughts and frequent crop failures devastated the national economy, which still relied heavily on agriculture. By 1932, Newfoundland's economy had completely collapsed, which led to a suspension of the constitution and the interim return of power to the British colonial office. Social welfare programs rapidly expanded during the 1930s, with much of the burden placed on the provincial and municipal governments.

1940s–1960s

Following World War II (1939–45), the question of Newfoundland's future status became an issue once again, with the campaign to join Canada led by J. R. Small-

Photo Credit: Government of Newfoundland and Labrador.

Glacial activity in Newfoundland created a rugged topography of deep fjords and rolling hills.

wood. In 1948, a public referendum was held on the subject, and Newfoundlanders voted in favor of joining the Canadian confederation. Newfoundland became Canada's newest province on 31 March 1949.

At the same time, consumer spending and immigration to Canada rapidly increased. Urbanization spread quickly by means of the National Housing Act, which made home ownership more easily available. Unemployment insurance and other social welfare programs were also created following the war. Under the leadership of Prime Minister Louis St. Laurent, old age pensions were increased in 1951 and a national hospital insurance plan was introduced in 1957.

During the 1950s and 1960s, the monitoring of northern Canadian airspace served a vital role in the defense of North America against a possible nuclear attack from the Soviet Union. But when ballistic missiles (which are launched in an arc toward their targets from great distances) replaced bombers as the means of delivering nuclear warheads, this strategy became obsolete.

1980s and 1990s

Newfoundland and the federal government disagreed on the development and revenue-sharing aspects of the vast Hibernia offshore oil and natural gas field during the early 1980s.

Canada's unity as a confederation has often been widely questioned. Most recently, the popular defeat of both the Meech Lake Accord of 1987 and the Charlottetown Accord of 1992 has failed to solve the issue of Québec's role in Canada. If Québec does eventually secede from Canada, the fate of the traditionally poorer maritime provinces would be uncertain. One or more might explore the possibility of admission to the United States.

The waters off the coast of Newfoundland became the scene of a tense confrontation on 9 March 1995 when Canadian ships pursued and seized the Spanish fishing trawler *Estai* in international waters after firing warning shots across its bow. Canadian authorities believed the vessel was engaged in irresponsible activities in its harvesting of turbot (a large food fish). As a result, both Canada and Spain sent warships to the area as tensions grew; Spain accused Canada of piracy since the *Estai* was seized in international waters. In April 1995, the European Union and Canada agreed to settle their differences by temporarily establishing a new higher turbot quota for European fishing vessels. The Canadian government also agreed to repeal the legislation that allows it to seize vessels in international waters.

12 PROVINCIAL GOVERNMENT

The structure of the provincial government reflects that of the federal government. For example, the provincial premier, as the majority party leader of the legisla-

ture, functions much like the Canadian prime minister. Provincial legislators, like their federal counterparts in Parliament, are elected to represent a constitutional jurisdiction and pass legislation. They do so as members of the 52-seat House of Assembly. A provincial lieutenant-governor approves laws passed by the legislature, much like the Governor General at the federal level. There is no provincial equivalent, however, to the federal Senate.

13 POLITICAL PARTIES

Local politics in Newfoundland from 1824 to the early 1900s was largely oriented around religious factions. From 1908 to 1932, the Newfoundland Fishermen's Protective Union (NFPU) was a dominant force in local politics. The Confederation Association, which played an instrumental role in Newfoundland's entry into the confederation in 1949, became the province's Liberal Party, while many who had opposed confederation allied themselves with the Progressive Conservative Party. The Liberal Party controlled provincial politics from the late 1940s to the late 1960s.

The most recent general election was held on 3 May 1993. Legislative seats in 1994 were held by 35 Liberals, 16 Progressive Conservatives, and 1 New Democrat.

Premiers of Newfoundland and Labrador

Term	Premier	Party
1949–72	Joseph Roberts Smallwood	Liberal
1972–79	Frank Duff Moores	Conservative
1979–89	Alfred Brian Peckford	Conservative
1989	Thomas Gerard Rideout	Conservative
1989–	Clyde Kirby Wells	Liberal

14 LOCAL GOVERNMENT

The Department of Municipal and Provincial Affairs Act grants the provincial government political power over the actions of the municipalities, except for the cities of St. John's, Corner Brook, and Mount Pearl. Although towns and communities have a large degree of freedom in financial affairs, the provincial government routinely inspects municipal finances. The incorporated cities, towns, and municipalities have the power to collect taxes; provide basic public services, fire protection, and recreational services; and make bylaws. Elections for city and town councils occur every four years, while community councils are elected every other year. Newfoundland has 3 city governments, 177 town governments, and 136 community governments.

15 JUDICIAL SYSTEM

North America's first court of justice was established in Trinity in 1615. The Canadian Constitution grants provincial jurisdiction over the administration of justice, and allows each province to organize its own court system and police forces. The federal government has exclusive domain over cases involving trade and commerce, banking, bankruptcy, and criminal law. The Federal Court of Canada has both trial and appellate divisions for federal cases. The 9-judge Supreme Court of Canada is an appellate court that determines the constitutionality of both federal and provincial statutes. The Tax Court of Canada hears appeals of taxpayers against assessments by Revenue Canada.

In 1990, there were no homicides in Newfoundland; typically fewer than eight homicides are committed in the province during any given year, which would give Newfoundland a rate of less than one homicide per 100,000 persons. Breaking and entering offenses in 1989 numbered 274 per 100,000 people for businesses and 321 per 100,000 people for residences.

16 MIGRATION

In 1991, Newfoundland lost 1,961 residents from migration between provinces (10,767 entered the province and 12,728 left for other provinces). While Ontario was the province of destination for 47% of residents leaving Newfoundland to live in some other province in 1991, it was the province of origin for 59% of all incoming internal migration into Newfoundland that year.

17 ECONOMY

Since its first settlement, Newfoundland and Labrador has been highly dependent on its resource sector, especially fisheries. Coastal towns provided support for the vessels fishing the Grand Banks. The main industries today are mining, manufacturing, fishing, pulp and paper, and hydroelectricity. Other natural resources important to the local economy include iron ore from Labrador and the development of substantial offshore oil and natural gas reserves.

18 INCOME

The average family income in the province was c$38,141 in 1989. As of December

1992, average weekly earnings in the province amounted to c$520.16.

19 INDUSTRY

In addition to fish products and pulp and paper products, companies in the province also manufacture such items as boats, lumber, chemical and oil-based products, food and beverages, clothing, and footwear. In total, the province shipped about c$1.4 billion in manufactured products in 1992.

20 LABOR

As of 1993, Newfoundland had the lowest labor force participation rate of the population aged 15 and older—48.3%. In 1990 total provincial employment was around 201,000, of which services accounted for 70,000; trade, 38,000; manufacturing, 22,000; government, 19,000; primary industry, 18,000; utilities, 17,000; construction, 10,000; and finance, 6,000.

Of the four maritime provinces, Newfoundland has been the hardest hit by recent recessions and declines in the resource sectors. The province saw the average unemployment rate for 1992 jump from 18.4% in 1991 to 20.2% in 1992. This figure, however, does not include anglers and fish plant workers receiving compensation under an aid package for the northern cod fisheries, since they do not meet the federal government's definition of unemployed.

Newfoundland had the highest unionization rate among the maritime provinces in 1992 at 55.1%, compared to the national average of 37.4%. The New-

foundland Association of Public Employees is the province's largest union.

21 AGRICULTURE

Newfoundland's agriculture industry is small compared with other Canadian provinces. The output of the agriculture industry is mainly for local consumption, although some agricultural products such as blueberries are sold to markets outside the province. In 1991, Newfoundland had 2 grain farms, 32 miscellaneous field crop farms, 112 fruits and vegetables farms, and 126 specialty product farms.

22 DOMESTICATED ANIMALS

One of the earlier attempts at animal breeding in the province is the famous web-footed Newfoundland dog, which is descended from the crossing of the American black wolf (tamed by the Native people) with the great bear dogs brought over by the Vikings. Another dog breed, the Labrador Retriever, was originally bred in Labrador to retrieve waterfowl for hunters and fish for anglers.

Meat and dairy production is for local consumption. In 1991, Newfoundland had 72 dairy farms, 48 cattle farms, 47 poultry farms, 14 hog farms, and 19 livestock combination farms. Newfoundland exports a small quantity of furs, but commercial seal hunts are no longer held.

23 FISHING

The province was initially settled because of its rich fishing grounds on the "nose" and "tail" of the Grand Banks. The mainstay of the province's fishing industry has been groundfish (primarily cod). Other

A humpback whale "breaches"—drives its entire body out of the water—in Notre Dame Bay off the north coast of the island of Newfoundland.

important catches are flounder, redfish, capelin, shrimp, and crab. As of 1991, Newfoundland had 24,409 registered commercial fishers.

Protection of the rich fishery resources off the coast of Newfoundland has been an ongoing concern and one that has become more serious in recent years. In 1977, the Canadian government extended its fishery jurisdiction to 200 miles (125 kilometers) around the coast of the province in an attempt to gain better control of fishing activity. This move produced positive results in the 1980s, but in 1989 scientific studies revealed that some of the Atlantic's key groundfish stocks were in severe decline. Since that period, there have been several reductions in fishing quotas.

24 FORESTRY

Much of the island and southern and central Labrador is covered by a thick boreal forest of black spruce and balsam fir mixed with birch, tamarack, and balsam poplar. Northern Labrador is largely devoid of forest. The third largest traditional goods-producing industry is the newsprint industry. This industry consists primarily of three pulp and paper mills located in Corner Brook, Grand Falls, and Stephenville, which have undergone extensive modernization over the past decade.

25 MINING

The mining industry ships mineral products valued at approximately c$700 million a year, mostly iron ore from Labrador. Other minerals mined in the province are gold, asbestos, limestone, and gypsum. In 1992, the total value of mineral production was c$735.3 million, of which metals accounted for 94.9%; structural minerals, 4%; and nonmetals, 1.1%.

26 ENERGY AND POWER

Recently, the discovery of offshore oil and gas reserves has added a new dimension to the marine resources of the province. The Hibernia discovery in 1979 was Newfoundland's first significant oil find; reserves are estimated at 615 million barrels. Currently under way, Hibernia is the largest construction project in North America.

The province's largest utility industry is electric power. The largest hydroelectric facility is located in Churchill Falls, Labrador, with a total installed capacity of 5,403 megawatts. In 1991, electricity generated totaled 36.9 billion kilowatt hours and consumption within the province amounted to 9.5 billion kilowatt hours.

27 COMMERCE

Newfoundland's service sector has experienced substantial growth over the years. In 1992, the service sector accounted for over two-thirds of provincial gross domestic product (GDP).

28 PUBLIC FINANCE

The fiscal year runs from 1 April to 31 March. For fiscal year 1992/93, total revenues were c$3.4 billion; expenditures totaled c$3.5 billion. The largest expenditure areas were health, education, debt charges and other financial expenses, social welfare, general government, and transportation and communication.

29 TAXATION

The basic personal income tax rate in 1993 was 69%. The retail sales tax was 12%. Major consumption taxes were levied on gasoline and tobacco. In 1991, the average family in Newfoundland had a cash income of c$44,500 and paid c$16,598 in taxes.

Corporate income tax rates in 1993 were as follows: small business rate, 5%; manufacturing and processing corporate rate, 7.5%; general business rate, 16%; and capital tax rate, 3%.

30 HEALTH

In 1992 there were 6,918 live births in Newfoundland, for a rate of 11.9 per 1,000 residents (lowest among the provinces). The death rate in 1992 was 6.5 per 1,000 residents, with 3,798 deaths occurring that year. Therapeutic abortions in Newfoundland numbered 462 in 1990, for a rate of 3.2 per 1,000 females aged 15–44 and a ratio of 6.1 per 100 live births. Reported cases of selected diseases in 1990 included chicken pox, 1,338; campylobacteriosis, 130; salmonellosis, 127; gonococcal infections, 49; and giardiasis, 46. There were 6 new AIDS cases reported in 1990; in 1991, the total number of cases was 21.

As of 1993, Newfoundland had 38 hospitals and health centers. In the late 1980s, there were 31 general hospitals with 2,864 beds, and 11 pediatric, psychiatric, rehabilitation, and extended health care hospitals with 756 beds.

31 HOUSING

In 1990, the average resale value of a home in St. John's was c$88,939. The average rent for a two-bedroom apartment in St. John's in 1990 was c$544, while the metropolitan area apartment vacancy rate was 1.6%.

32 EDUCATION

In 1990/91, Newfoundland had 127,400 students enrolled in elementary and secondary schools throughout the province, down from 142,757 in 1985/86.

The Memorial University of Newfoundland at St. John's, founded in 1925, is the province's only university. In 1990/91, full-time university enrollment was 12,534 (11,769 undergraduate, 765 graduate), while part-time enrollment was 4,607 (4,057 undergraduate, 550 graduate). Enrollment in career programs in postsecondary community colleges in 1990/91 was 3,666.

33 ARTS

In 1990/91, Newfoundland's six performing arts companies gave 270 performances before a total attendance of 53,652. Several craft studios such as the Central Newfoundland Visual Arts Society in Grand Falls-Windsor exhibit local art work, which includes pottery, quilting, weaving, paintings, and photography.

34 LIBRARIES AND MUSEUMS

Museums in St. John's include the Provincial Museum, the Newfoundland and Labrador Museum of Transportation, the Royal Newfoundland Constabulary Museum, and the Memorial University Art Gallery. Other museums in Newfoundland include the regional museum in Grand Falls-Windsor and more than 40 other community museums and historic houses and sites.

35 COMMUNICATIONS

As of 1994, Newfoundland had 18 AM and 5 FM radio stations, and 4 television stations.

36 PRESS

Newfoundland has two daily newspapers: the *Evening Telegram* (St. John's) and *The Western Star* (Corner Brook).

37 TOURISM, TRAVEL, AND RECREATION

In recent years, Newfoundland's efforts to develop a solid tourism industry have increased. The province's rich cultural and historical heritage and unique character are considered to be major selling features to other Canadians and travelers from around the world. It is estimated that between 265,000 and 300,000 people visit the province each year, spending an estimated c$400 million.

38 SPORTS

Regattas are commonly held throughout the province, including the Royal St. John's Regatta, North America's oldest continuously held sporting event. The World Women's Fast Pitch Softball Tournament was held in St. John's in 1994.

39 FAMOUS NEWFOUNDLANDERS

Noted poet Edwin J. Pratt (1883–1964) was a native of Western Bay. Other important writers from the province include Cassie Brown (1919–86), born in Rose Blanche; Percy Janes (b.1922), from St. John's; and Kevin Major (b.1949), born in Stephenville.

Born in Bishop's Falls, Alex Faulkner (b.1935) was the first Newfoundlander to play in the National Hockey League (NHL).

40 BIBLIOGRAPHY

Bumsted, J. M. *The Peoples of Canada*. New York: Oxford University Press, 1992.

Jackson, Lawrence. *Newfoundland and Labrador*. Minneapolis: Lerner Publications, 1995.

LeVert, Suzanne. *Let's Discover Canada: Newfoundland*. New York: Chelsea House, 1992.

Sorensen, Lynda. *Canada: Provinces and Territories*. Vero Beach, Fla.: Rourke Book Co., 1995.

Wansborough, M. B. *Great Canadian Lives*. New York: Doubleday, 1986.

Weihs, Jean. *Facts about Canada, Its Provinces and Territories*. New York: H. W. Wilson, 1995.

White, Marian Frances. *Discover Canada: Newfoundland and Labrador*. Toronto: Grolier, 1994.

THE NORTHWEST TERRITORIES

ORIGIN OF NAME: The name "the North-Western Territories," initially assigned by the British government, once referred to all the lands held by the Hudson's Bay Company.

CAPITAL: Yellowknife.

NICKNAME: Canada's Last Frontier, Land of the Polar Bear, or North of Sixty.

ENTERED CONFEDERATION: 15 July 1870; reorganized into current form 1 September 1905.

MOTTO: The New North (unofficial).

COAT OF ARMS: The crest consists of two golden narwhals (representing marine life) on either side of a compass rose, which symbolizes the magnetic north pole. The white upper portion of the shield represents the polar ice pack and is crossed by a wavy blue band symbolic of the Northwest Passage. The wavy diagonal line symbolizing the treeline separates the red (the tundra of the north) from the green (the forested lands of the south). The historical economic resources of the land—mineral wealth and the fur industry—are represented respectively by gold bricks in the green portion and the head of a white fox in the red area.

FLAG: The territorial shield of arms centered on a white field, with two vertical blue panels on either side. The white symbolizes the snow and ice of the winter, while the blue represents the territory's lakes and waters.

FLORAL EMBLEM: Mountain avens.

TARTAN: The official tartan of the Northwest Territories is a registered design in shades of red, green, yellow, and blue.

TERRITORIAL BIRD: Gyrfalcon.

TREE: Jack pine.

MINERAL: Gold.

TIME: 8 AM AST = noon GMT; 7 AM EST = noon GMT; 6 AM CST = noon GMT; 5 AM MST = noon GMT.

1 LOCATION AND SIZE

At some time in its history, the Northwest Territories (NWT) has included all of Alberta, Saskatchewan, and the Yukon, and most of Manitoba, Ontario, and Québec. Today, the Northwest Territories remains the largest political subdivision in Canada, with 34.1% of the total area of the country. The NWT has a total area of 1,304,903 square miles (3,376,689 square kilometers), larger than the combined area of the states of Texas, Alaska, California, and New Mexico.

The Northwest Territories includes all of Canada north of the 60th parallel, except the Yukon and portions of Québec and Newfoundland. The NWT is bordered on the northwest and north by the Arctic Ocean and polar ice; on the northeast and east by Baffin Bay and Davis Strait; on the southeast by Hudson Strait and Hudson Bay; on the south by Manitoba, Saskatchewan, Alberta, and British Columbia; and on the west by the Yukon Territory. From the 60th parallel, the NWT stretches 2,212 miles (3,560 kilometers) to the North Pole; the territory is 2,645 miles (4,256 kilometers) long from east to west. The NWT covers 1,322,902 square miles (3,426,320 square kilometers) and includes the islands in Hudson, James, and Ungava Bays. Across the Kennedy Channel in the far northeast, Greenland lies less than 25 miles (40 kilometers) from the NWT's Ellesmere Island.

2 TOPOGRAPHY

Like the Yukon, the NWT can be divided into two broad geographical regions: the taiga (a boreal forest belt that circles the subarctic zone and is typified by stands of pine, aspen, poplar, and birch trees), and the tundra (a rocky arctic region where the cold climate has stunted vegetation). One of the most remarkable features of the NWT is the Mackenzie River, one of the world's longest at 2,635 miles (4,241 kilometers).

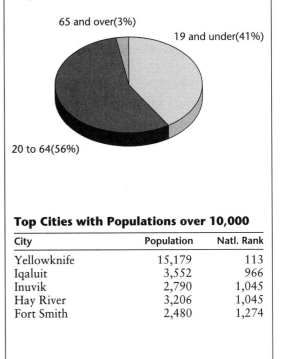

Northwest Territories Population Profile

Estimated 1994 population:		64,000
Population change, 1981–91:		26%
Leading ancestry group:		Inuit
Second leading group:		Dene
Population by ethnic group:		
Inuit:		37.4%
Dene:		16.7%
Métis:		7.1%
Non-Native:		38.8%
Urban/Rural populations:		
Urban:	21,157	36.7%
Rural:	36,492	63.3%
Estimated population density:		1 person per
		20.4 square miles
		(52.9 per square kilometer)

Population by Age Group

65 and over(3%)

19 and under(41%)

20 to 64(56%)

Top Cities with Populations over 10,000

City	Population	Natl. Rank
Yellowknife	15,179	113
Iqaluit	3,552	966
Inuvik	2,790	1,045
Hay River	3,206	1,045
Fort Smith	2,480	1,274

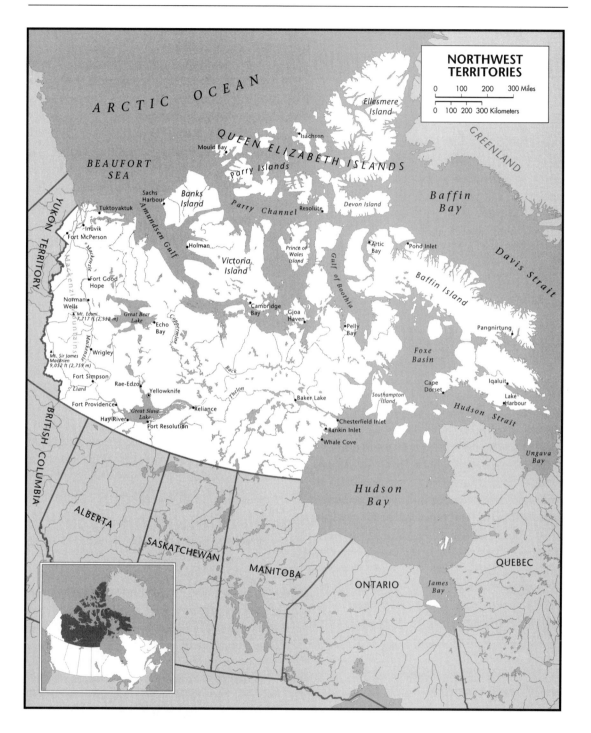

NORTHWEST TERRITORIES

0   100   200   300 Miles

0   100   200   300 Kilometers

ARCTIC OCEAN

Ellesmere Island

BEAUFORT SEA

QUEEN ELIZABETH ISLANDS

Isachsen

Mould Bay

Parry Islands

GREENLAND

Banks Island

Sachs Harbour

Tuktoyaktuk

Amundsen Gulf

Parry Channel

Resolute

Devon Island

Baffin Bay

YUKON TERRITORY

Inuvik

Fort McPerson

Holman

Prince of Wales Island

Artic Bay

Pond Inlet

Davis Strait

Victoria Island

Gulf of Boothia

Baffin Island

Fort Good Hope

Norman Wells

Mt. Eduni 7,717 ft (2,352 m)

Great Bear Lake

Echo Bay

Coppermine

Cambridge Bay

Gjoa Haven

Pelly Bay

Pangnirtung

Mackenzie Mountains

Mt. Sir James MacBrien 9,052 ft (2,759 m)

Wrigley

Back

Foxe Basin

Mackenzie

Fort Simpson

Liard

Rae-Edzo

Yellowknife

Thelon

Cape Dorset

Iqaluit

Lake Harbour

BRITISH COLUMBIA

Fort Providence

Hay River

Great Slave Lake

Fort Resolution

Reliance

Baker Lake

Southampton Island

Hudson Strait

Chesterfield Inlet

Rankin Inlet

Whale Cove

Ungava Bay

ALBERTA

SASKATCHEWAN

MANITOBA

Hudson Bay

QUEBEC

ONTARIO

James Bay

3 CLIMATE

There are two major climate zones in the NWT: subarctic and arctic. In the subarctic zone, average temperatures in January are -9°F (-23°C) and 70°F (21°C) in July, while average temperatures in the arctic zone range from -27°F (-33°C) in January to 50°F (10°C) in July. The average temperatures in Yellowknife are 8°F (-22°C) from November to March and 57°F (14°C) from June to August. As in the Yukon, the varying amounts of daylight over the year are an important influence on the climate: between 20 and 24 hours of daylight in June and up to 24 hours of darkness in December. The highest recorded temperature was 110°F (43°C) in 1991 at Coppermine and the lowest was -79.1°F (-61.7°C) at Fort Good Hope on 31 December 1910.

4 PLANTS AND ANIMALS

A short but intense summer produces many small but brilliant flowers, including purple mountain saxifrage and fireweed. The animal population in the NWT includes mammals such as the moose, musk ox, wolverine, black and brown bear, grizzly bear, polar bear, walrus, Dall's sheep, mountain goat, wood bison, caribou, wolf, and snowshoe hare. Bird species include grouse, ptarmigan, phalarope, Pacific loon, and peregrine falcon. Fish include lake trout, arctic grayling, arctic char, walleye, whitefish, and northern pike.

5 ENVIRONMENTAL PROTECTION

The NWT has 62 active solid waste disposal sites and about 500 abandoned sites. Annual generation of solid wastes is about 220,400 tons (200,000 metric tons) or 3.9 tons (3.5 metric tons) per person. There are also 20 hazardous waste sites. Releases of air pollution annually amount to 57,304 tons (52,000 metric tons) of smog-causing gases and 17,632 tons (16,000 metric tons) of gases that create acid rain. The Arctic Environmental Strategy introduced by the federal government in 1991 as part of its Green Plan involves northerners in projects to protect the arctic environment. It also supports communities in the development of their own plans to deal with environmental issues. About 3.5% of the territorial budget is spent on maintaining environmental and natural resources.

6 POPULATION

According to the 1991 census, the NWT had a population of 57,649; in 1994, the population was estimated at 64,000. Yellowknife, the capital, had a population of more than 15,000 in 1994. Other urban areas, and their 1991 populations include Iqaluit, 3,552; Hay River, 3,206; and Fort Smith, 2,480.

7 ETHNIC GROUPS

The NWT is the only place in Canada where most of the population (54.1%) are Aboriginals (Native Peoples); they live mostly in small communities. The largest Aboriginal group is the Inuit, which means "the preeminent people" in Inuktitut. In the western Arctic, the Dene have inhabited the forests and barrens for the past 2,500 years. Once nomads, today they live in communities, many still using tradi-

Photo Credit: Mike Beedell, *Economic Development & Tourism, GNWT.*

The summit of Mount Asgard in Auyuittuq National Park has been the goal of climbing expeditions from around the world. Auyuittuq means "the land that never melts."

tional skills of hunting, trapping, and fishing. There are four major Dene cultural groups: Chipewyan, Dogrib, Slavey (north and south) and Gwich'in (Loucheux). The Inuvialuit reside primarily around the Mackenzie River delta. The Métis are descendants of Dene and ethnic European parentage and comprise 7.1% of the territory's population. Other ethnicities found in the NWT include French, Scotch-Irish, and Pakistani.

8 LANGUAGES

The NWT has nine official languages, but English is the language used most often for business and commerce. In 1991, only 55.1% of the territory's residents claimed English as their native language (the lowest proportion in Canada after Québec), while 2.5% declared French as their mother tongue and 42.4% had other first languages (predominantly Inuktitut and Dene dialects). Inuit communities are often a mixture of people from different cultural and linguistic areas, but most have characteristic dialects. In general, the Inuit language is an active language, and most Inuit children learn Inuktitut as their mother tongue. The Dene have four linguistic groups: Chipewyan, Dogrib, Slavey (north and south) and Gwich'in (Loucheux).

9 RELIGIONS

In 1991, 50% of the population—about 28,800 people—was Protestant, including 18,450 Anglicans, 3,300 members of the United Church of Canada, 2,250 Pentecostals, 700 Baptists, 700 Lutherans, and less than 50 Presbyterians. The territory also had about 22,000 Catholics and almost 200 people of Eastern Orthodox faith. There were less than 100 people each of the following: Jews, Moslems, Buddhists, Sikhs, and Hindus. About 6,150 people had no religious affiliation in 1991.

10 TRANSPORTATION

Territorial highways are mostly all-weather gravel roads, with some paved sections; clouds of dust, flying gravel, soft spots, and long distances between service stations are common. In the north, the Dempster Highway (#8) connects Inuvik, on the Mackenzie River delta, with Dawson, Yukon, across the Richardson Mountains. In the south, the Mackenzie Highway (#1) provides access to Alberta via connecting roads leading from Yellowknife (#3), Hay River (#2), Fort Resolution (#6), and Fort Smith (#5). The Liard Highway (#7) provides entry to British Columbia. The Canol Road (#9) and the Nahanni Range Road also provide access from the Yukon, but terminate just inside the NWT border.

Ferry service is provided in the summer for Highways 1, 3, and 8, which cross major rivers; in the winter, motorists simply drive over the frozen rivers. During the freezing months of fall and thawing months of spring, however, crossings by vehicles are not possible.

Air Canada provides service to Yellowknife from Edmonton, Alberta. First Air, based in Iqaluit (Frobisher Bay), provides jet service to more than a dozen locations throughout the northern archipelago (group of islands), as well as Ottawa, Montreal, and Nuuk, Greenland. Air Inuit flies from Cape Dorset to points along the northwestern coast of Québec.

11 HISTORY

The ancestors of the Dene Indian people lived along the Mackenzie Valley in the Northwest Territories 10,000 years ago. The first Inuit are believed to have crossed the Bering Strait about 5,000 years ago, spreading east along the Arctic coast.

European Exploration and Settlement

The first European explorers were the Vikings, who sailed to the eastern Arctic about AD 1000. But the Englishman Martin Frobisher's expeditions in the 1570s were the first recorded visits to the Northwest Territories by an explorer. In 1610, Henry Hudson (another English explorer), while looking for a passage to Asia, landed briefly on the western shore of the bay that now bears his name. His discovery opened the door for further exploration of the interior of the continent.

With the arrival of the fur traders in the late 1700s and the whalers in the 1800s, life began to change substantially. The Europeans reshaped the North, bringing with them a new economy and way of life. Communities grew around trading posts, mission schools, and Royal Canadian Mounted Police stations with the arrival of fur traders, missionaries, and government officials.

In 1870, the British government transferred control of the North-Western Territories to Canada. Ten years later the British government annexed the islands of the arctic archipelago (large group of islands), which also became part of the Territories. In 1905, both Alberta and Saskatchewan were created from the Territories. Finally, in 1912, the provinces of Manitoba, Ontario, and Québec were enlarged and the Northwest Territories assumed its current boundaries.

Early 20th Century

During World War I (1914–18), Canada lost more than 68,000 soldiers. Returning veterans faced a bleak future of scarce low-paying jobs, while tariffs on imports kept prices for consumer goods high. During the 1920s, however, Canada experienced a period of rapid growth in industry. Transportation improvements—railways and roads—enabled businesses to flourish. Automobiles, telephones, electrical appliances, and other consumer goods became more widely available.

Just as in the United States, all of Canada suffered during the Great Depression. In addition to the problems with grain prices during the early 1920s, droughts and frequent crop failures devastated the national economy, which still relied heavily on agriculture. Social welfare programs rapidly expanded during the 1930s, with much of the burden placed on the provincial and municipal governments.

1940–1960s

By World War II (1939–45), mineral exploration and the military were playing a role in northern development, prompting a more active interest in the NWT by the rest of Canada. Following World War II, consumer spending and immigration to Canada rapidly increased. Urbanization spread quickly by means of the National Housing Act, which made home ownership more easily available. Unemployment insurance and other social welfare programs were also created following the war. Under the leadership of Prime Minister Louis St. Laurent, old age pensions were increased in 1951 and a national hospital insurance plan was introduced in 1957.

During the 1950s and 1960s, the monitoring of northern Canadian airspace served a vital role in the defense of North America against a possible nuclear attack from the Soviet Union. But when ballistic missiles (which are launched in an arc toward their targets from great distances) replaced bombers as the means of delivering nuclear warheads, this strategy became obsolete.

Aboriginal Land Claims (1970s–1990s)

As in the Yukon, the issue of settling Aboriginal land claims in the NWT emerged in the 1970s. In 1984, a final agreement was reached with the Inuvialuit of the western Arctic. The agreement provided some 2,500 people with 35,100 square miles (91,000 square kilometers) of land, financial compensation, social development funding, hunting rights, and a greater role in wildlife management, conservation, and environmental protection.

In 1992, the Gwich'in settled a comprehensive land claim that provided 8,657 square miles (22,422 square kilometers) of land in the northwestern portion of the NWT and 600 square miles (1,554 square kilometers) of land in the Yukon. The Gwich'in also received subsurface rights; a share in the resource royalties derived from the Mackenzie River Valley; tax-free capital transfers; hunting rights; a greater role in the management of wildlife, land, and the environment; and the right of first refusal on a variety of activities related to wildlife.

In 1993, a final agreement was reached with the Tungavik Federation of Nunavut—the largest comprehensive land claim to be settled in Canada. The agreement will provide some 17,500 Inuit of the eastern Arctic with 135,000 square miles (350,000 square kilometers) of land, financial compensation, the right to share in resource royalties, hunting rights, and a greater role in the management of land and the environment. The final agreement also commits the federal government to a process that will divide the NWT and create the new territory of Nunavut ("our land"), which is scheduled to come into formal existence in 1999.

12 PROVINCIAL GOVERNMENT

In both the NWT and the Yukon, political power rests with elected representatives. Although a federally appointed commissioner is technically in charge of the territorial administration, the role of that office has diminished, and it generally follows the lead of the elected territorial government. Executive power is held by a 24-seat elected assembly, whose members remain as political independents. This assembly then appoints an 8-person executive council, of which 1 is chosen as government leader for the territorial government. To help administer the vast area, the NWT is divided into three districts: Keewatin, Mackenzie, and Franklin.

13 POLITICAL PARTIES

Territorial legislators campaign as political independents.

Commissioners of Northwest Territories

Term	Commissioner
1905–19	Frederick D. White
1919–31	William Wallace Cory
1931–34	Hugh Howard Rowatt
1936–46	Charles Camsell
1947–50	Hugh Llewellyn Keenleyside
1950–53	Hugh Andrew Young
1953–63	Robert Gordon Robertson
1963–67	Bent Gestur Sivertz
1967–79	Stuart Milton Hodgson
1979–89	John Havelock Parker
1989–	Daniel Leonard Norris

Government Leaders of Northwest Territories

Term	Government Leader
1980–84	George Braden
1984–85	Richard Nerysoo
1985–87	Nick Gordon Sibbeston
1987–91	Dennis Glen Patterson
1991–	Nellie Joy Cournoyea

14 LOCAL GOVERNMENT

A village must have a total assessed value of c$10 million for the entire community to be incorporated; for a town, c$50 million; and for a city, more than c$200 million. Yellowknife is the sole city; there are also five town governments. Inuit resi-

Photo Credit: Douglas Walker, *Economic Development & Tourism, GNWT.*

Iqaluit, on Frobisher Bay, is an urban Inuit settlement. Iqaluit has recently been voted as the capital of the new eastern territory of Nunavut, which will gain autonomy in 1999.

dents in the eastern half of the NWT are currently working on establishing the self-governing region of Nunavut, which will gain autonomy in 1999 and will hold the same degree of political and economic sovereignty as the other territories.

15 JUDICIAL SYSTEM

The Canadian Constitution grants territorial and provincial jurisdiction over the administration of justice, and allows each territory and province to organize its own court system and police forces. The federal government has exclusive domain over cases involving trade and commerce, banking, bankruptcy, and criminal law. The Federal Court of Canada has both trial and appellate divisions for federal cases. The 9-judge Supreme Court of Canada is an appellate court that determines the constitutionality of both federal and territorial statutes. The Tax Court of Canada hears appeals of taxpayers against assessments by Revenue Canada.

The annual number of homicides varies but usually ranges from two to ten. Because of the small population, the NWT often has the highest homicide rate in Canada. Breaking and entering offenses in 1989 numbered 1,313 per 100,000 people for businesses and 1,337 per 100,000 people for residences; both rates were the highest in Canada.

16 MIGRATION

Some 20,000 to 30,000 years ago, the ancestors of the modern day Dene crossed a land bridge over the Bering Sea and dispersed throughout the Western Hemisphere. The Dene first migrated into what is now the NWT some 7,000 to 8,000 years ago. The Inuvialuit migrated into the NWT from Alaska in the 1800s, replacing the Mackenzie Inuit who were decimated by diseases introduced from migrant whalers.

In 1991, the NWT gained a net 59 residents from migration within Canada (4,341 people entered and 4,282 left). Of these migrants, Alberta was the province of origin for 31% of incoming residents and was the province of destination for 42% of departing NWT residents.

17 ECONOMY

The Aboriginal Peoples' traditional subsistence activities—fishing, hunting, and trapping—have an impact on the territorial economy. Sports fishing and big-game hunting also play a small role. Commercial fishery development in the NWT—both freshwater and saltwater—is being encouraged. Fur harvesting continues to be very important, supplementing the income of many Aboriginal families.

Inuit arts and crafts distribute a greater amount of income more widely than any other economic activity; 1 in 14 people of working age in the NWT earns some income by this means.

The settling of northern land claims sets the stage for increased economic activity in which all can share and have a voice. But even if development is welcome and necessary for economic prosperity, it must be managed so as not to threaten the fragile arctic ecosystem and the traditional life-styles of the northern peoples.

18 INCOME

In 1992, the average full-time worker in the NWT earned $42,268 per year, the highest in Canada.

19 INDUSTRY

Industry in the NWT centers on processing raw materials. Food products, wood, printing and publishing, nonmetallic mineral products, and chemical and chemical products are important manufacturing sectors. In 1990, the value of manufactured shipments for both the NWT and the Yukon was c$75.4 million.

20 LABOR

As of 1992, territorial employment was 20,770 persons, down 1% from 1991. The service sector employed an estimated 17,262 people in 1992 (down 2% from 1991) and employment in the goods-producing sector was 3,508 (up 5% from 1991). The largest employer in the NWT is the federal government.

Yellowknife was the scene of a bitter and violent strike in May 1992. More than 200 miners who were members of the Canadian Association of Smelter and Allied Workers (CASAW) were locked out by Vancouver-owned Giant Gold Mine after refusing a new contract. A bomb explosion on 18 September 1992 killed nine workers, six of whom were union members who had crossed the picket line. The mine has continued to operate amid negotiations between CASAW and the newly formed rival Giant Mines Employees Association, comprised of current and former Giant Mine workers.

21 AGRICULTURE

A brief but intense summer growing season (due to the midnight sun) limits local production of crops, of which seasonal berries and produce for home consumption are the most prominent. The territorial government is currently involved in a joint project with the University of Alberta to study the use of fiber optics to illuminate greenhouses with natural light on a year-round basis.

22 DOMESTICATED ANIMALS

For centuries, the Inuit and other Indigenous Peoples have bred dogs as draft ani-

Photo Credit: M. Milne, *Economic Development & Tourism, GNWT.*

The delta of the Mackenzie River is a haven for waterfowl and whales. The Mackenzie is part of the second longest river system in North America. The river was explored in 1789 by Sir Alexander Mackenzie, for whom it is named.

mals to carry packs and later to pull sleds. Before modern transportation was available, dog teams often served as the primary form of transportation during the winter months. Fur trapping is still practiced and is an important contributor to the economy.

23 FISHING

The Dene and Inuvialuit once depended on subsistence fishing to sustain their families and dog teams. Today, sport fishing is a popular activity and is a source of income from tourism. Principal species sought include lake trout, arctic grayling, arctic char, northern pike, walleye, whitefish, and inconnu.

24 FORESTRY

Although 151.8 million acres (61.4 million hectares)—or 58%—of the NWT is covered by forests, only 35.4 million acres (14.3 million hectares) of this land is useful for tree harvesting. The territorial government owns 83% of the forests and the federal government controls the remaining 17%.

25 MINING

With mineral production valued at more than c$800 million, mining is by far the largest private sector of the NWT economy. In 1992, the total value of mineral production was C$482.9 million, with metals accounting for nearly all of this amount. Production in 1992 included 199,140 tons (180,708 metric tons) of zinc, 43,132 tons (39,140 metric tons) of lead, 51,479 pounds (23,357 kilograms) of silver, and 30,413 pounds (13,799 kilograms) of gold.

26 ENERGY AND POWER

Oil and gas exploration and development are important to the territory's economy, but the industry is open to wide fluctuations in world markets. In 1991, crude oil and equivalent production totaled 69,074,184 cubic feet (1,956,000 cubic meters), valued at C$205 million. In 1991, electricity generated totaled 572 million kilowatt hours and consumption within the territory amounted to 532 million kilowatt hours.

27 COMMERCE

Inuit arts and crafts account for a great amount of retail income in the NWT, spread out over a wide geographical area. About one in 14 persons of working age in the NWT earns some income through the sales of craft items. Services related to tourism have become increasingly important sources of income.

28 PUBLIC FINANCE

The fiscal year runs from 1 April to 31 March. For fiscal year 1992/93, total revenues were C$1.2 billion, more than 80 percent coming from the government of Canada. Expenditures were also C$1.2 bil-

lion. Major expenditure areas were health, education, public works, social services, municipal and community services, NWT housing corporation, renewable resources, transportation, and economic development and tourism.

29 TAXATION

The NWT has no provincial sales tax, but a 7% tax is charged on most goods and services sold or provided.

30 HEALTH

In 1992 there were 1,554 live births in NWT, for a rate of 25 per 1,000 residents, the highest level in Canada. The death rate in 1992 was 4.3 per 1,000 residents, with 266 deaths occurring that year. Therapeutic abortions in NWT numbered 335 in 1990, for a rate of 24.3 per 1,000 females aged 15–44 (the highest rate in Canada) and a ratio of 21.1 per 100 live births. Reported cases of selected diseases in 1990 included gonococcal infections, 455; chicken pox, 361; giardiasis, 42; pertussis, 28; and salmonellosis, 28. There were no AIDS cases reported in 1990; in 1991, the total number of cases was 3.

Larger communities such as Yellowknife, Inuvik, Hay River, Fort Smith, and Iqaluit have well-equipped hospitals; smaller communities have nursing stations. Air ambulance (Medevac) service is available throughout the NWT and is coordinated by the local nursing stations. In the late 1980s, there were 4 general hospitals with 181 beds, and 14 pediatric, psychiatric, rehabilitation, and extended health care hospitals with 78 beds.

Photo Credit: Dan Heringa, *Economic Development & Tourism, GNWT.*

Inukshuk—the word means "like a person"—were built by the Inuits to simulate man and were placed in such a way as to lead or drive the caribou herds to a place of ambush. They are also used as landmarks.

31 HOUSING

As of October 1995, the average monthly rent for an apartment in Yellowknife ranged from c$648 for a studio apartment to c$1,240 for a three bedroom unit. Due to permafrost and a short construction season, the cost of building a house is more expensive in NWT than elsewhere in Canada. The Canadian Mortgage and Housing Association has estimated that a typical existing 1,200 square foot home costs c$206,575 in Yellowknife. As a result, many people live in mobile homes.

In 1995, of all the Yellowknife housing units for sale listed below c$175,000, 63.4% were mobile homes, 28.8% were condominiums, 5.2% were bungalow houses, and 2.6% were other types.

32 EDUCATION

All elementary and secondary schools in NWT are public; enrollment in 1990/91 was 14,079. The NWT has four education districts and nine boards of education. The Arctic College (with campuses in Yellowknife, Inuvik, Rankin Inlet, Cambridge Bay, Iqaluit, and Fort Smith) offers community college courses. Postsecondary community college enrollment in 1990/91 was 266, of which 255 were enrolled in career programs and 11 were in university transfer programs.

33 ARTS

Nearly every community in the NWT has artisans who produce clothing, accessories, tools, weavings, beadwork, or carvings. Studios are often found in the more populous areas of Pangnirtung, Iqaluit, Cape Dorset, Baker Lake, Rankin Inlet, Holman, Inuvik, Fort Laird, and Yellowknife. Inuvik is the site of the midsummer Great Northern Arts Festival, which draws artisans from throughout the territory.

34 LIBRARIES AND MUSEUMS

The NWT Public Library Services, based in Hay River, coordinates public library service throughout the territory. Member libraries are located in Arviat, Baker Lake, Cambridge Bay, Clyde River, Coppermine, Fort Norman, Fort Simpson, Fort Smith,

Hay River, Hay River Reserve, Igloolik, Inuvik, Iqaluit, Nanisivik, Norman Wells, Pangnirtung, Pond Inlet, Rankin Inlet, and Yellowknife. Museums in the NWT include the Prince of Wales Northern Heritage Centre in Yellowknife, the Northern Life Museum & National Exhibition Centre at Fort Smith, and the Nunatta Sunaqutangit Museum at Iqaluit.

35 COMMUNICATIONS

Yellowknife has 3 radio stations (2 AM and 1 FM). CABL-TV is a cable television station based in Yellowknife; Mackenzie Media Ltd. provides cable service to the capital.

36 PRESS

Periodicals and magazines published in the NWT include *Above & Beyond*, *Arctic Circle*, *News/North*, and *Up Here*.

37 TOURISM, TRAVEL, AND RECREATION

Recently, tourism has become increasingly important. The NWT offers a variety of landscapes of great natural beauty, which are well-suited to fishing, wildlife observation, and other outdoor activities. The NWT has five national parks: Auyuittuq National Park, on Baffin Island north of Pangnirtung; Nahanni National Park Reserve, west of the Liard River in the Mackenzie Mountains; Wood Buffalo National Park, west of Fort Smith and extending into Alberta; Ellesmere National Park, on northern Ellesmere Island; and Aulavik National Park, on northern Banks Island.

38 SPORTS

Local sporting organizations (for such sports as badminton, basketball, track and field, and volleyball) are popular in the territory, as are canoeing and kayaking.

39 FAMOUS PEOPLE FROM THE NORTHWEST TERRITORIES

Early English explorers who traveled the waterways of the NWT in search of a northwest passage included Sir Martin Frobisher (1539?–94) and Henry Hudson (d.1611). Famous early fur traders included Sir Alexander Mackenzie (b.Scotland, 1764–1820), who explored the Slave River and Great Slave Lake area, and American Peter Pond (1740–1807), who established the first trading post.

Nellie Joy Cournoyea (b.1940), from Aklavik, became the first woman head of government in Canada upon her 1991 election as government leader of the NWT. Ethel Blondin-Andrew (b.1951), from Fort Norman, became the first Native woman elected to the Canadian parliament in 1988. Actress Margot Kidder (b.1948) is a native of Yellowknife.

40 BIBLIOGRAPHY

Bumsted, J. M. *The Peoples of Canada*. New York: Oxford University Press, 1992.

Daitch, Richard W. *Northwest Territories*. Minneapolis: Lerner Publications, 1996.

Hancock, Lyn. *Discover Canada: Northwest Territories*. Toronto: Grolier, 1993.

Hancock, Lyn. *Nunavut*. Minneapolis: Lerner Publications, 1995.

LeVert, Suzanne. *Let's Discover Canada: Northwest Territories*. New York: Chelsea House, 1992.

Sorensen, Lynda. *Canada: Provinces and Territories*. Vero Beach, Fla.: Rourke Book Co., 1995.

Weihs, Jean. *Facts about Canada, Its Provinces and Territories*. New York: H. W. Wilson, 1995.

NOVA SCOTIA

ORIGIN OF PROVINCE NAME: The area was first called "Acadia" by French settlers and later "New Caledonia" (meaning "New Scotland" from the Latin name for northern Britain). The anglicized "Nova Scotia" name dates from 1621, when Sir William Alexander, a Scot, was given a charter to colonize the area.

NICKNAME: Bluenose Country or Canada's Ocean Playground.

CAPITAL: Halifax.

ENTERED CONFEDERATION: 1 July 1867.

SONG: "Farewell to Nova Scotia."

MOTTO: *Munit hæc et altera vincit* (One defends and the other conquers).

COAT OF ARMS: In the center, the provincial shield of arms displays (in a fashion similar to that of the provincial flag) the cross of St. Andrew, patron saint of Scotland, in blue on a white background. In the center of the cross are the Royal Arms of Scotland. Above the provincial shield is a royal helmet with a blue and silver scroll that represents the royal cloak. Two joined hands (one with a gauntlet and the other bare) are above the crest, supporting a branch of laurel which stands for peace and a branch of thistle representing Scotland. Above all, the provincial motto appears on a scroll. Supporting the shield are a white royal unicorn on the left representing England and an Aboriginal Canadian on the right holding an arrow. Beneath the shield is a grassy mound with mayflower entwined with the thistle of Scotland.

FLAG: The flag is based on the provincial shield of arms. It has a blue St. Andrew's Cross on a white field, with the Royal Arms of Scotland mounted at the center.

FLORAL EMBLEM: Trailing arbutus, also called mayflower.

TARTAN: Blue, white, green, red, and gold.

PROVINCIAL BIRD: None adopted.

TREE: Red spruce.

MINERAL: Stilbite.

GEMSTONE: Agate.

TIME: 8 AM AST = noon GMT.

1 LOCATION AND SIZE

Nova Scotia is one of Canada's Atlantic provinces and consists largely of a peninsula that is 360 miles (580 kilometers) in length. The peninsula is surrounded by four bodies of water—the Atlantic Ocean, the Bay of Fundy, the Northumberland Strait, and the Gulf of St. Lawrence. A narrow passage on the northwest (the Chignecto Isthmus) connects the province to New Brunswick. Its geographic location, together with large, ice-free, deepwater harbors, has been a key factor in the province's economic development.

With an area of 21,425 square miles (55,491 square kilometers), Nova Scotia is larger than Denmark, although somewhat smaller than Scotland, after which it is named. In size, it is the second smallest of the ten Canadian provinces. Its average width of 80 miles (128 kilometers) means that no part of the province is far from the sea. The highest point is North Barren Mountain, at 1,745 feet (531 meters) above sea level.

2 TOPOGRAPHY

The province is comprised of a peninsula, connected to the remainder of Canada by 17 miles (27 kilometers) of land, along with the island of Cape Breton (mainly highland country broken by lakes, rivers, and valleys), which is joined to the mainland by a 0.9-mile (1.4-kilometer) causeway. Nova Scotia is a mosaic of rugged headlands, tranquil harbors, and ocean beaches. Its indented shoreline stretches 6,478 miles (10,424 kilometers), while inland is a myriad of lakes and streams. The land is framed by the rocky Atlantic Uplands, the Cape Breton Highlands, and the wooded Cobequid Hills. The agricultural areas of Nova Scotia are predominantly lowlands. The northern coastal belt of low, level land stretches along the Northumberland Strait from the New Brunswick border to Cape Breton Island. When the glacial ice withdrew from coastal Nova Scotia 15,000 to 18,000 years ago, the ocean flooded ancient river valleys and carved out hundreds of small

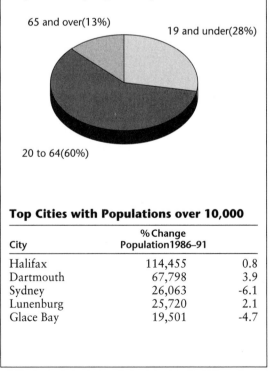

Nova Scotia Population Profile

Estimated 1996 population:		941,200
Population change, 1981–91:		6.2%
Population by ethnic origin:		
British origins:		43.5%
English:		28.5%
Scottish:		11.0%
Irish:		4.0%
Multiple origins:		40.8%
French:		6.1%
German:		2.8%
Black:		1.2%
Dutch:		1.0%
Aboriginal:		0.8%
Other single origins:		3.8%
Urban/Rural populations:		
Urban:	481,508	53.5%
Rural:	418,434	46.5%

Population by Age Group

65 and over(13%)

19 and under(28%)

20 to 64(60%)

Top Cities with Populations over 10,000

City	Population	% Change 1986–91
Halifax	114,455	0.8
Dartmouth	67,798	3.9
Sydney	26,063	-6.1
Lunenburg	25,720	2.1
Glace Bay	19,501	-4.7

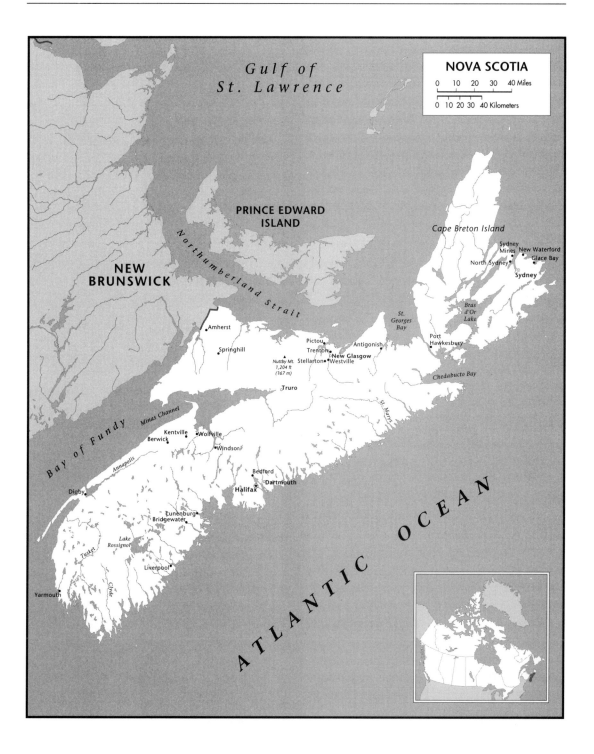

Gulf of
St. Lawrence

NOVA SCOTIA

0   10   20   30   40 Miles

0   10 20 30   40 Kilometers

PRINCE EDWARD
ISLAND

Cape Breton Island

NEW
BRUNSWICK

Northumberland Strait

Sydney
Mines   New Waterford
Glace Bay
North Sydney
Sydney

*Bras
d'Or
Lake*

*St.
Georges
Bay*

Port
Hawkesbury

Amherst

Springhill

Pictou
Trenton
▲ Nuttby Mt.   Stellarton   New Glasgow
1,204 ft   Westville
(367 m)

Antigonish

Chedabucto Bay

Truro

St. Marys

Bay of Fundy

Minas Channel

Kentville   •Wolfville
Berwick
•Windsor

Annapolis

Bedford
Dartmouth
Halifax

Digby

Lunenburg
Bridgewater

*Lake
Rossignol*

ATLANTIC   OCEAN

Tusket

Liverpool

Clyde

Yarmouth

protected harbors which later became fishing ports.

3 CLIMATE

Nova Scotia lies in the northern temperate zone and, although it is almost surrounded by water, the climate is classified modified continental rather than maritime. The temperature extremes of a continental climate, however, are moderated by the ocean. Because of cool currents of air and water from the Arctic alternating with warmer breezes from the Gulf Stream, extremes of summer and winter temperatures are not as evident as in central Canada. Average daily temperatures at the Halifax International Airport range from 21°F (-6°C) to 65°F (18.2°C) in July. The total average annual precipitation of 58.7 inches (1,490 millimeters) includes 107 inches (271 centimeters) of snowfall.

Only on rare occasions does the temperature rise above 90°F (32°C) or fall below 14°F (-10°C) in winter. The frost-free season ranges from 120 days in northern Nova Scotia to 145 days in the Annapolis Valley. The highest recorded temperature in Nova Scotia was 101°F (38.3°C) on 19 August 1935 at Collegeville, and the lowest was -42°F (-41.1°C) on 31 January 1920 at Upper Stewiacke.

4 PLANTS AND ANIMALS

Nova Scotia has more than 250 bird and mammal species. Deer, rabbit, pheasant, and ruffed grouse are prominent upland species, while beaver and waterfowl are common wetland species.

5 ENVIRONMENTAL PROTECTION

As in New Brunswick, the impact of drifting air pollution from industrial centers in the southeast (which results in acid rain falling in Nova Scotia and the other maritime provinces) is a local concern. Nova Scotia itself annually releases about 473,860 tons (430,000 metric tons) of nitrogen dioxide and carbon monoxide (gases that cause smog), 273,296 tons (248,000 metric tons) of sulfur dioxide and nitrogen oxide (gases that produce acid rain), and the equivalent of 5,224,582 tons (4,741,000 metric tons) of carbon dioxide. There are 50 landfills and 3 municipal incinerators. Although Nova Scotia generates about 2.6% of Canada's hazardous waste, the province has no hazardous waste disposal sites.

Nova Scotia has more than 400 companies with 2,500 employees in the environmental sector. These firms work in such specialties as remote sensing, geographic information systems, waste utilization, and water and wastewater treatment products and services. Nova Scotia Power Inc. is a world leader in the clean burning of coal for electricity generation, and has been approached by several Caribbean and Asian utilities for advice on how to control fossil fuel emissions.

6 POPULATION

As of 1996, almost all of the estimated 941,200 residents lived in close proximity to the coast. The population of Nova Scotia as of 1 July 1991 was estimated to be 918,100, compared to 892,100 at July 1986. The largest concentrations of popu-

In the autumn, the trees along the Cabot Trail in the Cape Breton region display bright blazing colors.

lation in 1991 were in the Halifax metropolitan area with a population of 320,501 (13th largest in Canada) and the Sydney urban area with 116,000. The Halifax metro area is the largest population area in Canada east of Québec City; Halifax functions as a regional headquarters for many government and private institutions. Major towns in Nova Scotia include Yarmouth, Kentville, Bridgewater, Truro, Amherst, and New Glasgow.

Residential growth is about evenly split between urban and rural areas, but the farm population is diminishing. Between 1986 and 1991 the rural portion of the population in Nova Scotia increased slightly from 46% to 46.5%, but the rural farm population declined by more than 2,000 people to 11,805.

7 ETHNIC GROUPS

Over 80% of Nova Scotia's population trace their ancestry either wholly or partly to the British Isles. Those with French origin rank second: 18% of residents have some French ancestry. The next largest groups by ancestry are German and Dutch. Residents of Nova Scotia are also of Polish, Italian, Jewish, and Lebanese descent. Over 15,000 residents of the province have African origins. Almost 22,000 residents have Amerindian origins, and primarily belong to the Micmac Nation. Almost 80% of the residents of

Nova Scotia in 1991 were born there and 15.5% in other parts of Canada, while 4.7% were born outside Canada.

8 LANGUAGES

In 1991, English was the first language of 93.5% of Nova Scotians, with French the mother tongue of 4.1% of the province's residents. While 8.6% of residents speak both English and French, 91.1% of the population speak only English and 0.2% speak only French.

9 RELIGIONS

In 1991, 54.1% of the population, or about 486,900 people, was Protestant, including 154,800 members of the United Church of Canada, 129,600 Anglicans, 99,900 Baptists, 31,500 Presbyterians, 11,700 Lutherans, and 10,800 Pentecostals. Nova Scotia also had about 334,800 Roman Catholics (37.2% of the population), about 2,700 people of Eastern Orthodox faith, and less than 1,800 people each of the following: Buddhists, Jews, and Hindus. More than 68,000 provincial residents professed no religious affiliation.

10 TRANSPORTATION

Nova Scotia has a network of 438 miles (705 kilometers) of railroad track serving major communities in the province. Both the Dominion Atlantic Railway, a subsidiary of Canadian Pacific, and Canadian National operate in the province. Unit trains are used for rapid delivery of containers between the Port of Halifax and central Canada and the United States. Total revenue freight handled by railways in Nova Scotia in 1990 was 23.8 million tons (21.6 million metric tons). Passenger rail service is provided by Via Rail from Halifax to Amherst and points west.

Nova Scotia has a network of 16,200 miles (26,000 kilometers) of highways, of which 8,400 miles (13,600 kilometers) are paved. During the 1980s a series of all-weather, controlled-access highways was constructed. Total motor vehicle registrations in 1992 included 421,443 passenger vehicles, 170,850 commercial vehicles, and 15,000 motorcycles and mopeds.

With a strategic location on the major North Atlantic shipping route, Nova Scotia ports are able to serve the eastern Canadian and north-central US markets for shipments of goods to world markets. The port of Halifax is in the forefront of this activity, handling approximately 16.5 million tons (15 million metric tons) of water-borne cargo in 1988 and almost 15.4 million tons (14 million metric tons) in 1992. Other harbor facilities at Halifax include 35 deepwater berths and, located in Woodside, the largest automobile distribution center in Canada. Approximately 175,000 vehicles were loaded or unloaded at this facility in 1993.

The port at the Strait of Canso can accommodate the world's largest supertankers. Sydney Harbour also has a full range of facilities and can handle vessels up to 44,080 tons (40,000 metric tons). In 1991, Nova Scotia's ports handled 23.6 million tons (21.4 million metric tons) of cargo, of which Halifax accounted for 16.3 million tons (14.8 million metric tons).

Urban transit in 1991 consisted of 218 buses which provided over 15.6 million passenger trips of over 6 million miles (9.7 million kilometers).

National and regional air service is provided at Yarmouth, Sydney, and Halifax International Airport. Air Canada, Canadian International Airlines, KLM, Air Nova, Air Atlantic, and Northwest Airlink provide regular scheduled service to all Canadian points and international service to Boston, New York, Bermuda, London, Glasgow, and Amsterdam. Several local airports have been developed throughout the province for the use of charter services, local commuting, and flying clubs. In 1991 the Halifax International Airport was the sixth busiest in Canada, handling a total of 63,757 flights with 2.3 million passengers. In 1991 the Sydney airport handled 8,439 flights and 140,000 passengers.

11 HISTORY

The Micmac Indians inhabited Nova Scotia long before the first explorers arrived from Europe. The first visitors were Norsemen in the early 11th century.

European Exploration and Settlement

In June 1497, Italian explorer John Cabot noted the rich fishing grounds in the area, and planted the English flag on the northern Cape Breton shore, when there were already 25,000 native Micmac Indians in Nova Scotia. It was the French, however, in 1605, under Pierre du Gua, Sieur de Monts, who established the first permanent settlement of Europeans north of the Gulf of Mexico at Port Royal. Samuel de Champlain accompanied him and organized the famous Order of Good Cheer, the first social club in North America.

In the 17th century, all of Nova Scotia, as well as parts of Québec, New Brunswick, and Maine, which made up an area known as Acadia, was settled by the French. In the early 1700s the English began to seriously contest the French ownership of the province. The English claim went back to 1621 when King James I granted the province to Sir William Alexander. King James named Nova Scotia "the Royal Province," and in 1625 a royal coat of arms was granted. From this crest came the Nova Scotia flag, which made it the first colony of Great Britain with its own flag. Control passed back and forth between the British and French until 1713, when all of Acadia was ceded to the British under the Treaty of Utrecht.

18th and 19th Centuries

For a century the Acadians, French-speaking settlers in the Minas Basin area, prospered in their trade with the New England states while England and France continued their battle for the territory. The French fortress at Louisbourg on Cape Breton Island was captured by the British and then handed back in 1748 under the Treaty of Aix-la-Chapelle. A year later the seat of government moved from Annapolis Royal to Halifax, when Governor Edward Cornwallis established a garrison and settlement there. British distrust in 1755 led to the expulsion to Louisiana and Virginia of all Acadians who would not swear allegiance to the British Crown. Louisbourg fell to the British for the last time in 1758.

After British control was firmly established in Nova Scotia, many of the Acadians returned.

In 1753, 2,000 Protestants from Germany founded the town and county of Lunenburg. In 1760, 22 shiploads of "New England Planters" (farmers from New England) arrived to occupy lands vacated by the Acadians. Seven years later, 7,000 more Planters settled mainly in the Annapolis Valley. In the 1770s, 11 shiploads of Yorkshiremen settled in Cumberland County where many of their descendants still farm the land. Following the American Revolution (1775–83), 25,000 British Loyalists arrived from the newly independent New England states of the United States of America; 10,000 of them founded the Town of Shelburne in 1783. The influx of the Loyalists doubled Nova Scotia's population, so in 1784 it was partitioned to create the colonies of New Brunswick and Cape Breton Island. After the War of 1812, several thousand blacks, including the Chesapeake Blacks, settled in the Halifax-Dartmouth area. Early in the 1800s, the Highland Scots started to arrive and within 30 years 50,000 had settled on Cape Breton Island and in Pictou and Antigonish counties.

In 1848, largely through the efforts of newspaper owner and patriot Joseph Howe, Nova Scotia became the first British colony to win responsible government. Nova Scotia was one of the four provinces that formed the new federation called the Dominion of Canada in 1867. At that time, the province was in the forefront of international shipbuilding, and the lumber and fish trades. Confederation helped to finance the railroad to Québec City, which opened the province to the interior of the continent. Both world wars emphasized the importance of Halifax, Nova Scotia's capital, as a staging point for convoys and confirmed it as one of the world's major military ports.

Early 20th Century

During World War I (1914–18), Canada lost more than 68,000 soldiers. Veterans returning to Nova Scotia faced a bleak future of scarce low-paying jobs, while tariffs on imports kept prices for consumer goods high. During the 1920s, however, Canada experienced a period of rapid growth in industry. Transportation improvements—railways and roads—enabled businesses to flourish. Automobiles, telephones, electrical appliances, and other consumer goods became widely available.

As in the United States, all of Canada suffered during the Great Depression. In addition to the problems with grain prices during the early 1920s, droughts and frequent crop failures devastated the national economy, which still relied heavily on agriculture. Social welfare programs rapidly expanded during the 1930s, with much of the burden placed on the provincial and municipal governments.

Following World War II (1939–45), consumer spending and immigration to Canada rapidly increased. Urbanization spread quickly by means of the National Housing Act, which made home ownership more easily available. Unemployment insurance and other social welfare

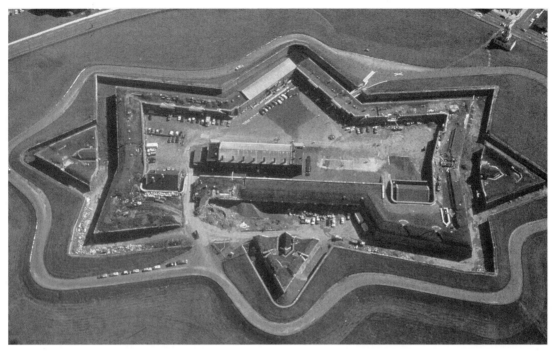

The Citadel Historic Park in Halifax.

programs were also created following the war. Under the leadership of Prime Minister Louis St. Laurent, old age pensions were increased in 1951 and a national hospital insurance plan was introduced in 1957.

Canada's unity as a confederation has often been widely questioned. Most recently, the popular defeat of both the Meech Lake Accord of 1987 and the Charlottetown Accord of 1992 has failed to solve the issue of Québec's role in Canada. If Québec does eventually secede from Canada, the fate of the traditionally poorer maritime provinces would be uncertain. One or more might explore the possibility of admission to the United States.

12 PROVINCIAL GOVERNMENT

The government of Nova Scotia consists of a 52-member elected House of Assembly and Lieutenant Governor who is the Queen's representative in the province. The lieutenant governor is appointed by the Governor General on the advice of the federal cabinet, acting on recommendation of the prime minister. The Legislative Assembly is elected by the people of Nova Scotia for a term of five years. It may be dissolved, however, at any time by the lieutenant governor on the advice of the premier of the province. Ministers of the

Executive Council, or Cabinet, are selected by the premier from elected representatives of the majority party.

13 POLITICAL PARTIES

Political parties first appeared in Nova Scotia in the 1830s. The Liberal Party was in the minority from 1836 to 1867 and was primarily against entry into the confederation. After 1867, however, it became the majority party and held power until 1956 (with brief interruptions in 1878, 1925, and 1928). After 1956, the Conservative Party took the majority until the 1970s.

The last general election was held in May 1993. The parties held the following number of seats in Nova Scotia's House of Assembly as of December 1993: Liberals, 41; Progressive Conservatives, 8; and New Democrats, 3.

Premiers of Nova Scotia

Term	Premier	Party
1867	Hiram Blanchard	Liberal
1867–75	William Annand	Anti-Confederation
1875–78	Philip Carteret Hill	Liberal
1878–82	Simon Hugh Holmes	Conservative
1882	John Sparrow David Thompson	Conservative
1882–84	William Thomas Pipes	Liberal
1884–96	William Stevens Fielding	Liberal
1896–1923	George Henry Murray	Liberal
1923–25	Ernest Howard Armstrong	Liberal
1925–30	Edgar Nelson Rhodes	Conservative
1930–33	Gordon Sydney Harrington	Conservative
1933–40	Angus Lewis Macdonald	Liberal
1940–45	Alexander Stirling MacMillan	Liberal
1945–54	Angus Lewis Macdonald	Liberal
1954	Harold Joseph Connolly	Liberal
1954–56	Henry Davies Hicks	Liberal
1956–67	Robert Lorne Stanfield	Conservative
1967–70	George Isaac Smith	Conservative
1970–78	Gerald Augustine Regan	Liberal
1978–90	John MacLennan Buchanan	Conservative
1990–91	Roger Stuart Bacon	Conservative
1991–93	Donald William Cameron	Conservative
1993–	John Patrick Savage	Liberal

14 LOCAL GOVERNMENT

Nova Scotia consists of 18 counties, of which 12 are separate municipalities and the other 6 are each separated into two districts. The 24 rural municipalities contain 39 incorporated towns and 3 cities. Towns must have a population of at least 1,500 in an area of less than 640 acres (1 square mile). In total, there are 66 municipal units in Nova Scotia—cities, towns, and rural municipalities—which have local governments with powers to enact bylaws governing such matters as zoning and planning.

15 JUDICIAL SYSTEM

The Canadian Constitution grants provincial jurisdiction over the administration of justice, and allows each province to organize its own court system and police forces. The federal government has exclusive domain over cases involving trade and commerce, banking, bankruptcy, and criminal law. The Federal Court of Canada has both trial and appellate divisions for federal cases. The 9-judge Supreme Court of Canada is an appellate court that determines the constitutionality of both federal and provincial statutes. The Tax Court of Canada hears appeals of taxpayers against assessments by Revenue Canada.

In 1990, there were 8 homicides in Nova Scotia, for a rate of 0.9 per 100,000 persons. Breaking and entering offenses in 1989 numbered 232 per 100,000 people for businesses and 517 per 100,000 people for residences.

[16] MIGRATION

The Micmac tribe inhabited Nova Scotia long before the first explorers arrived from Europe. In the 17th century, all of Nova Scotia (as well as parts of Québec, New Brunswick, and Maine, which made up an area known as Acadia) was settled by the French. In the next century, migration involved the forced deportations of Acadians (the descendants of the original French settlers) and their return, as well as an influx of British Loyalists from the American colonies following the American Revolution (1775–83). More recent immigrants to Nova Scotia in the 19th and 20th centuries have included Chinese, Indo-Chinese, African, Asian and eastern European groups. International migration, on a net basis, has not made a significant contribution to population change since the 1960s.

In 1991, Nova Scotia gained 987 residents from migration between provinces (22,148 people entered the province and 21,161 left for other provinces). Ontario was the province of origin for 39% of incoming internal migration and was the destination for 42% of all Nova Scotians leaving the province to live elsewhere in Canada that year.

[17] ECONOMY

Nova Scotia's economy is highly diversified. It has expanded from resource-based employment in agriculture, forestry, fishing, and mining to include many types of manufactured goods as well as business and personal services.

[18] INCOME

Per capita (per person) income for all Nova Scotians was estimated at c$18,956 for 1992. Average household income in Nova Scotia in 1992 was c$38,373, and average family income stood at c$46,872. The average weekly wage earned in the province in 1992 was c$491, but there were considerable variations in this average from one sector to another. The highest average weekly wage of c$778 was earned in the mining sector, followed by c$666 in public administration, c$627 in utilities, and c$580 for goods-producing industries, and only c$337 per week for the trade sector.

[19] INDUSTRY

The leading manufacturing industries in Nova Scotia are food and beverages (including the important fish processing sector); textiles; pulp, paper, and wood products; machinery; metal fabricating; primary metals; and transportation equipment. Approximately 41% of shipments from the province's manufacturers are destined for consumption within Nova Scotia, while 28% of shipments go to other provinces, and 31% is shipped to markets outside Canada.

[20] LABOR

The Nova Scotia labor force grew by 51,000 between 1983 and 1993. The overall participation rate increased from 57.5% to 59.8% in this period as more females actively sought employment. Within the service sector, the community, business, and personal services group is the largest employer with 33.8% of total provincial employment.

Unemployment in Nova Scotia increased to 14.6% in 1993 after having fallen to 9.9% in 1989 from 13.6% in 1985. While the provincial unemployment rate is lower than the average for the Atlantic Provinces, it is traditionally 2–3% higher than the national average. Nova Scotia has the lowest unionization rate of the four maritime provinces, at 30.4%.

21 AGRICULTURE

There were 3,980 farms in Nova Scotia in 1991. Total farm area was 981,064 acres (397,031 hectares), with 262,497 acres (106,231 hectares) of land area under crops. Farm cash receipts in 1992 totaled $312 million.

Nova Scotia has a highly specialized commercial agriculture sector dominated by horticultural crops. Export items include blueberries, apples and processed fruits, vegetables, and juices. A wide variety of vegetables are produced, with potatoes the most important one. Tobacco production in 1992 totaled 387 tons (351 metric tons), while production of grain—including milling wheat, feed wheat, barley, oats, and corn—was 2.2 million bushels in 1993. Production from the tree fruit industry in 1992 included 3.3 million bushels of apples, 60,000 bushels of pears, 4 million quarts (4.5 million liters) of strawberries, and 14,657 tons (13,300 metric tons) of blueberries.

Greenhouse operations numbered 174 in 1991 and covered 8,073,455 cubic feet (228,645 cubic meters). Total sales of these operations approached c$19 million. Vegetables accounted for 13.9% of total sales, while the remainder was made up of flowers and ornamental shrubs.

Production of maple syrup and maple products in 1992 was 26,000 gallons (118,000 liters) with a value of approximately c$933,000.

22 DOMESTICATED ANIMALS

More than 2,300 farms raise cattle in Nova Scotia, but they provide only a quarter of the beef consumed in the province. In 1992 there were 128,000 cattle on provincial farms, 120,000 hogs, and 30,000 sheep. In 1992, dairy product receipts were valued at c$84.2 million, followed by poultry and eggs at c$63.8 million, cattle at c$32.8 million, and hogs at c$23.5 million.

In 1991 Nova Scotia produced 19.5 million dozens of eggs, 3,973 tons (3,605 metric tons) of turkey meat, and 22,732 tons (20,628 metric tons) of fowl and chicken meat. Fur production in 1991 was valued at c$9.7 million. The most significant items were ranch mink and fox and wild muskrat, mink, and beaver.

23 FISHING

Fishing resources, particularly cod, have been hit by dwindling stocks in recent years. As a result, quotas are affecting those who make their living from fishing. Products of the sea include shellfish, such as lobster, deep-sea crab, and scallops; groundfish, such as cod, haddock, and halibut; and estuarial species, such as herring and mackerel. In 1992, of the approx-

Lunenberg is Nova Scotia's premier fishing port.

imately 20,000 workers in the province that were directly employed in fishing and fish processing, 16,487 were registered fishermen. The total landed value for all sea fish in 1993 was estimated at C$467.3 million, while the catch totaled 441,994 tons (401,083 metric tons).

24 FORESTRY

With 80.5% of the provincial land area covered by forest, forestry is of paramount importance to Nova Scotia. Total productive forest land in Nova Scotia exceeds 9.9 million acres (4 million hectares). Only 3.7 million acres (1.5 million hectares), or 37.6%, of this area is provincial Crown land, and a further 1.2% is under federal ownership; the majority of forest land is in the hands of a large number of individual owners, their holdings accounting for 47.4% of the total.

Predominant species include such softwoods as spruce, fir, and white pine, and such hardwoods as red maple, sugar maple, and yellow birch. Forest products take the form of pulp, newsprint paper, paperboard, hardboard, lumber, pulpwood, and Christmas trees. In 1993, forestry directly employed 3,700 persons, with 5,400 others in the forestry processing sector.

25 MINING

In 1993, mining activities employed 6,500 persons. The 5.7 million tons (5.2 million metric tons) of gypsum mined in Nova Scotia in 1992 represented 77.7% of the Canadian total. The principal markets for gypsum are the New England and south Atlantic states of the United States where it is primarily used in the production of wallboard, with other markets in central Canada and many foreign countries. The province also has major deposits of salt, limestone, and anhydrite. The estimated value of mineral production for 1992 was c$540 million for the province, representing an increase of 21.1% over the 1988 total. Other types of mining activity involve barite, crushed stone, horticultural peat, and sand and gravel.

26 ENERGY AND POWER

The mining sector is dominated by coal—production of 4,959 tons (4,500 metric tons) in 1992 was valued at c$265 million (accounting for 49.1% of the total value of all minerals). More than 60% of this coal is used to generate electricity within the province. The largest coal reserves are near Sydney. Substantial reserves of fuel-grade peat also exist in several southwestern counties.

Development of the Cohasset Panuke oilfield, to the southwest of Sable Island, began in 1990. Production started in 1992 with shipments valued in excess of c$100 million. Substantial gas reserves have been discovered off the coast of Nova Scotia. The Venture Project, in the vicinity of Sable Island, is expected to be developed if world prices rise to a sufficient level. The project is expected to cost c$3 billion.

Total net energy generated in Nova Scotia in 1992 approximated 9.7 billion kilowatt hours; thermal generation accounted for almost 91% of this total. In 1981, coal represented 49% and oil 51% of all thermal power generation. During the 1980s, Nova Scotia Power Inc. adopted an operating plan based on conversion to coal generation from imported oil. By 1992 the dependence on oil-fired generation was cut to less than 25%.

The concept of using tides to generate electricity was first proposed in the late 1800s. With the opening of the Annapolis Tidal Generating Station at the mouth of the Annapolis River in 1984, this goal became a reality. It was built as a small-scale tidal project to test and evaluate the potential of the Straflo turbine for possible future use within a massive tidal project on the Minas Basin.

27 COMMERCE

Nova Scotia's foreign exports totaled c$2.3 billion in 1992. More than half of these exports consisted of products of the forest and the sea. Exports of food products are largely in the form of fish, bakery, and dairy products, fruits and fruit preparations, fish meal, and feed. Fabricated materials—primarily paper and paperboard, wood pulp, industrial oils and chemicals, metals and metal-fabricated basic products, and wood-fabricated materials—were the next most significant group of goods exported. The United States market accounted for 68.7% of total Nova Scotia exports in 1992; the European Economic Community, 17.5%; and Japan, 4.5%.

Retail sales in Nova Scotia for 1992 totaled c$6.1 billion. Retail trade per capita (per person) in Nova Scotia increased from c$3,787 in 1982 to c$6,645 in 1992, a growth of 75.5% over the 10-year period.

28 PUBLIC FINANCE

The fiscal year runs from 1 April to 31 March. For fiscal year 1992/93, total revenues were c$4.4 billion; expenditures totaled c$5.5 billion. The largest expenditure areas were health, education, interest on debt, transportation and communication, social services, and resource development.

29 TAXATION

Taxation rates for provincial residents include a retail sales tax of 11% to cover most physician and hospital costs. A major consumption tax was levied on gasoline. The personal income tax rate for Nova Scotia residents is 59.5% of the federal basic tax, while the corporation tax is 16% of taxable income and 5% for small businesses. For the 1994 taxation year a surtax of 20% was applied on provincial tax payable between c$7,000 and c$10,499, and 30% on provincial tax payable of c$10,500 and over.

30 HEALTH

The annual number of births in the province has remained fairly steady recently at about 12,000 (11,874 in 1992; a rate of 12.9 per 1,000 residents), while deaths have increased from an annual level of 7,000 to 7,500 (7,544 in 1992; a rate of 8.2 per 1,000 residents) since the mid-1980s. Therapeutic abortions in Nova Scotia numbered 1,871 in 1990, for a rate

of 8.7 per 1,000 females aged 15–44 and a ratio of 14.5 per 100 live births. The decline in birth rates, which began in the early 1960s, has resulted in a shift in the age distribution of the population. Extended life expectancy has also contributed to an increasingly older population. Between 1976 and 1993 the proportion of the total population under 15 years of age declined from 26.8% to 20.1%, while the number of people over 65 years of age increased from 9.7% to 12.7% of the total. Reported cases of selected diseases in 1990 included chicken pox, 852; salmonellosis, 336; gonococcal infections, 310; campylobacteriosis, 223; and giardiasis, 119. There were 17 new AIDS cases reported in 1990; in 1991, the total number of cases was 81.

Hospitals and maternity wards are provided to communities throughout the province, with regional hospitals providing some of the more specialized requirements. As of 1993, Nova Scotia had 51 hospitals and health centers. In the late 1980s, there were 44 general hospitals with 4,928 beds, and 5 pediatric, psychiatric, rehabilitation, and extended health care hospitals with 920 beds. The Victoria General Hospital in Halifax is the overall referral hospital for the province and in many instances for the Atlantic Region. The Izaak Walton Killam Hospital provides similar regional specialization for children. Psychiatric facilities are available in Dartmouth and Sydney.

31 HOUSING

The 1991 Census enumerated 324,375 occupied dwellings in Nova Scotia, of

Photo Credit: Canadian Tourism Commission photo.

Humpback whales near Brier Island. Many whales, dolphins, porpoises, and seals travel through the Bay of Fundy along Nova Scotia.

which 70.6% were owner-occupied and the remaining 29.4% were rented units. The most significant difference in cost of living from one area to another is the cost of housing or rent. In January 1993 the estimated price of a three-bedroom bungalow was c$128,000 in Halifax's Clayton Park, c$96,000 in Dartmouth East, c$123,000 in Bedford, and c$82,000 in Sackville. A comparable house in other parts of the province would generally be priced in the ic$70,000–c$85,000 range. Rental rates for a modern two-bedroom apartment average approximately c$629 per month in Halifax City, compared to c$561 in Dartmouth and c$430–c$470 in the larger towns of the province.

32 EDUCATION

Elementary and secondary schools offer free instruction from primary through grade 12. School attendance is compulsory from 6 to 16 years of age. During the 1992/93 academic year almost 169,000 students were enrolled in elementary, junior high, and senior high schools.

Eleven regional vocational schools, the Institute of Technology, the Adult Vocational Training Campuses in Dartmouth and Sydney, the Nautical Institute in Port Hawkesbury, and the College of Geographic Sciences in Lawrencetown have been integrated into the province's Community College System. Three other vocational schools are associate members of the Community College System. Enrollment in career programs in postsecondary community colleges in 1990/91 was 2,692.

Halifax is the center for several universities, including Dalhousie, Saint Mary's, Mount Saint Vincent, King's College, and the Technical University of Nova Scotia. The Technical University provides bachelor's and master's degrees in engineering and architecture and a doctorate degree in engineering. Other facilities in the Halifax metro area include the Nova Scotia College of Art and Design, the Atlantic School of Theology, and the Maritime School of Social Work. Other areas of the province are served by Université Ste. Anne at Church Point, Acadia University in Wolfville, St. Francis Xavier in Antigonish, and the University College of Cape Breton in Sydney. Other specialized facilities throughout the province include the Cox Institute of Agricultural Technology, the Nova Scotia Agricultural College, and the Nova Scotia Teachers College, all in Truro, and the Coast Guard College at Point Edward. In 1990/91, full-time university enrollment was 27,009 (24,694 undergraduate, 2,315 graduate), while part-time enrollment was 8,371 (6,808 undergraduate, 1,563 graduate).

33 ARTS

The Rebecca Cohn Auditorium in Halifax is center stage for Symphony Nova Scotia and other musical and theatrical performances. The Neptune Theatre provides professional repertory theater in Halifax. Art galleries are found throughout the province, and the Art Gallery of Nova Scotia has renovated a historic building for its new headquarters. The site is close to the Nova Scotia College of Art and Design in downtown Halifax. In 1990/91, Nova Scotia's eight performing arts companies gave 1,141 performances before a total attendance of 357,162.

34 LIBRARIES AND MUSEUMS

Historical houses, sites, and museums attract tourists and residents who wish to examine the history of the province. These include the Fortress of Louisbourg, the Port Royal Habitation, Fort Anne, the Halifax Citadel, the Alexander Graham Bell Museum, Sherbrooke Village, Ross Farm, the Maritime Museum of the Atlantic, the Nova Scotia Museum of Natural History, and many more.

35 COMMUNICATIONS

The number of telephone access lines in use in Nova Scotia increased 3.4% between 1989 and 1991 and numbered over 512,000 in 1991 (including both residential and business telephones). All local telephone service is provided by Maritime Telegraph and Telephone, which is a private company, while long distance service is now being offered by both Maritime and other companies. As of 1994, Nova Scotia had 18 AM and 11 FM radio stations, and 6 television stations.

36 PRESS

Halifax has two daily newspapers: *The Chronicle-Herald* and *The Mail-Star*. Other daily papers are published in Sydney, Amherst, Dartmouth, New Glasgow, and Truro.

37 TOURISM, TRAVEL, AND RECREATION

Recreational activities in Nova Scotia are often centered on the seacoast because of its proximity to most of the population. While the water is on the cool side along the Atlantic coast, the beaches on the Northumberland Strait enjoy some of the warmest waters north of the Gulf of Mexico. Kejimkujik National Park and Cape Breton Highlands National Park are administered by the federal government, while smaller provincial parks are located throughout the province.

Tourism is an important sector in the provincial economy. Total tourism receipts exceed c\$800 million and over 30,000 are employed in the many aspects of the industry. More than a million persons visit the province each year, with almost one quarter of these coming from outside Canada.

New construction and renovations have modernized and expanded the accommodations sector in the past five years. In 1992 there were 682 establishments providing 13,025 rooms, an increase of 1,074 rooms since 1988.

Festivals, exhibitions, and various other celebrations throughout the province attract both residents and tourists. A few of the most notable events include: the Annapolis Valley Apple Blossom Festival, the Antigonish Highland Games, the Nova Scotia Provincial Exhibition, the Joseph Howe Festival, the Nova Scotia Fisheries Exhibition and Fishermen's Reunion, and the Buskers Festival. Halifax is also host to the Nova Scotia International Tattoo (a military drill held outdoors to music) in late June.

38 SPORTS

Sailing, wind surfing, and canoeing are all enjoyed extensively throughout the province. In winter the lakes become a skater's paradise, and the hills and mountains of areas such as Martock, Cape Smokey, and Wentworth attract downhill skiers. Virtually all towns and many smaller communities have arenas, bowling alleys, gymnasiums, tennis courts, ball diamonds, playing fields, and curling rinks (curling is a game imported from Scotland in which large rounded stones with attached handles are slid down an ice-covered playing area toward a circular target). Golf courses abound and are available within short distances of all communities.

Spectator sports are available in the major towns, with the Halifax Metro Centre Stadium attracting professional sporting and other touring entertainment events.

39 FAMOUS NOVA SCOTIANS

Nova Scotia was the birthplace of three Canadian prime ministers: Sir John Thompson (1845–94), Sir Charles Tupper (1821–1915), and Sir Robert Borden (1854–1937).

Famous Nova Scotian entertainers include actress Joanna Shimkus (b.1943) and singers Clarence Eugene "Hank"

Snow (b.1914), Anne Murray (b.1945), and Carole Baker (b.1949).

Noted novelists born in Nova Scotia include Hugh MacLennan (1907–90), Alden Nowlen (1933–83), and Joan Clark (b.1934).

40 BIBLIOGRAPHY

Bumsted, J. M. *The Peoples of Canada.* New York: Oxford University Press, 1992.

LeVert, Suzanne. *Let's Discover Canada: Nova Scotia.* New York: Chelsea House, 1992.

Lotz, Jim. *Discover Canada: Nova Scotia.* Toronto: Grolier, 1991.

Sorensen, Lynda. *Canada: Provinces and Territories.* Vero Beach, Fla.: Rourke Book Co., 1995.

Thompson, Alexa. *Nova Scotia.* Minneapolis: Lerner Publications, 1995.

Wansborough, M. B. *Great Canadian Lives.* New York: Doubleday, 1986.

Weihs, Jean. *Facts about Canada, Its Provinces and Territories.* New York: H. W. Wilson, 1995.

ONTARIO

ORIGIN OF PROVINCE NAME: Derived from the Iroquois Indian word *Kanadario*, meaning "sparkling water" or "beautiful lake."

CAPITAL: Toronto.

ENTERED CONFEDERATION: 1 July 1867.

MOTTO: *Ut incepit fidelis sic permanet* (Loyal it began, loyal it remains).

COAT OF ARMS: In the center, the provincial shield of arms displays in the upper third the cross of St. George (a red cross on a white background) and in the lower two-thirds three gold maple leaves on a green background. Above the shield is a black bear standing on a gold and green bar. Supporting the shield is a brown moose on the left and a brown Canadian deer on the right. Beneath the shield the provincial motto appears.

FLAG: The flag has a red field, with the Union Jack displayed in the upper quarter on the left side and the provincial shield of arms centered in the right half.

FLORAL EMBLEM: White trillium.

PROVINCIAL BIRD: Common loon (unofficial).

TREE: Eastern white pine.

GEMSTONE: Amethyst.

TIME: 7 AM EST = noon GMT; 6 AM CST = noon GMT.

1 LOCATION AND SIZE

Ontario, five times as large as France, covers some 412,579 square miles (1,068,580 square kilometers) and is bordered on the north by Hudson Bay; on the east by Québec; on the south by the St. Lawrence River, the Great Lakes, and the US state of Minnesota; and on the west by Manitoba.

2 TOPOGRAPHY

Three main geological regions make up Ontario: the Great Lakes-St. Lawrence Lowlands, the Canadian Shield, and the Hudson Bay Lowlands. The Hudson Bay Lowlands are narrow coastal plains bordering Hudson Bay and James Bay; the land is wet and covered by scrub growth.

The Canadian Shield, covering the rest of northern Ontario from Lake Superior to Hudson Bay, and extending into the southern part of the province, is a vast rocky plateau. Although the soil is poor and not well suited to large-scale farming, there is a wealth of minerals, forests, and water power. The Canadian Shield and the Hudson Bay Lowlands cover 90% of the province's territory. Four of the five Great Lakes are the most visible results of the ice age in Ontario, providing the longest fresh water beach in the world. The biggest, Lake Superior, is the world's largest body of fresh water. About 68,490 square miles (177,390 square kilometers), or one-sixth of Ontario's terrain, is covered by some

400,000 lakes and 37,000 miles (59,000 kilometers) of rivers.

The Great Lakes-St. Lawrence Lowlands comprise the rest of southern Ontario. Here is where most of Ontario's population can be found; it is also the area with the most of province's industry, commerce, and agricultural lands.

The short Niagara River, which flows from Lake Erie into Lake Ontario is the site of Niagara Falls (at the Ontario-New York border), which drains some 800,000 gallons (3,000,000 liters) of water per second over its 187-foot (57-meter) drop. The highest point in Ontario is found at Ishpatina Ridge in the Timiskaming District, at an elevation of 2,274 feet (693 meters).

3 CLIMATE

The relatively temperate climate is more severe east of the Great Lakes. Mean annual summer temperatures reach 72°F (22°C) in the south, where the temperate climate and fertile soils nurture a major agricultural industry. This relatively small area has more than half of Canada's best agricultural land. At Winisk, average daily temperatures reach only 54–59°F (12–15°C) in July, dropping to -13°F (-25°C) in January. The warmest recorded temperature in Ontario was 108°F (42.2°C) on 20 July 1919 at Biscotasing; the coldest was -73°F (-58.3°C) on 23 January 1935 at Iroquois Falls.

4 PLANTS AND ANIMALS

The relatively temperate climate of the south is hospitable for a wide variety of

Ontario Population Profile

Estimated 1996 population:	11,189,000
Population change, 1981–91:	16.9%
Population by ethnic origin:	
Multiple origins:	33.7%
British origins:	25.2%
French:	5.2%
Italian:	4.8%
German:	2.9%
Chinese:	2.7%
Dutch:	1.8%
Portuguese:	1.7%
East Indian:	1.7%
Polish:	1.5%
Black:	1.5%
Jewish:	1.3%
Ukrainian:	1.0%
Greek:	0.8%
Filipino:	0.8%
Aboriginal:	0.7%
Other single origins:	12.7%

Population by Age Group

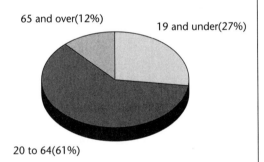

65 and over(12%)

19 and under(27%)

20 to 64(61%)

Top Cities with Populations over 10,000

City	Population	% Change 1986–91
Toronto	635,395	3.8
North York	562,564	1.1
Scarborough	524,598	8.2
Mississauga	463,388	23.9
Hamilton	318,499	3.8
Ottawa	313,987	4.4
Etobicoke	309,993	2.3
London	303,165	12.6
Brampton	234,445	24.4
Windsor	191,435	-0.9

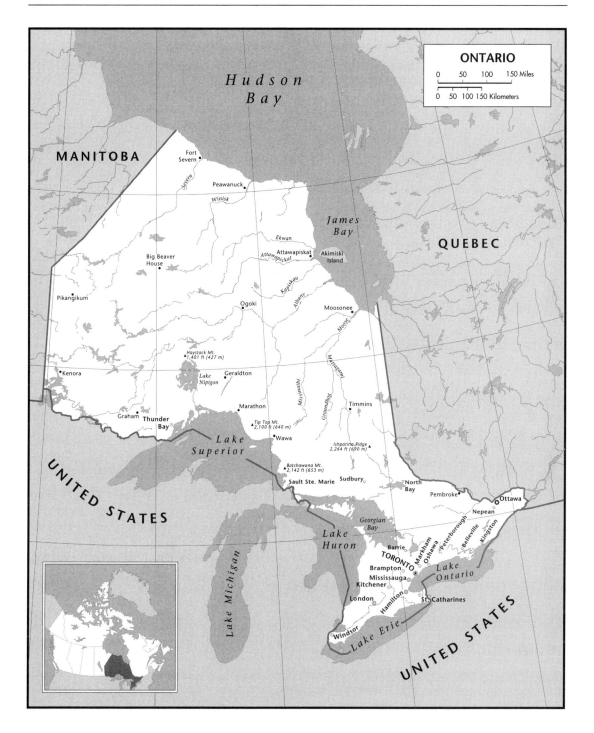

ONTARIO

0   50   100   150 Miles

0   50 100 150 Kilometers

Hudson Bay

MANITOBA

Fort Severn

Severn

Peawanuck

Winisk

James Bay

QUEBEC

Ekwan

Big Beaver House

Attawapiskat

Attawapiskat

Akimiski Island

Pikangikum

Kapiskau

Albany

Ogoki

Moosonee

Moose

Haystack Mt.
▲1,401 ft (427 m)

Missinaibi

Mattagami

Kenora

Lake Nipigon

Geraldton

Marathon

Groundhog

Timmins

Tip Top Mt.
▲2,100 ft (640 m)

Wawa

Ishpatina Ridge
2,264 ft (690 m)

Lake Superior

UNITED STATES

Batchawana Mt.
▲2,142 ft (653 m)

Sault Ste. Marie

Sudbury

North Bay

Pembroke

Ottawa

Nepean

Georgian Bay

Graham

Thunder Bay

Lake Huron

Barrie

Peterborough

Belleville

Kingston

Lake Michigan

TORONTO

Markham

Oshawa

Brampton

Mississauga

Lake Ontario

Kitchener

London

Hamilton

St. Catharines

Windsor

Lake Erie

UNITED STATES

native as well as imported European plants. Many migratory flying species annually traverse Ontario: Point Pelee is a yearly site for the autumnal exodus of monarch butterflies, and Aylmer is the annual layover location for 60,000 migrating tundra swans headed for the Arctic. Muskie and trout are common stream and lake fish species. Woodland caribou, moose, muskrats, beavers, eagles, and wolves inhabit the northern reaches of the province. Polar bears live in the far north along Hudson Bay.

5 ENVIRONMENTAL PROTECTION

The Ministry of Natural Resources (MNR) is responsible for the management of provincial parks, forests, fisheries, wildlife, minerals, and Crown lands and waters, which comprise 87% of Ontario's area. The MNR also develops policies on forestry, fisheries, wildlife, parks, and land and water issues. These policies aim to sustain Ontario's natural resources for future generations. The MNR has helped create several partnership arrangements in resource management that show to the public the social costs and benefits of resource development. Some of these partnerships include the Wildlife Working Group, the Strategic Plan for Ontario Fisheries, and the Forest Management Agreements. Ontario's Chapleau Game Preserve is the largest in the world.

6 POPULATION

With an estimated 1996 population of 11,189,000 people, Ontario is Canada's most heavily populated province. The Canadian Shield and the Hudson Bay Lowlands cover 90% of the province's territory, but are home to only 10% of Ontario's population. Toronto, Ontario's capital and Canada's largest city, had a metropolitan area population of 3,893,046 in 1991. Ottawa, the bilingual, bicultural national capital, sits at the junction of the Gatineau, Rideau, and Ottawa Rivers; together with Hull, Québec, the metropolitan population in 1991 was 920,857, ranking it fourth in Canada. Other metropolitan areas and their 1991 populations (and national rankings) include: Hamilton, 599,760 (9th); London, 381,522 (10th); St. Catharines-Niagara, 364,552 (11th); Kitchener, 356,421 (12th); Windsor, 262,075 (15th); Oshawa, 240,104 (16th); Sudbury, 157,613 (21st); and Thunder Bay, 124,427 (25th).

7 ETHNIC GROUPS

About one-third of Ontario's population is of British origin, and many individuals are of mixed British and French ancestry. Other heritages for those reporting a single ethnic origin include French, Italian, German, Dutch, Chinese, Portuguese, South Asian, Jewish, and Polish. In 1991, Ontario had almost 250,000 people of Aboriginal (native) or Métis origin. Six Nations of the Grand River, which consists of 13 different groups, has the largest native band in Canada.

8 LANGUAGES

In 1991, English was the mother tongue of 74.5% of Ontario's residents, while French was the primary language of 5% of Ontarians and the remaining 20.5% had other first languages. English is the only

Photo Credit: Canadian Tourism Commission photo.

The CN Tower and Skydome in Toronto. With a population of about four million, Toronto is Canada's largest city and headquarters for many Canadian corporations.

official language, but Ontario's French speakers play an essential part in the province's cultural life and are the largest language minority. The provincial government provides services in French in the regions where the French-speaking population is sufficiently high. Toronto has more Italian speakers than any city outside of Italy.

9 RELIGIONS

In 1991, 44.4% of the population, or about 4,477,700 people, was Protestant, including 1,422,000 members of the United Church of Canada, 1,069,000 Anglicans, 423,600 Presbyterians, 272,300 Baptists, 231,900 Lutherans,

and 231,900 Pentecostals. Ontario also had about 3,580,100 Catholics (3,539,800 Roman Catholics and 40,300 Ukrainian Catholics), who made up 35.5% of the population. There were about 191,600 people of Eastern Orthodox faith, 181,500 Jews, 151,300 Moslems, 110,900 Hindus, 70,600 Buddhists, and 50,400 Sikhs. Some 1,280,800 provincial residents professed no religious affiliation in 1991.

10 TRANSPORTATION

Northern Ontario's towns were built because of the railway, and today rails and roads carry the products of the mines and mills southward. Further north, travel is often limited to air and water.

In 1990, Ontario had 4,756,885 passenger cars; 1,118,629 trucks, truck tractors, and buses; and 124,838 motorcycles and mopeds, for a total of 6,000,352 registered motor vehicles (35% of Canada's total).

Access to the Great Lakes and the St. Lawrence Seaway helps make waterborne traffic an important part of the province's transportation system. In 1991 Ontario's ports handled 74.7 million tons (67.8 million metric tons) of cargo.

Public transportation is well-developed in the metropolitan Toronto area. Toronto Transit operates the subway system, with streetcar and bus service available as well. The provincial government operates the GO (Government of Ontario) commuter train service, connecting Toronto to Richmand Hill, Georgetown, and Bradford in the north; to Whitby in the east; and to Hamilton in the west. Urban transit in 1991 consisted of 4,631 buses, 269 trolley coaches, 291 light-rail vehicles, 620 heavy rail vehicles, and 309 other vehicles. These vehicles together provided over 685.4 million passenger trips of over 218.9 million miles (352.2 million kilometers).

International air service is available from Ottawa as well as Pearson International Airport in Toronto. In 1991 Pearson served 17.2 million passengers, making it Canada's busiest airport, and ranking it 15th in the world for amount of international passenger traffic.

11 HISTORY

Sailing into the large bay that bears his name, Henry Hudson became the first European to touch the shores of present-day Ontario in 1610. In 1613, Samuel de Champlain and Ètienne Brûlé made the first contacts with the aboriginal people in the southern part of the province.

In 1774, the British ruled over southern Ontario, then part of the British colony of Québec. Under the Constitutional Act of 1791, "Québec" was divided in two and Ontario renamed Upper Canada. This became necessary with the tremendous influx of Loyalist refugees after the American Revolution (1775–83).

In 1840, the Act of Union saw Upper and Lower Canada reunited, this time with the name Canada. The two regions, Canada West and Canada East, took part in the 1864 confederation debate. When the Dominion of Canada was created in 1867, the regions became the separate provinces of Ontario and Québec.

Early 20th Century

During World War I (1914–18), Canada lost more than 68,000 soldiers. Veterans returning to Ontario faced a bleak future of scarce low-paying jobs, while tariffs on imports kept prices for consumer goods high. As in the prairie provinces, Ontarian farmers had prospered from high wheat prices during World War I, but with the end of the war global grain markets collapsed and wheat prices fell 50% by 1920. Affected farmers organized the United Farmers Movement in Ontario in 1919 to protest the low farm product prices and

Photo Credit: Canadian Tourism Commission photo.

Niagara Falls, along the border of the United States, drains about 800,000 gallons (3 million liters) of water per second from the short Niagara River.

high transportation rates, and played an important role in provincial politics of the 1920s.

During the 1920s, grain prices recovered and Canada experienced a period of rapid growth in industry, with heavy industry developing across southern Ontario. Transportation improvements—railways and roads—enabled businesses to flourish. Automobiles, telephones, electrical appliances, and other consumer goods became widely available.

Just as in the United States, all of Canada suffered during the Great Depression. In addition to the problems with grain prices during the early 1920s, droughts and frequent crop failures devastated the national economy, which still relied heavily on agriculture. Social welfare programs rapidly expanded during the 1930s, with much of the burden placed on the provincial and municipal governments.

1940s–1990s

Following World War II (1939–45), consumer spending and immigration to Canada rapidly increased. Urbanization spread quickly by means of the National Housing Act, which made home ownership more easily available. Unemployment insurance and other social welfare programs were also created following the war. Under the leadership of Prime Minister Louis St. Laurent, old age pensions were increased in 1951 and a national hospital insurance plan was introduced in 1957. The St. Lawrence Seaway, completed in 1959, was an important development for the expansion of commerce in Ontario and eastern Canada by permitting oceangoing ships access to the center of the nation.

During the 1950s and 1960s, the monitoring of northern Canadian airspace served a vital role in the defense of North America against a possible nuclear attack from the Soviet Union. But when ballistic missiles (which are launched in an arc toward their targets from great distances) replaced bombers as the means of delivering nuclear warheads, this strategy became obsolete.

Canada's unity as a confederation has often been widely questioned. Most recently, the popular defeat of both the Meech Lake Accord of 1987 and the Charlottetown Accord of 1992 has failed to solve the issue of Québec's role in Canada. If Québec does eventually secede from Canada, Canada would lose 25% of its population and much of its economic strength; also it would likely no longer have the ability to be as assertive in world affairs. Moreover, the ability for the remainder of Canada to stay unified would be in serious doubt.

12 PROVINCIAL GOVERNMENT

The structure of the provincial government reflects that of the federal government. For example, the provincial premier, as the majority party leader of the legislature, functions much like the Canadian prime minister. Provincial legislators, like their federal counterparts in Parliament, are elected to represent a constitutional jurisdiction and pass legislation. They do so as members of the 130-seat Legislative Assembly, 30 members of which represent metropolitan Toronto. A provincial lieutenant-governor approves laws passed by the legislature, much like the Governor General at the federal level. There is no provincial equivalent, however, to the federal Senate.

13 POLITICAL PARTIES

The Liberal Party was the principal political group in the 1800s, and held power continuously during from 1848 to 1905. After 1905, the Conservative Party dominated, reaching a high point in 1929 by winning 92 of 112 seats. During the late 1910s and early 1920s, the United Farmers of Ontario (UFO) controlled a considerable minority of seats. After 1943, the province began to see three parties vie for power; from the 1940s to 1960s, the Co-operative Commonwealth Federation (CCF) and later the New Democratic Party (NDP) irregularly won control over a sizable minority of seats. Finally in 1990, the NDP won control of the Legislative Assembly.

The most recent general election was held on 7 September 1990. The parties held the following number of seats in Ontario's Legislative Assembly in 1994: New Democratic Party, 70; Liberal Party, 34; Progressive Conservative Party, 21; and Independent, 4; with 1 seat vacant.

Premiers of Ontario

Term	Premier	Party
1867–71	John Sandfield Macdonald	Liberal-Conser.
1871–72	Edward Blake	Liberal
1872–96	Oliver Mowat	Liberal
1896–99	Arthur Sturgis Hardy	Liberal
1899–1905	George William Ross	Liberal
1905–14	James Pliny Whitney	Conservative
1914–19	William Howard Hearst	Conservative
1919–23	Ernest Charles Drury	United Farmers
1923–30	George Howard Ferguson	Conservative
1930–34	George Stewart Henry	Conservative
1934–42	Mitchell Frederick Hepburn	Liberal
1942–43	Gordon Daniel Conant	Liberal
1943	Harry Corwin Nixon	Liberal
1943–48	George Alexander Drew	Conservative
1948–49	Thomas Laird Kennedy	Conservative
1949–61	Leslie Miscampbell Frost	Conservative
1961–71	John Parmenter Robarts	Conservative
1971–85	William Grenville Davis	Conservative
1985	Frank Miller	Conservative
1985–90	David Robert Peterson	Liberal
1990–	Robert Keith Rae	New Democratic

14 LOCAL GOVERNMENT

The populous regions of southern Ontario are divided into counties, regional municipalities, the Municipality of Metro Toronto, the District Municipality of Muskoka, and the Restructured County of Oxford. Cities and towns within counties are not under the jurisdiction of county governments. Restructured municipalities have about 66% of Ontario's population and contain fewer but larger incorporated municipalities than those of the counties. Restructured units provide more extensive services than do counties, such as water supply, sewage treatment, waste management, regional planning, social services, long-term financing, and police services.

Northern Ontario is divided into 10 territorial districts (which are not considered unified municipal units), and has 1 regional municipality (Sudbury). The far northern parts on Ontario are not organized into any municipal units.

15 JUDICIAL SYSTEM

The Canadian Constitution grants provincial jurisdiction over the administration of justice, and allows each province to organize its own court system and police forces. The federal government has exclusive domain over cases involving trade and commerce, banking, bankruptcy, and criminal law. The Federal Court of Canada has both trial and appellate divisions for federal cases. The 9-judge Supreme Court of Canada is an appellate court that determines the constitutionality of both federal and provincial statutes. The Tax Court of Canada hears appeals of taxpayers against assessments by Revenue Canada.

Provincial courts, under the Ministry of the Attorney General, are divided into seven regional offices plus the metropolitan Toronto district.

In 1990, there were 180 homicides in Ontario, for a rate of 1.9 per 100,000 persons. Breaking and entering offenses in 1989 numbered 359 per 100,000 people for businesses and 611 per 100,000 people for residences.

16 MIGRATION

Ontario's first immigrants arrived about 10,000 years ago, during the last ice age. The European explorers encountered the Iroquois and Algonquin descendants of those first migrants in the 17th century. From 1779 on, waves of English, Scottish, and Irish immigrants followed one another, moving up the St. Lawrence and populating the country. Today, immigration continues to be important to Ontario, and there are large numbers of people of Italian, German, Chinese, Dutch, Portuguese, Indian, and Polish origin.

In 1991, Ontario lost 6,604 residents from migration between provinces (82,995 people entered the province and 89,599 left for other provinces). As Canada's most populous province, Ontario is both the primary origin and primary destination for internal migration. In 1991, Québec was the leading province of origin for people entering Ontario from other provinces, accounting for 32% of the incoming internal migration. British Columbia was the principal destination for Ontarians leaving to live elsewhere in Canada, accounting for 26% of outgoing internal migration in 1991.

17 ECONOMY

Ontario is Canada's most productive province having generated some 40% of the country's gross domestic product (GDP) in 1992. The main industries are manufacturing, finance, construction, tourism, agriculture, and forestry.

18 INCOME

Average family income in the province was c$55,286 in 1989. As of December 1992, average weekly earnings in the province amounted to c$583.25. Average weekly earnings in the manufacturing sector in mid-1990 were c$525.17, and c$504.51 in the electrical products industries.

19 INDUSTRY

Toronto is Canada's leading producer of manufactured goods. The headquarters of a large number of Canadian companies are also found in Toronto. Automobiles are Ontario's major manufacturing industry and are its most important export; the auto industry employed 136,000 people and provided 26% of Canada's total exports in 1989. In 1990, the value of manufactured shipments totaled c$156 billion. The leading contributors were: transportation equipment, c$41.8 billion; food products, c$15.4 billion; chemicals and chemical products, c$12.8 billion; electrical and electronic products, c$11.6 billion; fabricated metal products, c$10.4 billion; and primary metal products, c$10.1 billion.

20 LABOR

As of 1993, 65.9% of Ontarians age 15 and older participated in the labor force. In 1992, Ontario had 38.3% of Canada's total labor force. That year, employment was down 1.2% to 4.7 million and the unemployment rate reached a record 10.8%. In 1990, of the 4.9 million employed persons, services engaged 1.6 million people; manufacturing, 960,400; trade, 842,800; transportation, communications, and other utilities, 343,000; finance, insurance, and real estate, 338,100; construction, 323,400; government, 303,800; agriculture, 107,800; and fishing, trapping, forestry, and mining, 49,000.

In 1992, the Ontario Legislature passed revisions to the Ontario Labour Relations Act which went into effect on 1 January

1993. Organized labor generally approved of the bill, but many businesses opposed it, claiming plant investment would decline as a result. The most important change is one that prohibited employers from hiring replacement workers (scabs) if 60% of employees support a strike. Major unions in Ontario include the Canadian Autoworkers Union, the United Food and Commercial Workers Union, the Ontario Public Service Employees Union, and the Ontario Nurses' Association.

21 AGRICULTURE

In 1991, the total land area of farms in Ontario exceeded 13.5 million acres (5.4 million hectares), of which 8.4 million acres (3.4 million hectares) was under crops. Some 529 farms in Ontario were exclusively devoted to growing wheat in 1991; 11,432 produced other small grains, 3,746 grew fruits and vegetables, 3,535 grew other field crops, and 7,312 produced specialty crops. Field crop production in 1992 included wheat, 1,385,765 tons (1,257,500 metric tons); barley, 671,779 tons (609,600 metric tons); oats, 202,217 tons (183,500 metric tons); dry beans, 47,937 tons (43,500 metric tons); and rye, 27,991 tons (25,400 metric tons). Some 15 wineries in the Niagara Peninsula have produced wines of international acclaim; 80% of the national wine production comes from this area.

22 DOMESTICATED ANIMALS

As of 1991, Ontario had 16,853 cattle farms, 9,757 dairy farms, 3,830 hog farms, 1,583 poultry farms, and 1,921 livestock combination farms.

23 FISHING

As of 1991, Ontario had about 1,500 registered freshwater commercial anglers. Sport fishing is a popular activity on Ontario's rivers and lakes.

24 FORESTRY

In 1991, Ontario had 104.3 million acres (42.2 million hectares) of timber productive forest, of which provincial ownership accounted for 86%; private lands, 13%; and federal areas, 1%. The provincial government licenses logging rights. Of the total timber productive forest volume of 134.6 billion cubic feet (3.77 billion cubic meters), 63% consists of broad-leaved species and 37% is coniferous (cone-bearing evergreen trees or shrubs). Principal types include spruce, popular, birch, pine, and maple. Many Ontario towns have at least one industry connected to forestry. The forest industry accounts for about 5.8% of Ontario's annual exports.

25 MINING

Mining has always played an important role in the development of Ontario's economy. Extraction of gold, nickel, copper, uranium, and zinc represents a multibillion-dollar business. Production in 1992 included salt, 7,326,096 tons (6,648,000 metric tons); copper, 284,919 tons (258,547 metric tons); zinc, 210,286 tons (190,822 metric tons); nickel, 136,847 tons (124,181 metric tons); uranium, 1,089 tons (988 metric tons); silver, 468,749 pounds (212,681 kilograms); and gold, 161,549 pounds (73,298 kilograms). In 1992, the value of mineral production was c$4.7 billion (highest in Canada), of which metals accounted for 75.7%; structural minerals, 19.3%; and nonmetals, 5%. Thunder Bay has the largest open pit gemstone mine in North America; all types of amethyst are found there.

26 ENERGY AND POWER

The Bruce Nuclear Power Station in Bruce Township opened in 1967 as Canada's first nuclear power-generating plant, and became fully operational in 1969. As of the early 1990s, five of Canada's seven nuclear power plants were in Ontario. In 1991, crude oil production totaled 8,298,790 cubic feet (235,000 cubic meters), valued at c$36 million.

In 1991, electricity generated totaled 142.4 billion kilowatt hours and consumption within the province amounted to 134.1 billion kilowatt hours. Electrical power in Ontario is relatively inexpensive.

27 COMMERCE

Southern Ontario's heavy population density makes the region the most commercially active in Canada for supermarkets, motor vehicle dealers, general merchandise stores, and gasoline service stations. Ontario's proximity to key US markets puts the province's products less than a day's drive away from a large portion of American consumers.

28 PUBLIC FINANCE

The fiscal year runs from 1 April to 31 March. For fiscal year 1992/93, total revenues were c$45.9 billion; expenditures totaled c$59.02 billion. The largest expenditure areas were health, social services, education, interest on debt, and colleges and universities.

29 TAXATION

The basic personal income tax rate in 1993 was 58%, with high income surtaxes of 20–30%. The retail sales tax was 8%. Major consumption taxes were levied on gasoline and tobacco. In 1991, the average family in Ontario had a cash income of c$59,500 and paid c$28,595 in taxes.

Corporate income tax rates in 1993 were as follows: small business rate, 9.5%; manufacturing and processing corporate rate, 13.5%; general business rate, 15.5%; and capital tax rate, 0.3–1.12%.

30 HEALTH

In 1992 there were 150,593 live births in Ontario, for a rate of 14.2 per 1,000 residents. The death rate in 1992 was 6.9 per 1,000 residents, with 73,206 deaths occurring that year. Therapeutic abortions in Ontario numbered 31,224 in 1990, for a rate of 13.4 per 1,000 females aged 15–44 and a ratio of 20.7 per 100 live births. Reported cases of selected diseases in 1990 included gonococcal infections, 6,148; campylobacteriosis, 5,768; salmonellosis, 3,605; giardiasis, 3,462; amoebiasis, 1,007; syphilis, 979; pertussis, 850; measles, 741; tuberculosis, 704; and type B hepatitis, 656. There were 437 new AIDS cases reported in 1990; in 1991, the total number of cases was 2,058.

As of 1993, Ontario had 307 hospitals and health centers. In the late 1980s, there were 188 general hospitals with 42,824 beds, and 39 pediatric, psychiatric, reha-

Photo Credit: Canadian Tourism Commission photo.

Students playing cricket at Trinity College in Port Hope. As a member of the British Commonwealth, Canadian customs have often been influenced by British culture.

bilitation, and extended health care hospitals with 8,088 beds.

31 HOUSING

In 1990, the average resale value of a home in Toronto was c$254,890; in Mississauga, c$224,449; in Hamilton, c$165,742; and in Ottawa, c$141,562. The average rent for a two-bedroom apartment in Toronto in 1990 was c$683, while the metropolitan area apartment vacancy rate was 0.9%. Average 1990 monthly rents (and the metropolitan area apartment vacancy rate) for other cities included Windsor, c$618 (2.2%); Oshawa, c$605 (1.6%); Thunder Bay, c$581 (0.9%); London, c$549 (2.8%); St.

Catharines-Niagara, c$527 (1.9%); Hamilton, c$522 (1.2%); Kitchener, c$522 (1.3%); and Sudbury, c$506 (0.7%).

32 EDUCATION

In 1990/91, Ontario had 2,009,090 students enrolled in its elementary and secondary schools (39% of the nation's total), with 1,932,755 students in public schools, 66,347 in private schools, 9,266 in federal schools, and 722 in schools for the blind and the deaf.

The University of Toronto, founded in 1827, is the largest university in Canada: in 1990/91, it had 37,649 full-time students with a full-time teaching faculty of 3,116. Other universities in Ontario (with location and year founded) and their 1990/91 full-time enrollments include: York University (North York, 1959), 23,451; University of Western Ontario (London, 1878), 18,593; University of Waterloo (1957), 17,260; University of Guelph (1964), 14,999; University of Ottawa (1848), 14,895; Carleton University (Ottawa, 1942), 14,511; Queen's University (Kingston, 1841), 12,914; McMaster University (Hamilton, 1887), 12,266; Ryerson Polytechnical Institute (Toronto, 1948), 12,013; University of Windsor (1857), 10,335; Brock University (St. Catharines, 1964), 5,597; Laurentian University (Sudbury, 1960), 4,500; Lakehead University (Thunder Bay, 1965), 4,248; Trent University (Peterborough, 1963), 3,701; and the Royal Military College of Canada (Kingston, 1876), 790. In 1990/91, full-time university enrollment was 216,441 (191,901 undergraduate, 24,540 graduate), while part-time enrollment was 105,477 (92,601 undergraduate, 12,876 graduate). Enrollment in career programs in postsecondary community colleges in 1990/91 was 99,466.

33 ARTS

Toronto is well-known for its impressive theatrical productions, which recently have included *The Phantom of the Opera* and *Miss Saigon*; more than 115 professional companies perform plays, cabaret, opera, and dance in Toronto. Toronto also boasts North America's largest film festival which is held each year in September. In 1990/91, Ontario's 124 performing arts companies gave 12,956 performances before a total attendance of 5,025,269.

34 LIBRARIES AND MUSEUMS

The Metropolitan Toronto Reference Library is Canada's largest public library, with more than 4 million items in its collections.

The Royal Ontario Museum in Toronto is Canada's largest, with over 6 million examples of works of art, artifacts, and scientific treasures. Toronto also has the Art Gallery of Ontario, which houses over 15,000 paintings, prints, drawings, and sculptures, including the world's largest public collection of Henry Moore sculptures. Other museums in Toronto include the Gardiner Museum of Ceramic Art, the Museum for Textiles, the Bata Shoe Museum, Canada's Sports Hall of Fame, and the Hockey Hall of Fame. Ottawa has many national museums, including the Canadian Museum of Civilization, the National Gallery of Canada, the Canadian War Museum, the Canadian Museum of Nature, the National Museum of Science and Technology, the Agricultural Museum, and the National Aviation Museum. The Seagram Museum in Waterloo is devoted to both spirits and wines.

35 COMMUNICATIONS

As of 1994, Ontario had 78 AM and 71 FM radio stations, and 28 television stations. Toronto is the headquarters of several broadcasting and cable networks, including the Canadian Broadcasting Corporation, the Canadian Television Network, the Family Channel, First Choice,

Much Music, The Sports Network, Vision TV, and the Youth Channel.

36 PRESS

Nearly 50 daily newspapers are published in Ontario, with Toronto accounting for six: *The Toronto Sun*, *The Toronto Star*, *The Financial Post*, *The Globe and Mail*, *The Korean Times* (in Korean), and *El Popular* (in Spanish). *The Toronto Star*, *The Globe and Mail*, and the *Toronto Sun* were three of the four largest circulating newspapers in Canada in 1991. Ottawa's three daily newspapers are *Le Droit* (French-language), *The Ottawa Citizen*, and the *Ottawa Sun*. International Thomson, a multinational publishing corporation, is headquartered in Toronto and is Canada's largest media company.

37 TOURISM, TRAVEL, AND RECREATION

Tourism is an important sector of the Ontario economy. In 1990, tourist spending of more than c$9.5 billion generated about c$13.4 billion in total revenue for the province and more than 320,000 person-years of employment.

Toronto's Canadian National Exhibition, with crafts and exhibits from around the world, draws thousands of tourists every August. Its Symphony of Fire is the largest fireworks display in the world, while the Caribana is the world's largest Caribbean festival. Ottawa annually holds the largest tulip festival in the world, and Fergus is the site of the biggest Scottish festival in North America.

38 SPORTS

The Sky Dome, the world's first stadium with a completely retractable roof, is the home of Major League Baseball's Toronto Blue Jays, who in 1992 became the first Canadian team to win the World Series. The Blue Jays were baseball's champions again in 1993. Ontario has two teams in the National Hockey League(NHL): the Toronto Maple Leafs and the Ottawa Senators. The Maple Leafs were the Stanley Cup winners in 1932, 1942, 1945, 1947–49, 1951, 1962–64, and 1967; the Senators won it in 1909, 1911, 1920, 1921, 1923, and 1927. The Canadian Football League (CFL) fields three teams in Ontario: the Hamilton Tiger-Cats, CFL champions in 1957, 1963, 1965, 1967, 1972, and 1986; the Ottawa Rough Riders, CFL champions in 1960, 1968, 1969, 1973, and 1976; and the Toronto Argonauts, CFL champions in 1983 and 1991.

Ontario has more than 500 public golf courses; the only Professional Golf Association (PGA) Tour event outside the United States is held near Toronto. Kenora's Lake of the Woods Regatta in August is the largest freshwater sailing regatta in the world. Snowmobiling across the province's 21,000 miles (33,789 kilometers) of snowmobile trails is a popular winter activity.

39 FAMOUS ONTARIANS

Ontarians Sir John A. Macdonald (b.Scotland, 1815–91) and Alexander Mackenzie (b.Scotland, 1822–92) served as Canada's first and second prime ministers, respectively. Other prime ministers native to Ontario have included Arthur Meighen

Toronto is the home of the Blue Jays professional baseball team. In 1992, the Blue Jays became the first Canadian team to win the World Series.

(1874–1960), Mackenzie King (1874–1950), John Diefenbacker (1895–1975), and Lester Pearson (1897–1972), who received the Nobel Peace Prize in 1957.

Military figures include General Sir Arthur Currie (1875–1933), Canadian infantry commander in World War I, and the World War I flying ace Roy A. Brown (1893–1944), who is credited with shooting down Captain Manfred von Richthofen ("the Red Baron"), Germany's leading war hero, on 21 April 1918.

Ontario has been the birthplace of many prominent figures in entertainment and the arts including actors and actresses Mary Pickford (b.Gladys Smith, 1893–1979), Cecilia Parker (b.1909), Robert Beatty (b.1909), Hume Cronyn (b.1911), Lou Jacobi (b.1913), Lorne Greene (1915–87), Ann Rutherford (b.1917), Don Harron (b.1924), John Colicos (b.1928), Christopher Plummer (b.1929), Eugene Levy (b.1946), John Candy (1950–94), Kate Nelligan (b.1951), Dan Aykroyd (b.1952), Rick Moranis (b.1953), Hart Bochner (b.1956), and Corey Haim (b.1972); directors David Cronenberg (b.1943) and Norman Jewison (b.1926); comedians Frank Shuster (b.1916), Rich Little (b.1938), Martin Short (b.1951), and Howie Mandel (b. 1955); musicians and singers Teresa Stratas (b.1938), Gordon Lightfoot (b.1938), Sylvia Tyson (b.1940), Paul Anka (b.1941), Neil Young (b.1945), Geddy Lee (b.1953), Dan Hill (b.1954), and Jeff Healey (b.1966); pianist Glenn Gould (1932–82); classical guitarist Liona Boyd (b.England, 1949); Big Band leader Guy Lombardo (1902–77); artists Frank Carmichael (1890–1945), Jack Bush (1909–77), and Ken Danby (b.1940); prima ballerinas Melissa Hayden (b.1923) and Karen Kain (b.1951); broadcasters and journalists Knowlton Nash (b.1927), Morley Safer (b.1931), Barbara Frum (b.1938), and Peter Jennings (b.1938); and television host Alex Trebek (b.1940).

Noted Ontarian authors include novelists Morley Callaghan (1903–90), Robertson Davies (b.1913), Elizabeth Smart (1913–86), Timothy Findley (b.1930), Howard Engel (1933–85), Sylvia Fraser (b.1935), Matt Cohen (b.1942), and Joan Barfoot (b.1946); playwrights Mazo De la Roche (1879–1961), James Reaney (b.1926), and Paul Quarrington (b.1953); humorist and historian Stephen Leacock (b.England, 1869–1944); children's author Dennis Lee (b.1939); "subjective nonfiction" writer Farlay Mowat (b.1921); short story writer Alice Munro (b.1931); poets Pauline Johnson (1861–1913), John McCrae (1872–1918), Al Purdy (b.1918), David Helwig (b.1938), Margaret Atwood (b.1939), Gwendolyn MacEwen (1941–87), and M. T. Kelly (b.1946); and writer/journalists June Callwood (b.1924), and Silver Donald Cameron (b.1937).

Famous Ontarians in science include physiologist Sir Frederick Grant Banting (1891–1941), who received the 1923 Nobel Prize in medicine for his codiscovery of insulin. Alexander Graham Bell (b.Scotland, 1847–1922), inventor of the telephone, was raised in Brantford.

James Naismith (1861–1939), inventor of basketball, was born in Almonte. Hockey stars from Ontario include Frank Selke (1893–1985), Leonard Patrick ("Red") Kelly (b.1927), Alex Peter Delvecchio (b.1931), Robert Marvin "Bobby" Hull Jr. (b.1939), Ed Giacomin (b.1939), Barclay Plager (1941–89), Phil Esposito (b.1942), Robert "Bobby" Orr (b.1948), Douglas Bradford "Brad" Park (b.1948), Larry Clark Robinson (b.1951), and Wayne Gretzky (b.1961).

40 BIBLIOGRAPHY

Barnes, Michael. *Ontario*. Minneapolis: Lerner Publications, 1995.

Bumsted, J. M. *The Peoples of Canada*. New York: Oxford University Press, 1992.

LeVert, Suzanne. *Let's Discover Canada: Ontario*. New York: Chelsea House, 1991.

MacKay, Kathryn. *Discover Canada: Ontario*. Toronto: Grolier, 1991.

Sorensen, Lynda. *Canada: Provinces and Territories*. Vero Beach, Fla.: Rourke Book Co., 1995.

Wansborough, M. B. *Great Canadian Lives*. New York: Doubleday, 1986.

Weihs, Jean. *Facts about Canada, Its Provinces and Territories*. New York: H. W. Wilson, 1995.

PRINCE EDWARD ISLAND

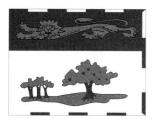

ORIGIN OF PROVINCE NAME: Prince Edward Island was originally called *Abegweit* ("lying down flat," or "cradled by the waves") by the Micmac Indians. Europeans called it the Island of Saint John in 1763; in 1799 the island was renamed Prince Edward Island, in honor of Prince Edward of England.

NICKNAME: The Garden Province, The Million Acre Farm, or Spud Island. Called by most residents simply "The Island."

CAPITAL: Charlottetown.

ENTERED CONFEDERATION: 1 July 1873.

SONG: "The Island Hymn."

MOTTO: *Parva sub ingenti* (The small under the protection of the great).

COAT OF ARMS: Consists primarily of a shield, which displays in the upper third a golden lion against a red background, and in the lower two-thirds a large oak tree (representing Canada) and three smaller oak trees (representing the three counties of Prince Edward Island) growing from a green island, all on a white background. Beneath the shield the provincial motto appears on a scroll.

FLAG: The design of the flag is similar to that of the shield in the coat of arms, with the addition of a fringe of alternating red and white.

FLORAL EMBLEM: Lady's slipper.

TARTAN: Reddish-brown, green, white, and yellow.

PROVINCIAL BIRD: Blue jay.

TREE: Northern red oak.

TIME: 8 AM AST = noon GMT.

1 LOCATION AND SIZE

Prince Edward Island (PEI), one of Canada's four Atlantic Provinces, is the smallest of the ten provinces in both size and population. The island is crescent shaped, measures 139 miles (224 kilometers) from tip to tip, is 4 to 40 miles (6 to 64 kilometers) wide. Its total area is 2,185 square miles (5,660 square kilometers). It is situated in the Gulf of St. Lawrence and is separated from Nova Scotia and New Brunswick by the Northumberland Strait.

2 TOPOGRAPHY

The province has numerous lakes and rivers, most of which are quite small, and is known for its red soil, sand dunes and 500 miles (800 kilometers) of beaches. The highest point is 499 feet (152 meters) above sea level at Springton, Queen's County.

3 CLIMATE

The climate is generally temperate, with chilly winters and mild summers. The most precipitation occurs between November and January. Average temperatures for Charlottetown are 19°F (-7°C) in January and 64°F (18°C) in July. The highest recorded temperature on PEI was 98°F (36.7°C) on 19 August 1935 at Charlottetown, while the lowest was -60°F (-51.1°C) on 26 January 1884 at Kilmahumaig.

[4] PLANTS AND ANIMALS

The temperate maritime climate is hospitable for a wide variety of native and imported European plants. Many species of clams, snails, and seaweeds are found along the coast, as well as seals, seagulls, and various migratory bird species.

[5] ENVIRONMENTAL PROTECTION

As in New Brunswick, the drift of air pollution from industrial centers in central Canada and New England over PEI is a prominent environmental problem. PEI has 41 landfills and 1 municipal incinerator. Total solid waste generation is about 115,269 tons (104,600 metric tons) per year, or 0.9 tons (0.8 metric tons) per person. Water usage per person is the lowest in Canada. Emissions of air pollution are minimal; annual carbon dioxide equivalent releases are about 471,656 tons (428,000 metric tons).

[6] POPULATION

Prince Edward Island's estimated 1996 population of 137,100 is fairly evenly divided between urban and rural dwellers. Approximately 60% of the population is rural and 7% of the total population of

Prince Edward Island Population Profile

Estimated 1996 population:		137,100
Population change, 1981–91:		5.9%
Population by ethnic origin:		
Multiple origins:		43.7%
British origins:		43.5%
English:		22.7%
Scottish:		12.8%
Irish:		7.8%
French:		9.1%
Dutch:		1.0%
German:		0.5%
Aboriginal:		0.3%
Other single origins:		1.9%
Population by age group:		
19 and under:	39,385	30.4%
20–64:	73,305	56.5%
65 and over:	17,075	13.1%
Urban/Rural populations:		
Urban:	51,813	39.9%
Rural:	77,952	60.1%

Population by Age Group

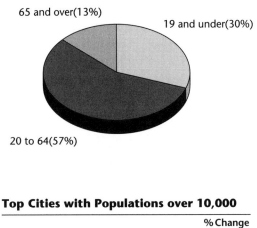

65 and over(13%)

19 and under(30%)

20 to 64(57%)

Top Cities with Populations over 10,000

City	Population	% Change 1986–91
Charlottetown	15,396	-2.4

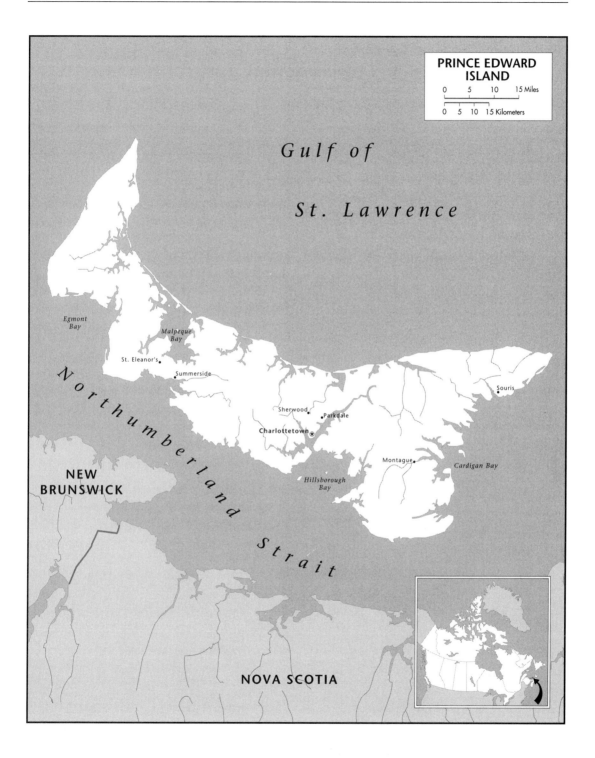

129,765 lived on farms in 1991. The island population is quite young—about 38% of all residents are under 25. About 49% of the population is in the 25–64 age group. Charlottetown, with a 1991 population of 15,396, is the only city in the province; the Charlottetown urban area had a 1991 population of 57,472 (the 50th largest in Canada). Summerside, population 7,474, is the second largest municipality. Other municipalities include Montague (1,901), Souris (1,333), Kensington (1,332) and Tignish (893).

7 ETHNIC GROUPS

Approximately 80% of the population is of British ancestry (mostly Scottish or Irish), and about 15% is of French descent.

8 LANGUAGES

As of 1991, English was the first language of 94.2% of the island's residents, while 4.5% claimed French as their mother tongue and 1.3% had other first languages.

9 RELIGIONS

Prince Edward Island is the only province where the numbers of Protestants and Catholics are nearly the same. In 1991, 48.4% of the population, or about 62,800 people, was Protestant, including 26,300 members of the United Church of Canada, 11,200 Presbyterians, 6,700 Anglicans, 5,300 Baptists, 1,300 Pentecostals, and less than 150 Lutherans. Roman Catholics comprised 47.3% of the population, or about 61,400 people. The province also had less than 150 each of the following:

people of Eastern Orthodox faith, Sikhs, and Jews. About 5,200 provincial residents professed no religious affiliation in 1991.

10 TRANSPORTATION

The movement of goods to and from the province is carried out largely by truck, since rail service to PEI was discontinued in 1989. The province's highway system is comprised of 2,360 miles (3,798 kilometers) of paved highways and 938 miles (1,510 kilometers) of unpaved or clay roads. In 1990 PEI had 84,716 registered motor vehicles, consisting of 59,970 passenger cars; 23,176 trucks, truck tractors, and buses; 1,512 motorcycles and mopeds; and 58 other vehicles. SMT Limited operates twice daily bus service between Charlottetown, Summerside, and Moncton, New Brunswick, for connection with Via Rail passenger train services and other bus services.

In October 1993, the Strait Crossing Development Corp. was awarded a contract to build a 8-mile (13-kilometer) bridge across the Northumberland Strait, thus linking PEI with the mainland. The bridge will be entirely financed, designed, and built by the private sector and is expected to be ready for traffic by 1997.

Modern car ferries currently link the island to New Brunswick and Nova Scotia. Service is provided year-round between Borden, PEI, and Cape Tormentine, New Brunswick. During the winter months, powerful ice-breaking ferries maintain the service. Ferry service is operated from late April to mid-December between Wood Islands, PEI, and Caribou,

Photo Credit: Tourism PEI.

Rustico Harbour, on the island's north coast, is a part of the Prince Edward Island National Park.

Nova Scotia. A third ferry service links Souris, PEI, with Grindstone in the Magdalen Islands of Québec from 1 April to 31 January. Ports on PEI handled 912,456 tons (828,000 metric tons) of cargo in 1991.

Air travel between Charlottetown and other centers, including Toronto, is provided by Air Nova and Air Atlantic to connect with Air Canada and Canadian Airlines International flights at Halifax, Nova Scotia. Air Canada also provides daily jet service between Charlottetown and Toronto, Ontario. Prince Edward Air provides daily scheduled service to Halifax from Summerside and Charlottetown. Atlantic Island Airways provides daily scheduled service to Toronto and Ottawa.

11 HISTORY

There is evidence that the ancestors of the Micmac Indians lived on the island 10,000 years ago. Most likely they migrated in before the Northumberland Strait was covered by water.

European Settlement

Europeans first encountered the island when Jacques Cartier landed there in 1534; he described it as "the most beautiful stretch of land imaginable." In spite of his enthusiastic description, it was a long time before the island was settled. No permanent colony existed until the French established one in 1719; 30 years later, the population numbered a mere 700.

The population of the island multiplied after the British deported the Acadians from Nova Scotia in 1755. By the time Louisbourg fell to the British in 1758, the island's population had risen to 5,000.

In 1766 Captain Samuel Holland prepared a topographic map of the island, then known as the Island of Saint John. He divided the island into 67 parcels of land, which he distributed at random to a group of British landowners. The absentee landlords, many of whom never set foot on the island, gave rise to numerous problems. Some refused to sell their lands to their tenants, while others demanded extremely high purchase or rental prices.

In 1769 the Island of Saint John became a separate colony, and in 1799 it was given its present name, in honor of Prince Edward of England. Prince Edward Island is known as the cradle of confederation, since Charlottetown, its capital, was the site of the 1867 conference that set Canadian confederation in motion. The island, however, waited until 1873 to join the Dominion of Canada.

Early 20th Century

During World War I (1914–18), Canada lost more than 68,000 soldiers. Veterans returning to PEI faced a bleak future of scarce low-paying jobs, while tariffs on imports kept prices for consumer goods high. During the 1920s, however, Canada experienced a period of rapid growth in industry. Transportation improvements—railways and roads—enabled businesses to flourish. Automobiles, telephones, electri-cal appliances, and other consumer goods became widely available.

As in the United States, all of Canada suffered during the Great Depression. In addition to the problems with grain prices during the early 1920s, droughts and frequent crop failures devastated the national economy, which still relied heavily on agriculture. Social welfare programs rapidly expanded during the 1930s, with much of the burden placed on the provincial and municipal governments.

1940s–1990s

Following World War II (1939–45), consumer spending and immigration to Canada rapidly increased. Urbanization spread quickly by means of the National Housing Act, which made home ownership more easily available. Unemployment insurance and other social welfare programs were also created following the war. Under the leadership of Prime Minister Louis St. Laurent, old age pensions were increased in 1951 and a national hospital insurance plan was introduced in 1957.

Canada's unity as a confederation has often been widely questioned. Most recently, the popular defeats of both the Meech Lake Accord of 1987 and the Charlottetown Accord of 1992 has failed to solve the issue of Québec's role in Canada. If Québec does eventually secede from Canada, the fate of the traditionally poorer maritime provinces such as PEI would also be uncertain. One or more might explore the possibility of admission to the United States.

Photo Credit: Gord Johnston.

In 1864 Province House in Charlottetown was the site of the first meeting to discuss the formation of Canada as a federal union.

12 PROVINCIAL GOVERNMENT

Three different levels of government exist on Prince Edward Island—federal, provincial, and municipal. The provincial parliament is known as the Legislative Assembly and consists of 32 members elected from 16 dual member electoral districts (in 1893, the Legislative Council and the Assembly were merged). At the federal level, the island is represented by 4 Members of Parliament in the House of Commons and four Senators in the Senate of Canada. As part of a constitutional monarchy, the province also has a lieutenant governor who is the Queen's provincial representative.

13 POLITICAL PARTIES

From 1769 to the early 1800s, the informal political groups of PEI concentrated on settling land disputes and rivalries within the government, church, and militia. By 1870 however, labor union and church problems had proven so divisive that there were no stable political parties on the island. Since the development of local political parties was immature when PEI entered the confederation in 1873, the evolution of provincial political parties on the island closely resembled that of the federal parties. As a result, third parties have never played a serious role in Island politics.

The most recent general election was held on 29 March 1993, which gave power to 31 Liberals and 1 Progressive Conservative.

Premiers of Prince Edward Island

Term	Premier	Party
1873	James Colledge Pope	Conservative
1873–76	Lemuel Cambridge Owen	Conservative
1876–79	Louis Henry Davies	Liberal
1879–89	William Wilfred Sullivan	Conservative
1889–91	Neil McLeod	Conservative
1891–97	Frederick Peters	Liberal
1897–98	Alexander Bannerman Warburton	Liberal
1898–1901	Donald Farquharson	Liberal
1901–08	Arthur Peters	Liberal
1908–11	Francis Longworth Haszard	Liberal
1911	Herbert James Palmer	Liberal
1911–17	John Alexander Mathieson	Conservative
1917–19	Aubin-Edmond Arsenault	Conservative
1919–23	John Howatt Bell	Liberal
1923–27	James David Stewart	Conservative
1927–30	Albert Charles Saunders	Liberal
1930–31	Walter Maxfield Lea	Liberal
1931–33	James Davis Stewart	Conservative
1933–35	William Parnell MacMillan	Conservative
1935–36	Walter Maxfield Lea	Liberal
1936–43	Thane Alexander Campbell	Liberal
1943–53	John Walter Jones	Liberal
1953–59	Alexander Wallace Matheson	Liberal
1959–66	Walter Russell Shaw	Conservative
1966–78	Alexander Bradshaw Campbell	Liberal
1978–79	William Bennett Campbell	Liberal
1979–81	John Angus McLean	Conservative
1981–86	James Matthew Lee	Conservative
1986–93	Joseph Atallah Ghiz	Liberal
1993–	Catherine Sophia Callbeck	Liberal

14 LOCAL GOVERNMENT

Charlottetown is the province's only incorporated city. PEI also has 8 towns and 81 communities. There is no minimum population requirement for the incorporation of a municipality.

15 JUDICIAL SYSTEM

The Canadian Constitution grants provincial jurisdiction over the administration of justice, and allows each province to organize its own court system and police forces. The federal government has exclusive domain over cases involving trade and commerce, banking, bankruptcy, and criminal law. The Federal Court of Canada has both trial and appellate divisions for federal cases. The 9-judge Supreme Court of Canada is an appellate court that determines the constitutionality of both federal and provincial statutes. The Tax Court of Canada hears appeals of taxpayers against assessments by Revenue Canada.

No more than 1 homicide per year usually occurs on the island, which would give PEI a rate of 0.8 homicides per 100,000 persons. Breaking and entering offenses in 1989 numbered 285 per 100,000 people for businesses and 256 per 100,000 people for residences.

16 MIGRATION

In 1991, PEI lost 1,553 residents from migration between provinces (3,169 people entered the province and 4,722 left for other provinces). While Ontario was the province of origin for 31% of incoming internal migration into PEI in 1991, Nova Scotia was the province of destination for 31% of those leaving the island to live elsewhere in Canada that year.

17 ECONOMY

The PEI economy is more diverse than is often realized and today the largest and fastest growing sectors in terms of employment are in the service sector. The traditional sectors of agriculture and fishing dominate goods production, while food processing dominates manufacturing.

Tourism is also an important contributor to the local economy.

18 INCOME

The annual personal income per capita (per person) was c$18,159 in 1993. Average family income in the province was c$38,854 in 1989. As of December 1992, average weekly earnings in the province amounted to c$457.74.

19 INDUSTRY

Most of PEI's industrial activity involves the processing of agricultural and fisheries products. In recent years, technology-intensive industry has become more important, especially in the medical, electronics, and agricultural fields. Specialized manufacturing industries have been established in the province producing goods such as diagnostic medical kits, optical frames, and steel and aluminum cookware. PEI also has a growing number of firms in the aerospace industry. In 1990, the value of manufactured shipments was c$396.4 million, of which food products accounted for 72%.

20 LABOR

There were 65,000 people in the labor force in 1993; the participation rate for those over 15 years of age was 62.5%. Of the total employment of 55,000 in 1990, services engaged about 19,000; trade, 9,000; agriculture, 5,000; government, 5,000; manufacturing, 5,000; utilities, 4,000; and other sectors, 8,000. Prince Edward Island saw an increase in its unemployment rate from 16.8% in 1991 to 17.7% in 1992; as of March 1993, it stood at 17.4%. Problems in the potato and tourism sectors contributed to the rise in unemployment.

The Employment Standards Act, revised in 1992, gives women 17 weeks of unpaid maternity leave and 17 weeks of unpaid parental leave (although many women collect unemployment insurance benefits during that time), allows for three days of unpaid leave after the death of a family member, and entitles workers to statutory holiday pay. The Act also makes it mandatory for employers to establish a policy on sexual harassment and to post that policy.

21 AGRICULTURE

Prince Edward Island's rich red soil and temperate climate make it an ideal location for mixed farming. Some 46% of the total land area is devoted to agriculture. In fact, the island is often called the "Million Acre Farm," or "the Garden Province." In 1991, of the 639,680 acres (258,875 hectares) devoted to agriculture, 381,788 acres (154,103 hectares) were in crops. Annual farm cash receipts exceed c$222 million. Potatoes are the major source of farm income, contributing an average of more than 30% of the total farm cash receipts; much of the annual potato harvest is shipped to the populous areas of Ontario. Field crop production in 1992 included barley, 137,750 tons (125,000 metric tons); oats, 23,142 tons (21,000 metric tons); and wheat, 19,615 tons (17,800 metric tons). There are approximately 5,000 people employed in agriculture with about 2,400 farms.

22 DOMESTICATED ANIMALS

As of 1991, PEI had 498 dairy farms, 488 cattle farms, 203 hog farms, 23 poultry farms, and 83 livestock combination farms.

23 FISHING

Fishing and related industries are of major importance to the Prince Edward Island economy. They contribute in excess of c$210 million annually. The landed value of the catch fluctuates annually, but reaches as high as c$80 million. Lobster fishing accounts for two-thirds to three-quarters of the annual fishing income. In 1993, the total landing was 51,413 tons (46,654 metric tons), valued at c$69 million.

Although lobster is the primary species caught off Prince Edward Island, about 30 other fish and seafood species are caught, notably cultivated "Island Blue" mussels, snow crab, groundfish, herring, mackerel, the giant bluefin tuna, and the renowned Malpeque oysters. Irish Moss, a seaplant, is widely harvested for its extract, carrageenan, which is used heavily in the food industry.

There are approximately 5,300 professional fishermen and helpers working from some 1,500 fishing vessels. More than 2,500 Islanders are employed in the fish processing industry, working at factories and facilities around the province.

24 FORESTRY

There are some 692,000 acres (280,000 hectares) of forested land on Prince Edward Island. Though timber quality has suffered from poor harvesting in the past, soil and site potential for forest production is excellent.

During 1993, some 104,000 cords of roundwood were burned for heating, the equivalent of about c$17 million worth of imported oil. Additionally, 36 million board feet of lumber, worth c$14 million was sawn in the Island's 50 sawmills. Pulpwood sales during 1993 accounted for 19,000 cords going to markets in Nova Scotia, New Brunswick, and Newfoundland. Also in 1993, fuel chip use accounted for 13,000 cords (or 33,000 Green Metric tons) of wood fiber.

25 MINING

Mining on Prince Edward Island is limited to mostly sand and gravel. The value of production in 1992 was c$3.4 million.

26 ENERGY AND POWER

Prince Edward Island relies upon the mainland for its electricity. In 1991, electricity generated totaled 71 million kilowatt hours and consumption within the province amounted to 682 million kilowatt hours.

27 COMMERCE

Due to its small population and isolation, retail trade on PEI relies on tourism and local recreation.

28 PUBLIC FINANCE

The fiscal year runs from 1 April to 31 March. For fiscal year 1992/93, total revenues were c$747.9 million; expenditures totaled c$839.8 million. The largest

A potato field on Prince Edward Island. Potatoes are the major source of farm income, usually accounting for 30% of total farm receipts.

expenditure areas were health and social services, education, interest on debt, transportation and public works, and industry.

29 TAXATION

The basic personal income tax rate in 1993 was 59.5%, with high income surtaxes of 10%. The retail sales tax was 10%. Major consumption taxes were levied on gasoline and tobacco. In 1991, the average family in PEI had a cash income of c$42,000 and paid c$15,512 in taxes.

Corporate income tax rates in 1993 were as follows: small business rate, 7.5%; manufacturing and processing corporate rate, 7.5%; general business rate, 16%; and capital tax rate, 3%.

30 HEALTH

In 1992 there were 1,850 live births in Prince Edward Island, for a rate of 14.2 per 1,000 residents. The death rate in 1992 was 8.6 per 1,000 residents, with 1,114 deaths occurring that year. Therapeutic abortions in PEI numbered 51 in 1990, for a rate of 1.7 per 1,000 females aged 15–44 and a ratio of 2.5 per 100 live births; both the rate and ratio were the lowest in Canada. Reported cases of selected diseases in 1990 included campylobacteriosis, 90; salmonellosis, 72; pertussis, 31; giardiasis, 18; and gonococcal infections, 10. There were no AIDS cases reported in 1990; in 1991, the total number of cases was 3.

Prince Edward Island had nine hospitals and health centers in 1993. In the late 1980s, there were seven general hospitals with 690 beds, and one specialty hospital with 63 beds.

31 HOUSING

PEI had 42,829 households in 1989, of which 31,592 occupied single dwelling units, 9,852 lived in multiple units, and 1,385 resided in other units. In 1993 there were 645 housing starts (down from more than 1,100 in 1988) and 674 housing completions. Private and public investments in housing intended for 1994 amounted to c$119.2 million.

32 EDUCATION

The public school system in the province provides free education for students from grades 1 to 12. In 1993 there were 24,418 students and 1,449 teachers in the elementary-secondary system. Of the 69 schools in operation, three are private schools, and one is Aboriginal-operated. Provincial public schools are organized into 5 regional administrative units with elected school boards. Approximately 2% of the students receive their education in the French language, while an additional 15% are enrolled in French immersion programs.

The province has one university and one college of applied arts and technology. The University of Prince Edward Island (UPEI) offers undergraduate programs in arts, science, education, music, business administration, and nursing. Total enrollment in 1993 at UPEI consisted of 2,691 full-time and 776 part-time students. A professional program in veterinary medicine (DVM) has 200 students along with a graduate program in veterinary medicine with 25 students. The primary purpose of Holland College is to provide training for students seeking employment at semiprofessional levels in business, applied arts, technology, and vocational areas. Each year approximately 1,200 full-time and 4,100 part-time students register in postsecondary programs within Holland College, which also offers extensive academic, vocational, and career preparation programs to approximately 1,000 full-time and 2,500 part-time students annually.

Annual expenditures on education for the province exceeded c$179.3 million in the 1993/94 government fiscal year.

33 ARTS

The Victoria Playhouse near Charlottetown and the Britannia Hall Theatre in Tyne Valley feature concerts and plays. Dinner theater is also popular in Charlottetown, Summerside, and Mont-Carmel. In 1990/91, PEI's five performing arts companies gave 601 performances before a total attendance of 122,621.

34 LIBRARIES AND MUSEUMS

The Confederation Centre Public Library serves the province, with 22 branch libraries around the island. The Robertson Library of the University of Prince Edward Island is the main academic library. Other special libraries in Charlottetown include

This house inspired the setting for Lucy Maud Montgomery's popular novel Anne of Green Gables.

the Government Services Library, the PEI School of Nursing Library, and the Stewart McKelvey Stirling Scales Law Library. The Prince Edward Island Museum & Heritage Foundation operates five historic museums across the province. The Confederation Centre Art Gallery & Museum in Charlottetown features 15,000 pieces with a special focus on the development of Canadian art over the past two centuries.

35 COMMUNICATIONS

There are 3 AM and 2 FM radio stations operating in the province. CBC provides television and FM radio services from a studio in Charlottetown, while television programs of the CTV network are fed to the province via a repeater station. Radio-Canada offers French FM radio and UHF-TV from Moncton through repeater stations situated on the island. Cable and pay television service is provided to approximately 29,000 (69%) of the island's households. Telephones and telecommunications services are provided to 72,346 subscribers by the Island Telephone Co. Ltd., a member of Stentor. Cellular telephone service is now available as well.

36 PRESS

Readers have a choice of three local daily newspapers and three weekly papers (one French-language). The largest daily newspapers on PEI are the *Guardian and*

Patriot of Charlottetown and the *Journal Pioneer* of Summerside.

37 TOURISM, TRAVEL, AND RECREATION

Tourism is extremely important to the economy of Prince Edward Island. In 1993, expenditures from nonresident tourists amounted to c$121 million. There were approximately 690,000 visitors to PEI during the 1993 tourism season.

Prince Edward Island offers a number of activities relating to history, culture, cuisine, sport, and recreation. PEI offers visitors scenic hiking trails, great golf courses, lobster suppers, live theater, historic properties, and picturesque landscapes. Finally, the island's 500 miles (800 kilometers) of beaches attract more than 665,000 visitors yearly for relaxation and water sports, including bluefin tuna fishing.

38 SPORTS

Golf and hiking are popular warm-weather activities, while skiing and hockey are prominent winter sports. Harness racing draws spectators year-round.

39 FAMOUS PRINCE EDWARD ISLANDERS

George H. Coles (1810–75), one of the fathers of confederation, was born in PEI and as its premier initially delayed the province's joining the confederation until 1873.

The most renowned PEI author was novelist Lucy Maud Montgomery (1874–1942), who made the island internationally famous in *Anne of Green Gables* and other related stories.

The Island's sports heroes include George Godfrey (1852–1901), American Black Heavyweight Champion and one of the leading heavyweight boxers of the 1880s; Michael Thomas (1883–1954), a Micmac Indian who was one of Canada's best long-distance runners; and Joe O'Brien (1917–84), considered one of harness racing's best drivers ever.

40 BIBLIOGRAPHY

Bumsted, J. M. *The Peoples of Canada.* New York: Oxford University Press, 1992.

Campbell, Kumari. *Prince Edward Island.* Minneapolis: Lerner Publications, 1996.

Kessler, Deirdre. *Discover Canada: Prince Edward Island.* Toronto: Grolier, 1992.

LeVert, Suzanne. *Let's Discover Canada: Prince Edward Island.* New York: Chelsea House, 1991.

Sorensen, Lynda. *Canada: Provinces and Territories.* Vero Beach, Fla.: Rourke Book Co., 1995.

Wansborough, M. B. *Great Canadian Lives.* New York: Doubleday, 1986.

Weihs, Jean. *Facts about Canada, Its Provinces and Territories.* New York: H. W. Wilson, 1995.

QUÉBEC

ORIGIN OF PROVINCE NAME: From an Algonquin Indian word meaning "narrow passage" or "strait," referring to the narrowing of the St. Lawrence River at what is currently Québec City.

NICKNAME: La Belle Province (The Beautiful Province).

CAPITAL: Québec City.

ENTERED CONFEDERATION: 1 July 1867.

MOTTO: *Je me souviens* (I remember).

COAT OF ARMS: Consists of a shield with a royal crown above and a golden scroll with blue borders bearing the provincial motto below. The upper third of the shield has three white upright fleur-de-lis on a blue background, the middle third has a gold leopard on a red background, and the lower third a sugar maple sprig on a gold background.

FLAG: The flag of Québec, also known as the "fleurdelisé" flag, consists of a white cross on a sky-blue field, with an upright fleur-de-lis centered in each of the four quarters.

FLORAL EMBLEM: White garden (madonna) lily.

PROVINCIAL BIRD: Snowy owl.

TREE: Yellow birch.

TIME: 8 AM AST = noon GMT; 7 AM EST = noon GMT.

1 LOCATION AND SIZE

Québec is almost entirely surrounded by water. It is bordered on the north by the Hudson Strait; on the east by Labrador (the mainland portion of the province of Newfoundland); on the southeast by the Gulf of St. Lawrence; on the south by New Brunswick and the US states of Maine, New Hampshire, Vermont, and New York; on the southwest and west by Ontario; and on the west and northwest by James Bay and Hudson Bay. Québec has an area of 594,857 square miles (1,545,680 square kilometers), three times that of France and seven times that of Great Britain. It is the largest of Canada's provinces.

2 TOPOGRAPHY

From north to south, Québec takes in three main geographical regions: the Canadian Shield, the St. Lawrence lowlands, and the Appalachian Mountains. Extending from the shores of the Canadian Arctic to the Laurentians, the Canadian Shield covers about 60% of the land mass, and is the world's oldest mountain range. The highest point in Québec is located in this region; it is Mount D'Iberville—elevation 5,420 feet (1,652 meters) above sea level—located in the Torngat Mountains in extreme northeastern Québec.

The St. Lawrence River, the province's dominant geographical feature, links the

Atlantic Ocean with the Great Lakes. The St. Lawrence lowlands are dotted with more than a million lakes and rivers. To the south, the foothills of the Appalachians separate Québec from the United States. Québec's tens of thousands of lakes and rivers account for 16% of the world's fresh water supply.

3 CLIMATE

Southern Québec, along the St. Lawrence River, has a temperate continental climate, while the bay and Gulf of St. Lawrence have a temperate maritime climate. Permafrost reigns in the northern part of the Canadian Shield; only dwarf birches and lichen are able to grow there. Average temperatures for January are 16°F (-8.7°C) in Montréal, 10°F (-12.1°C) in Québec City, 8°F (-13.2°C) in Baie-Comeau, and -10°F (-23.3°C) in Kuujjuak. In July, average temperatures are 71°F (21.8°C) in Montréal, 66°F (19.1°C) in Québec City, 62°F (16.8°C) in Baie-Comeau, and 53°F (11.4°C) in Kuujjuak. The warmest recorded temperature in Québec was 104°F (40°C) on 6 July 1921 at Ville Marie and the coldest was -66°F (-54.4°C) on 5 February 1923 at Doucet.

4 PLANTS AND ANIMALS

The relatively temperate climate of the south is hospitable for a wide variety of native as well as imported European plants. A myriad of migratory ducks and geese annually fly across Québec, and large colonies of local bird species inhabit the numerous islands in the Bas-Saint-Laurant region of the St. Lawrence River. Several species of whale seasonally cruise

Québec Population Profile

Estimated 1996 population:	7,361,300
Population change, 1981–91:	7.1%
Population by ethnic origin:	
French:	73.6%
Multiple origins:	10.1%
British:	4.1%
English:	2.3%
Irish:	1.2%
Scottish:	0.6%
Italian:	2.5%
Jewish:	1.1%
Aboriginal:	0.9%
Greek:	0.7%
Black:	0.6%
Portuguese:	0.5%
Chinese:	0.5%
Other single origins:	5.4%

Population by Age Group

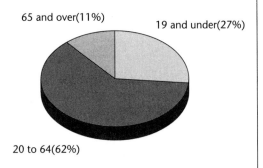

65 and over(11%)
19 and under(27%)
20 to 64(62%)

Top Cities with Populations over 10,000

City	Population	% Change 1986–91
Montréal	1,017,666	0.2
Laval	314,398	10.6
Québec City	167,517	1.8
Longueuil	129,874	3.5
Gatineau	92,284	18.8
Montréal Nord	85,516	-5.3
Sherbrooke	76,429	2.6
Saint-Hubert	74,027	11.8
LaSalle	73,804	-2.4
Saint-Leonard	73,120	-3.7

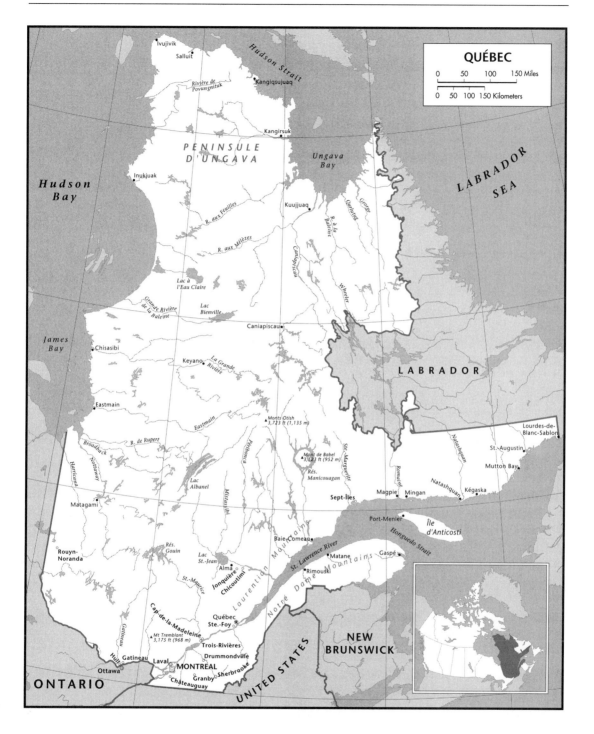

QUÉBEC

0   50   100   150 Miles

0   50   100   150 Kilometers

Ivujivik
Salluit
Hudson Strait
Kangiqsujuaq
Rivière de Povungnituk
Kangirsuk
PENINSULE D'UNGAVA
Ungava Bay
LABRADOR SEA
Inukjuak
Hudson Bay
Kuujjuaq
R. aux Feuilles
R. à la Baleine
Koksoak
George
R. aux Mélèzes
Caniapiscau
Wheeler
Lac à l'Eau Claire
Lac Bienville
Grande Rivière de la Baleine
Caniapiscau
James Bay
Chisasibi
Keyano
La Grande Rivière
LABRADOR
Eastmain
Eastmain
Broadback
R. de Rupert
Monts Otish
3,723 ft (1,135 m)
Péribonca
Mont de Babel
3,123 ft (952 m)
Ste.-Marguerite
Rés. Manicouagan
Natashquan
Lourdes-de-Blanc-Sablon
St.-Augustin
Mutton Bay
Harricana
Nottaway
Lac Albanel
Mistassibi
Romaine
Natashquan
Kégaska
Matagami
Magpie Mingan
Sept-Îles
Rouyn-Noranda
Rés. Gouin
Lac St.-Jean
Port-Menier
Île d'Anticosti
Baie-Comeau
Honguedo Strait
St.-Maurice
Alma
Jonquière
Chicoutimi
Laurentian Mountains
St. Lawrence River
Matane
Gaspé
Notre Dame Mountains
Rimouski
Cap-de-la-Madeleine
Québec
Ste.-Foy
Mt Tremblant
3,175 ft (968 m)
Trois-Rivières
Drummondville
Gatineau
Laval
MONTREAL
Sherbrooke
Hull
Gatineau
Ottawa
Granby
Chateauguay
ONTARIO
UNITED STATES
NEW BRUNSWICK

through the St. Lawrence straits. Muskie and trout are common stream and lake fish species. Seals are common to Îles-de-la Madeleine and the waters of the Gulf of St. Lawrence. Woodland caribou, moose, muskrats, beavers, eagles, and wolves inhabit the northern reaches of the province. Polar bears live in the far north along Hudson Bay.

5 ENVIRONMENTAL PROTECTION

Québec has 576 landfills, 3 municipal incinerators, and 11 hazardous waste sites. Annual generation of solid wastes is about 5.6 million tons (5.4 million metric tons), or 0.9 tons (0.8 metric tons) per person; Québec produces about 22.2% of Canada's hazardous waste. Annual air pollution emissions include about 2,769,326 tons (2,513,000 metric tons) of nitrogen dioxide and carbon monoxide (gases that cause smog), 1,028,166 tons (933,000 metric tons) of sulfur dioxide and nitrogen oxide compounds (gases that produce acid rain), and the equivalent of 19,127,414 tons (17,357,000 metric tons) of carbon dioxide.

The Montréal Protocol is an international treaty that seeks to reduce and eliminate the consumption of substances believed to deplete the ozone layer. The protocol came into force on 1 January 1989 and has been ratified by 46 other nations to reduce the global consumption of chlorofluorocarbons (CFCs) and halons to 1986 levels. In June 1990, representatives of 55 nations met to augment some of the treaty's provisions and accelerate the rate of phasing out five of the CFCs specified in the treaty from 50% to 100% by the year 2000.

6 POPULATION

Québec's estimated 1996 population of 7,361,000 is equivalent to nearly 25% of the national total. Almost 80% of Quebeckers live in urban centers located along the St. Lawrence. Montréal and its suburbs had a population of 3,127,242 in 1991, ranking second in the nation. Québec City, North America's oldest fortified city and Québec's capital, is a seaport with a metropolitan population of 645,550 in 1991 (eighth in Canada). Other metropolitan areas and their 1991 populations (and national rankings) include: Chicoutimi-Jonquière, 160,928 (20th); Sherbrooke, 139,194 (22d); and Trois-Rivières, 136,303 (23d).

7 ETHNIC GROUPS

Québec has more than five million people of French origin, 350,000 of British origin, about 137,000 Aboriginals (Native Peoples, including Mohawk, Cree, Montagnais, Algonquin, Attikamek, Micmac, Huron, Abenaki, and Naskapi), and 7,200 Inuit. Ten distinct Aboriginal nations in Québec have been recognized by the federal Indian Act; the largest native band in the province is at Kahnawake. Montréal is one of Canada's most ethnically diverse metropolitan areas, with large Italian, Greek, Portuguese, and Chinese communities, as well as a notable South American, Arab, and Asian population.

Ethnic divisions between francophones (speakers of French) and anglophones (speakers of English) have recently been

Photo Credit: Canadian Tourism Commission photo.

Québec City is North America's oldest fortified city and Québec's capital.

replaced by tensions between ethnic Europeans and Aboriginals. In 1990, some Mohawks protested the rezoning of a burial ground in Oka, resulting in armed confrontation and a three-month siege by federal troops.

8 LANGUAGES

Most of North America's francophones live in Québec. French is the mother tongue of 82.2% of Quebeckers, while 9.7% cite English as their mother tongue. In addition to French and English, some 35 other languages are spoken by provincial residents, with Italian, Greek, and Spanish the most prevalent. Each Aboriginal nation uses its own language, with the exception of the Abenakis, Huron-Wendats, and Malecites.

In 1977, Québec's National Assembly adopted the Charter of the French Language, with the aim of making French the language of the government, judicial system, and all official signs, as well as the customary language of work, instruction, communications, commerce, and business.

9 RELIGIONS

With the overwhelming majority of its residents Roman Catholic, Québec is unique to Canada. In 1991, 86% of the population was Roman Catholic, or about 5,930,500 people. Only 5.9% of the population, or about 406,900 people, was

Protestant, including 96,500 Anglicans, 62,100 members of the United Church of Canada, 27,600 Baptists, 10,800 Pentecostals, 20,700 Presbyterians, and 13,800 Lutherans. Québec also had about 96,500 Jews, 89,600 people of Eastern Orthodox faith, 48,300 Moslems, 34,500 Buddhists, 13,800 Hindus and 6,900 Sikhs. Just under 4% of the population, or about 27,500 people, professed no religious affiliation in 1991, the lowest such rate in Canada.

10 TRANSPORTATION

The St. Lawrence River's 2,330 miles (3,750 kilometers) of navigable length has been the transportation focus in Québec for 400 years. The expansion of farming, logging, and mining at the end of the 1800s helped with the original construction of the major arteries of the road system. Road transport is controlled by the Ministère des Transports du Québec (MTQ), while sea, air, and rail transport are mainly under federal control.

Railroads in 1992 consisted of 4,631 miles (7,453 kilometers) of track, about 9% of the Canadian total, with 86% operated by Canadian National (CN) and Canadian Pacific (CP). The preferred method of transport by manufacturers is often via railway, since much of Québec's exports are bulky natural resources (such as pulp and paper, lumber, and ore). The National Transportation Act of 1987 mandated the abandonment of unprofitable rail lines. As a result, much freight traffic has recently been switched from rail to road in Québec.

Most of the highway system was built in the 1960s, and today serves 80% of Québec's population, linking urban centers and connecting to the networks of Ontario and New England. In 1991, Québec had 77,227 miles (124,279 kilometers) of roads, with 2,894 miles (4,658 kilometers) of freeways. In 1992, Québec had 4,129,832 licensed drivers, 3,023,128 registered passenger vehicles, 60,249 motorcycles, and 1,001,997 registered commercial vehicles. During the winter, massive snow clearing and de-icing operations are necessary to keep roads open. In 1992/93, winter road maintenance cost c$165.6 million, or 34.7% of all road maintenance expenditures.

Mass transit in Québec annually carries 522 million passengers by bus, metro, and commuter train. Public transportation companies serve about 3.5 million people and have almost 95% of the urban bus fleet. The MTQ is legally required by the Education Act to subsidize school busing, which in 1992/93 required the daily use of 10,000 vehicles for 680,000 pupils, and cost c$408 million. Ferries to the Côte-Nord region operate weekly from April to January. Ferries throughout Québec carried 5,009,154 passengers and 1,713,077 vehicles in 1992.

Québec has some 300 landing sites, public and private airports, seaplane bases, and heliports. Major international commercial air facilities are Dorval International and Mirabel International, both in the Montréal area. In 1992 Dorval handled 5.5 million passengers (39% international traffic), while Mirabel handled 2.4 million passengers (96% international passengers). Other important commercial airports are at Québec City, Sept-Îles, Val-d'Or, Bagotville-Saguenay, Rouyn-Noranda, Mont-Joli, and Baie-Comeau. In 1993, the MTQ completed the construction of 13 new airports for remote communities north of the 55th parallel, a region with virtually no roads. The MTQ also provides floatplane, skiplane, and helicopter service for remote areas in the Côte-Nord region.

11 HISTORY

Québec was originally inhabited by members of the Algonquin and Iroquois Aboriginal Peoples. The northern part of the province was, and still is, inhabited by the Inuit (previously known as "Eskimos").

European Settlement

The European history of Québec began with the arrival of French explorer Jacques Cartier in 1534. In the following years, a thriving fur trade was established, the Europeans developed relatively friendly relations with the Aboriginal People, and French and English colonists developed an ongoing rivalry.

Founded in 1608, Québec City became the capital of New France. During the French regime, the fortified city was an important center of trade and development. Today it is regarded as the cradle of French civilization in America, and was named a World Heritage City by the United Nations Educational, Scientific, and Cultural Organization (UNESCO) in 1985.

French-English rivalry in North America culminated with the Seven Years' War, which saw the fall of Québec City to British forces in 1759. With the Treaty of Paris in 1763, New France became a colony of Britain. In 1774, under the Québec Act, Britain granted official recognition to French civil laws, guaranteed religious freedom, and authorized the use of the French language.

In 1791, the colony was divided in two to reflect the large influx of Loyalists who, wishing to remain British subjects, fled north after the American Revolution (1775–83), to settle in western Québec. This led to the creation of Upper Canada (now Ontario) and Lower Canada (Québec). After rebellions in both regions in 1837, the two were reunited by the Act of Union in 1840 and became the Province of Canada. In 1867, Québec became a founding member of the new Dominion of Canada.

Early 20th Century

During World War I (1914–18), Canada lost more than 68,000 soldiers. Veterans returning to Québec faced a bleak future of scarce low-paying jobs, while tariffs on imports kept prices for consumer goods high. Local farmers, as in other provinces, had prospered from high wheat prices during World War I. With the war's end, however, global grain markets collapsed and wheat prices fell 50% by 1920.

For a long time, Québec's rural roots and domination by the Roman Catholic Church made it a traditional agrarian (of agricultural groups) society. With the advent of Canada's period of rapid growth in industry between 1920 and 1940, urbanization and higher living standards came to the province. The recovery of grain prices during the 1920s helped the province's fortunes, as well. At the same time, transportation improvements—railways and roads—enabled businesses to flourish. Automobiles, telephones, electrical appliances, and other consumer goods became widely available.

Just as in the United States, all of Canada suffered during the Great Depression. In addition to the problems with grain prices during the early 1920s, droughts and frequent crop failures devastated the national economy, which still relied heavily on agriculture. Social welfare programs rapidly expanded during the 1930s, with much of the burden placed on the provincial and municipal governments. The Union Nationale, established by Maurice Duplessis, came to power in Québec in the 1930s but was unsuccessful at reversing the economic havoc of the Depression.

1940s–1960s

Following World War II (1939–45), consumer spending and immigration to Canada rapidly increased. Urbanization spread quickly by means of the National Housing Act, which made home ownership more easily available. Unemployment insurance and other social welfare programs were also created following the war. Under the leadership of Prime Minister Louis St. Laurent, old age pensions were increased in 1951 and a national hospital insurance plan was introduced in 1957. The St. Lawrence Seaway, completed in 1959, was an important development for eastern Canada by permitting oceangoing ships access to the center of the nation.

During the 1950s and 1960s, the monitoring of northern Canadian airspace served a vital role in the defense of North America against a possible nuclear attack from the Soviet Union. But when ballistic missiles (which are launched in an arc toward their targets from great distances) replaced bombers as the means of delivering nuclear warheads, this strategy became obsolete.

Beginning in 1960, Québec entered a period of transition: the "Quiet revolution." It was an era marked by rapid economic expansion, increased cultural pride, and the changing of political institutions to meet the needs of contemporary society. In 1967, Canada's centennial (100th) anniversary, the world's fair was held in Montréal. The Quiet Revolution was also the beginning of a period of political tension and disputes between Québec and the federal government as the province sought to assume greater control over its economy and society. Regrettably, it was through acts of terrorism that the issue of Québec's status in Canada was brought into wide view. In October 1970 terrorists belonging to the Front de Libération du Québec (FLQ) kidnapped James Cross, the British Trade Commissioner, and killed Québec cabinet minister Pierre Laporte. As a result, Prime Minister Pierre Trudeau invoked the War Measures Act to declare a state of emergency and impose martial law.

1970s–1990s

In 1976, Quebeckers elected the Parti Québécois (PQ), a party wanting independence for Québec. The PQ made French the sole, official language of Québec, and, in 1980, conducted a referendum on negotiating an arrangement for sovereignty-association with Canada. The referendum was defeated by a majority of Québec citizens.

Throughout Québec's history, the survival of the French language, culture, and institutions in Québec and also in the rest of Canada has been central to the concerns of Québec's residents. This French heritage has traditionally been the motive for treating Québec's place in the Canadian confederation differently than that of the other provinces. Québec's French heritage also gives Canada its bilingual character and cultural richness.

Canada's unity as a confederation has often been widely questioned. Most recently, the popular defeats of both the Meech Lake Accord of 1987 and the Charlottetown Accord of 1992 have failed to solve the issue of Québec's role in Canada. If Québec does eventually secede from Canada, Canada would lose 25% of its population and much of its economic strength; also it would likely no longer have the ability to be as assertive in world affairs. Moreover, the ability of the remainder of Canada to stay unified would be in serious doubt. For example, the fate of the traditionally poorer maritime provinces to the east would be uncertain, and one or more might explore the possibility of admission to the United States.

12 PROVINCIAL GOVERNMENT

The parliamentary system is based both on the French and British systems. Québec's National Assembly is the chief parliamentary body, with 125 elected representative members. The National Assembly's prime minister is the majority party leader (an elected member of parliament) who serves a term of five years, at the end of which time he or she must call an election. The prime minister selects and presides over the 30 members of the executive cabinet.

13 POLITICAL PARTIES

In theory, Québec has a multiparty system, but in reality there are two main parties (Liberal and Conservative), with one or two others receiving a small proportion of votes. Since the 1940s, various splinter groups such as the nationalist Bloc Populaire, the créditiste Union des Electeurs, the separatist Rassemblement pour l'Indépendance Nationale, Ralliement Nationale, and more recently Parti Québécois have occasionally challenged the traditional two-party rule. Since 1939, the Liberal Party has been especially popular among the urban electorate.

In 1976, the province's voters elected into majority power the Parti Québécois (PQ), a party wanting independence for Québec. The PQ made French the sole, official language of Québec, and, in 1980, conducted a referendum on negotiating an arrangement for sovereignty-association with Canada. The referendum was defeated by a majority of Québec citizens.

The most recent general election was held on 12 September 1994, in which the Parti Québecois defeated the ruling Liberal Party, giving the following party seat status: Parti Québecois, 77; Liberal Party, 47; and Parti Démocratique, 1.

Premiers of Québec

Term	Premier	Party
1867–73	Pierre-Joseph-Olivier Chauveau	Conservative
1873–74	Gèdèon Ouimet	Conservative
1874–78	Charles-Eugène Boucher de Boucherville	Conservative
1878–79	Henri-Gustav Joly de Lotbinière	Liberal
1879–82	Joseph-Adolphe Chapleau	Conservative
1882–84	Joseph-Alfred Mousseau	Conservative
1884–87	John Jones Ross	Conservative
1887	Louis-Olivier Taillon	Conservative
1887–91	Honoré Mercier	Liberal
1891–92	Charles-Eugène Boucher de Boucherville	Conservative
1892–96	Louis-Olivier Taillon	Conservative
1896–97	Edmund James Flynn	Conservative
1897–1900	Félix-Gabriel Marchand	Liberal
1900–05	Simon-Napoléon Parent	Liberal
1905–20	Jean-Lomer Gouin	Liberal
1920–36	Louis-Alexandre Taschereau	Liberal
1936	Joseph-Adélard Godbout	Liberal
1936–39	Maurice Duplessis	Union nationale
1939–44	Joseph-Adélard Godbout	Liberal
1944–59	Maurice Duplessis	Union nationale
1959–60	Paul Sauvé	Union nationale
1960	J. Antonio Barrette	Union nationale
1960–66	Jean Lesage	Liberal
1966–68	Daniel Johnson	Union nationale
1968–70	Jean-Jacques Bertrand	Union nationale
1970–76	Robert Bourassa	Liberal
1976–85	René Lévesque	Parti québécois
1985	Pierre-Marc Johnson	Parti québécois
1985–94	Robert Bourassa	Liberal
1994	Daniel Johnson	Liberal
1994–	Jacques Parizeau	Parti québécois

14 LOCAL GOVERNMENT

Québec is divided into 16 administrative regions, 95 regional county municipalities, and 3 urban communities (Montréal, Québec City, and Outaouais). Rural municipalities are classified as villages, parishes, townships, united townships, not designated, and Indian reserves. Cities and towns are both often referred to as "villes." Special municipal legislation calls for more governmental autonomy for Montréal, Québec City, and the Cree and Northern villages organized under the James Bay Agreement in 1975.

15 JUDICIAL SYSTEM

The Canadian Constitution grants provincial jurisdiction over the administration of justice, and allows each province to organize its own court system and police forces. The federal government has exclusive domain over cases involving trade and commerce, banking, bankruptcy, and criminal law. The Federal Court of Canada has both trial and appellate divisions for federal cases. The 9-judge Supreme Court of Canada is an appellate court that determines the constitutionality of both federal and provincial statutes. The Tax Court of Canada hears appeals of taxpayers against assessments by Revenue Canada.

The judiciary is independent of legislative or executive powers, and administers the Civil Code of Québec and the Canadian Penal Code. The Civil Code of Québec is based on the Napoleonic Code, which was developed in France.

In 1990, there were 174 homicides in Québec, for a rate of 2.6 per 100,000 persons. Breaking and entering offenses in 1989 numbered 383 per 100,000 people for businesses and 987 per 100,000 people for residences.

16 MIGRATION

Since the end of World War II, more than 650,000 immigrants from over 80 countries have moved to Québec, particularly to the city of Montréal. Italians and Eastern Europeans were traditionally the largest immigrant groups to Québec, but since 1960 the ranks of new Quebeckers have been swollen by Portuguese, Haitians, Lebanese, South Americans, and Southeast Asians. In 1968, the Québec government created its own department of immigration, the only such provincial office in Canada. In 1992, Québec admitted more than 48,000 immigrants (20% of the Canadian total), with 50% from Asia and 17% from Europe. Québec also admitted 11,000 refugees and 8,000 foreign professionals in 1992.

In 1991, Québec lost 12,259 residents from migration between provinces (28,291 people entered the province and 40,550 left for other provinces). Ontario was the province of origin for 64% of incoming internal migration into Québec in 1991 and was the destination for 66% of Québec's residents who left the province to live elsewhere in Canada that year.

17 ECONOMY

Québec's economy is highly industrialized and quite diversified. The province has abundant natural resources and energy, along with well-developed agriculture, manufacturing, and service sectors. The service sector is by far the largest sector of the economy, followed by manufacturing; finance, insurance, and real estate; public administration and defense; retail trade; wholesale trade; transportation; utilities; agriculture, forestry, fishing, and mining; communications; and warehousing.

The inflation rate in Québec in 1993 was 1.4%, one of the lowest rates among the industrialized nations. The savings rate among households rose from 7.2% in 1988 to 10.7% in 1992.

18 INCOME

The average hourly wage for a worker in Québec in 1993 was c$14.40, 9.3% less than the national average and 15.1% less than Ontario's average. Wages in the manufacturing sector increased by 1.8% in 1993. Average family income in the province was c$44,868 in 1989. As of December 1992, average weekly earnings in the province amounted to c$545.87.

19 INDUSTRY

Québec's manufacturing sector produces a wide variety of high quality products for export, such as air traffic control equipment, software, subway trains, helicopters, compact discs, air purifiers, and toys. More than 60% of the province's manufacturing firms are small or medium-sized companies. Montréal accounts for 70% of Québec's manufacturing production and is especially strong in space and aeronautics, telecommunications, energy, and transportation. In 1992, the value of manufacturers' shipments totaled c$68.6 billion, of which food and beverages accounted for c$11.8 billion; textiles and apparel, c$6.7 billion; paper, c$6.6 billion; primary metal processing, c$5.7 billion; transportation equipment, c$5.4 billion; chemical products, c$5.3 billion; electrical and electronic products, c$4.5 billion; metal products, c$3.3 billion; and other industries, c$19.3 billion.

20 LABOR

The number of legal working age people in Québec totaled 5,476,000 in 1993, with a participation rate of 62.2%. In 1993, Québec's labor force numbered around 3,404,000, with 2,959,600 employed and about 444,400 unemployed, giving an unemployment rate of 13.1%. In 1993, nearly 75% of all jobs were in services. By sector, 36.5% of the jobs were in social, cultural, commercial, and personal services; 17.6% in manufacturing; 16.6% in trade; 7.5% in public administration; 7.5% in transportation, communications, and utilities; 6.1% in finance, insurance, and real estate; 4.5% in construction; 2.4% in agricultural activities accounted; and 1.2% in fishing, forestry, and mining.

Overall unionization levels for Québec showed a slight increase in 1992 to 49.7%. As of September 1992, 982,599 employees were covered by collective bargaining agreements, 4,207 more than in 1991. Memberships in Québec's largest unions in 1992 were: the Québec Federation of Labor, 450,000; the Confederation of National Trade Unions, 235,000; and the Québec Teachers' Union, 110,000.

21 AGRICULTURE

In 1991, Québec had over 8.4 million acres (3.4 million hectares) in farms, of which 3.9 million acres (1.6 million hectares) were in crops. Field crop production in 1992 included barley, 611,610 tons (555,000 metric tons); oats, 325,090 tons (295,000 metric tons); and wheat, 134,444 tons (122,000 metric tons). In 1991, there were 94 wheat farms, 2,423 other small grain farms, 2,091 fruits and vegetables farms, 1,903 other field crop farms, and 5,355 specialty product farms. Crop production in 1992 included carrots, 125,000 tons (113,430 metric tons); green cabbage, 64,463 tons (58,497 metric tons); onions, 48,918 tons (44,390 metric tons); apples, 100,057 tons (90,796 metric tons); strawberries, 10,957 tons (9,943 metric tons); potatoes, 473,860 tons (430,000 metric tons); corn for grain, 1,575,860 tons (1,430,000 metric tons); barley, 617,120 tons (560,000 metric tons); oats, 304,152 tons (276,000 metric tons); wheat, 134,224 tons (121,800 metric tons); tobacco, 3,405 tons (3,090 metric tons); tame hay, 4,738,600 tons (4,300,000 metric tons); and fodder corn, 991,800 tons (900,000 metric tons). Cash receipts for all crops in 1992 totaled c$715.6 million.

22 DOMESTICATED ANIMALS

Dairy, beef, pork, and poultry production significantly contribute to provincial self-sufficiency in food. As of 1991, Québec had 12,952 dairy, 6,583 cattle, 2,308 hogs, 912 poultry, and 405 livestock combination farms. Québec also had 34 mink and 106 fox farms in 1992. Hog production in 1992 amounted to nearly 4.7 million head, with cash receipts totaling c$521.3 million. The 1992 slaughter of 276,000 head of cattle and 347,000 calves generated cash receipts of c$375.7 million. Receipts from the 63,200 sheep and 15,300 lambs slaughtered in 1992 came to c$6.6 million. The value of shipments from poultry production in 1992 totaled c$546.5 million. Québec's 505,000 dairy cows generated more than 661.8 million gallons (2.5 billion liters) of milk in 1992, with cash receipts of C$1.19 billion. Egg production in 1992 amounted to 68.9 million dozen, valued at C$63.4 million. Québec's 36,397 beehives produced 1,586 tons (1,439 metric tons) of honey in 1992, valued at C$5.7 million. Cash receipts for all livestock products in 1992 totaled C$2.42 billion.

23 FISHING

Commercial fishing in Québec benefits from some of the most productive fishing areas in the Atlantic as well as large consumer markets for fish and fish products. As of 1991, Québec had 5,303 registered marine commercial anglers and 240 freshwater commercial fishers. In 1993, total landings amounted to 61,168 tons (55,506 metric tons) and were valued at nearly C$88 million, fifth among the provinces. About 75% of the annual provincial fisheries production is exported, especially crustaceans and shellfish. In 1992, there were 379 licensed fish farms that produced 376 tons of trout, 60 tons of salmon, and 87 tons of mussels.

24 FORESTRY

Québec's forests are equal in area to those of Sweden and Norway combined. About 50% of Québec's lands are covered with commercial forests, of which 75% is softwood. Major softwood species include white, black, and red spruce as well as balsam fir and eastern white pine. Common hardwood species include sugar and red maple, trembling aspen, paper and yellow birch, and American beech. Forestry product processing in Québec is diversified and includes furniture and lumber, wood chip mills, sawmills, and particle board and plywood plants. Québec's pulp and paper industry produces about 16% of the world's newsprint, equivalent to the entire US production.

25 MINING

Québec is one of the world's 10 leading mineral producers. Metallic minerals predominate and include gold, copper, zinc, silver, iron, and asbestos. Production amounts for 1992 include zinc, 112,219 tons (101,832 metric tons); copper, 101,510 tons (92,114 metric tons); silver, 303,213 pounds (137,574 kilograms); and gold, 98,175 pounds (44,544 kilograms). The total value of mineral production in 1992 was C$2.63 billion, to which metals contributed 62%; nonmetals, 21.8%; and structural minerals, 16.2%. Due in part to inexpensive energy resources, Québec is one of the world's chief exporters of aluminum; annual production is around 2.4 million tons (2.2 million metric tons).

26 ENERGY AND POWER

Consumption of natural gas increased from 5% of total energy usage in 1971 to 16% in 1991. Québec's natural gas comes from enormous Canadian reserves that make up 60% of the North American supply. The industrial sector accounts for 60% of natural gas consumption in Québec, and the federal government has recently encouraged industrial conversion from oil to natural gas.

Québec has enormous hydroelectric resources; electricity output increased 132% between 1971 and 1991, with hydroelectricity now accounting for about 42% of Québec's total energy supply. Hydroelectricity is controlled by Hydro-Québec, a state-owned company that distributes electricity throughout Québec, the maritime provinces, and to much of New England. In 1991, electricity generated totaled 143 billion kilowatt hours and consumption within the province amounted to 149.4 billion kilowatt hours.

27 COMMERCE

In 1992, trade with the rest of Canada amounted to c$70 billion, of which 70% was with Ontario. Such trade has grown since 1987 thanks to several agreements that have helped to encourage trade between the provinces.

International trade totaled c$60 billion in 1992. In 1992, North America was the destination of 76.3% of Québec's exports; Europe, 14.6%; Asia and Oceania, 5.3%; Africa and the Middle East, 2%; and Latin America, 1.8%. Major export areas for Québec include the forest industry (printing, lumber and paper), mining (aluminum and iron ore) and transportation equipment manufacturing.

28 PUBLIC FINANCE

The fiscal year runs from 1 April to 31 March. For fiscal year 1992/93, total revenues were c$39.1 billion; expenditures totaled c$44.6 billion. The largest expenditure items were health and social services, education, finance, income security, health insurance, transport, and municipal affairs.

29 TAXATION

Unlike other provinces, Québec administers and collects its own corporate and personal income taxes. The retail sales tax was 8% in 1993. Major consumption taxes in 1993 were levied on gasoline and tobacco. In 1991, the average family in Québec had a cash income of c$45,500 and paid c$20,226 in taxes.

Corporate income tax rates in 1993 were as follows: small business rate, 5.75%; general business rate, 8.9%; and capital tax rate, 0.56–1.12%. Corporations in Québec have one of the lowest overall tax rates on profits in North America.

30 HEALTH

In 1992 there were 96,146 live births in Québec, for a rate of 13.4 per 1,000 residents. The death rate in 1992 was 6.8 per 1,000 residents, with 48,824 deaths occurring that year. Therapeutic abortions in Québec numbered 14,438 in 1990, for a rate of 8.8 per 1,000 females aged 15–44 and a ratio of 14.7 per 100 live births. Reported cases of selected diseases in 1990 included campylobacteriosis, 2,151; gonococcal infections, 1,966; salmonellosis, 1,962; pertussis, 1,626; hepatitis type B, 1,039; giardiasis, 688; shigellosis, 418; tuberculosis, 405; hepatitis type A, 315; and syphilis, 200. There were 436 new AIDS cases reported in 1990; in 1991, the total number of cases was 1,654.

Life expectancy at birth in Québec is 80.5 years for females and 73.2 years for males. Québec's 712 health establishments in 1991/92 consisted of 140 hospitals with

31,791 beds; 440 reception and long-term care centers, with 56,289 beds; and 132 rehabilitation centers, with 15,311 beds. Québec has about 7 hospital beds per 1,000 inhabitants (greater than either the national Canadian or US ratio), and about 433 persons per physician; physicians numbered 15,279 in 1987.

31 HOUSING

In 1990, the average resale value of a home in Montréal was c$111,956. The average rent for a two-bedroom apartment in Québec City in 1990 was c$485, while the metropolitan area apartment vacancy rate was 6.1%. Average 1990 monthly rents (and metropolitan area apartment vacancy rates) for other cities included Montréal, c$475 (5.9%); Chicoutimi-Jonquiére, c$422 (6.2%); Sherbrooke, c$395 (10.5%); and Trois Rivières, c$379 (8.1%).

32 EDUCATION

Schooling is available in both French and English. In 1992/93, Québec had 2,745 public elementary and secondary schools administered by 158 school boards, with a student population of 1,039,128. The Mininstère de l'Éducation (ME) is responsible for determining which educational services are to be provided in the school system. Historically public schools were either Roman Catholic or Protestant. In the early 1990s, however, legislation was passed to eliminate the religious nature of the schools and to reorganize the system into French-language and English-language schools. Private schools numbered just 308 in 1992/93, with 101,416 students; the ME subsidized 187 of the private schools in 1993/94 through grants of over c$289 million. In addition, some 4,000 pupils attend federal schools, and about 600 are enrolled in schools for the blind and the deaf. In 1993/94, the Québec government spent over c$10 billion on education, or 24.8% of its total budget.

In 1993, more than 45% of the working population held a postsecondary diploma or university degree. The ME is responsible for managing higher education at Québec's 47 public colleges, which had 150,458 students in 1992; about 45% of students enrolled in these colleges are in career programs, while 55% are in university transfer programs. These public colleges as well as 10 other institutions operated by the government (such as music conservatories, farm technology institutes, and the Institut de tourisme et d'hotellerie) charge no tuition. Québec also has 61 private colleges (with a 1992 enrollment of 21,007), of which 27 receive funding from the government.

The Université du Québec in Québec City, founded in 1968, is the second-largest university in Canada and the nation's largest French-language higher education institution; full-time enrollment in 1990/91 was 29,312. Other universities (with location and year founded) and their 1990/91 full-time enrollments include: Université Laval (Québec City, 1852), 23,763; McGill University (Montréal, 1821), 19,335; Université de Montréal (1920), 18,180; Concordia University (Montréal, 1974), 13,715; Université de Sherbrooke (1954), 10,125; and Bishop's

A lake near Mont Ste. Marie. The lowlands near the St. Lawrence River are dotted with more than one million lakes and rivers.

University (Lennoxville, 1843), 1,685. Four of the province's seven universities offer courses taught in French (Université Laval, Université de Montréal, Université de Sherbrooke, and Université du Québec); the other three offer instruction in English (McGill, Bishop's, and Concordia). Total university enrollment in 1992/93 was 256,956.

33 ARTS

Québec, with the Grands Ballet Canadiens, is well-known for its numerous dance companies, and a North American center for dance. Montréal annually hosts the Festival international de nouvelle danse, which attracts dance professionals from around the world. Montréal also has some 50 theaters and 20 permanent theater companies that stage traditional works as well as a repertory from Québec's avant-garde playwrights. Québec also offers several yearly music festivals, including a classical music competition, the Festival international de Lanaudière, and the International Jazz Festival, all in Montréal; the Festival d'été de Québec (a summer music festival) is held in Québec City. Cinema productions by the National Film Board of Canada in Québec have recently included Denys Arcand's *The Decline of the American Empire* and *Jesus of Montréal,* and Frédérick Back's *The Man Who Planted Trees.* In 1990/91, Québec's 129 performing arts companies gave 10,602 performances before a total attendance of 3,803,217.

34 LIBRARIES AND MUSEUMS

Québec had 165 public library systems in 1992, with 929 branches. The Université du Québec and McGill University maintain large academic libraries in Montréal. Other academic libraries include those of Université de Sherbrooke and Université Laval (Québec City).

The Musée du Québec in Québec City is one of Canada's most prominent museums, with a distinguished collection of 17th–19th century art as well as a collection of contemporary art. Montréal has some 20 museums and many art galleries, including the McCord Museum of Canadian History and the International Museum of Cartoon Art.

35 COMMUNICATIONS

As of 1994, Québec had 42 AM and 55 FM radio stations, and 29 television stations. In 1993, radio broadcasts totaled 137,089,000 hours, 66% FM and 34% AM. Television operations in the province handled 174,533,000 hours of programming, of which 77.3% was Canadian francophone programming. Montréal produces 65% of the world's French-language television programming and original productions. Montréal is also Canada's main routing center for international telecommunications connections—including one of the world's first digital telephone switching systems.

36 PRESS

Québec has 11 daily newspapers, with 9 published for French speakers and 2 for speakers of English. Montréal's dailies are *Le Journal de Montréal, La Presse, Le Devoir,* and *The Gazette*; Québec City has *Le Journal de Québec* and *Le Soleil*. More than 500 publications are printed in Québec, with over 400 in French and 75 in English. Québec has about 100 publishers and a dozen annual book fairs.

37 TOURISM, TRAVEL, AND RECREATION

Québec is famous for its expansive system of large urban parks; the province maintains 20 parks and wildlife reserves. The taiga and tundra of the north is a popular destination for adventurous travelers. Montréal's Botanical Garden, the second largest in the world, has ornate Chinese and Japanese gardens. Also in Montréal, the Biôdome exhibits four distinct ecosystems, and has become the city's most popular tourist destination since its opening in June 1992. Casinos are located in Montréal and Charlevoix. Besides traditional hotel, motel, and inn accommodations, Québec's tourist accommodations include a wide variety of vacation centers, bed-and-breakfasts, and youth hostels. Tourists in Québec numbered more than 20 million in 1992, of which 75.5% were Québécois, 11.7% were Canadians visiting from other provinces, and 12.9% were foreigners. Travelers and tourists spent c$4.7 billion in the province in 1992.

38 SPORTS

Professional sports teams include the Montréal Canadiens of the National Hockey League (NHL) and the Montréal Expos of Major League Baseball, the first franchise the league awarded outside the United States. The Canadiens are the best-known team in hockey and have won the NHL championship (the Stanley Cup) a record 23 times—the earliest in 1924 and the most recent in 1993. The Montréal Alouettes, a former team of the Canadian Football League, won the Grey Cup in 1970, 1974, and 1977. Major sporting events in Québec include an international tennis tournament, the Formula 1 Grand Prix, the Grand Prix cycliste des Amériques, the Valleyfield International Regatta, the international swim across Lac Saint-Jean, and the Harricana snowmobile rally from southern Québec to James Bay. Montréal hosted the summer Olympics in 1976.

Popular summer recreational activities include sailing, golf, cycling, swimming, and tennis. Downhill skiing on world-class slopes, cross-country skiing, and ice hockey and skating are popular winter activities.

39 FAMOUS QUÉBÉCOIS/ QUÉBECKERS

Early explorers included Jacques Cartier (b.France, 1491–1557), who navigated up the St. Lawrence River. Geographer Samuel de Champlain (b.France, 1570–1635), the "Father of New France," also led expeditions and organized settlements. Étienne Brûlé (b.France, c.1592–c.1633) was the first European explorer to live among the Aboriginal people and translated the Huron language. Louis de Buade, Comte de Palluau et de Frontenac (b.France, 1622–98) was the greatest of the French royal governors and promoted French expansion into North America by establishing fur-trade posts and defending them against the Iroquois and the English. Louis Jolliet (1645–1700) was commissioned by Frontenac to explore the Mississippi River. Fur trader James McGill (b.Scotland, 1744–1813) was the founder of the university in Montréal that bears his name.

Sir John Abbott (1821–93), Canada's first native-born prime minister, was from St. Andrews, Lower Canada (Québec). Other prominent political leaders from Québec include Canadian prime ministers Sir Wilfred Laurier (1841–1919), Louis St. Laurant (1882–1973), Pierre Trudeau (b.1919), Brian Mulroney (b.1939), and Jean Chrétien (b.1934). René Lévesque (1922–87) led the separatist Parti Québécois to power in 1976 and served as Québec's premier until 1985. Lucien Bouchard (b.1938) is the leader of the Bloc Québécois, a political party that desires the independence of Québec from Canada.

Famous entertainers from Québec include actors Glenn Ford (b.1916), Joseph Wiseman (b.1918), Madeleine Sherwood (b.1926), William Shatner (b.1931), John Vernon (b.1932), Michael Sarrazin (b.1940), Geneviève Bujold (b.1942), and Robert Joy (b.1951); director and producer Paul Almond (b.1931); pianist Oscar Peterson (b.1925); operatic singer Maureen Forrester (b.1930) and baritone Louis Quilico (b.1931); and sing-

Rafting on the River Rouge. Québec's lakes and rivers account for 16% of the world's fresh water supply.

ers Leonard Cohen (b.1934), Burton Cummings (b.1947), and Corey Hart (b.1962).

Noted francophone Québecois authors include novelists Yves Thériault (1915–83), Roger Lemelin (b.1919), and Hubert Aquin (1929–77); and poets François-Xavier Garneau (1809–66), Octave Crémazie (1827–79), Émile Nelligan (1879–1941), Gratien Gélinas (b.1909), Anne Hébert (b.1916), and Roch Carrier (b.1937). Famous anglophone authors include critic Northrop Frye (1912–91), novelists Constance Beresford-Howe (b.1922), Mordecai Richler (b.1931); short story writer Mavis Gallant (b.1922);

and poet F. R. Scott (1899–1985). Distinguished Québec authors known for their works in both French and English include novelist Marie-Claire Blais (b.1939), poet and novelist Nicole Brossard (b.1943), and playwright Michel Tremblay (b.1942). Sculptor Akeeaktashuk (1898–1954) was one of the first Inuit artists to receive individual acclaim.

Québec has been the home of many great hockey players, including Maurice "Rocket" Richard (b.1921), Jacques Plante (b.1929), Jean Beliveau (b.1931), Bernie "Boom Boom" Geoffrion (b.1931), Rodrique "Rod" Gilbert (b.1941), Yvan Serge Cournoyer (b.1943), Bernard Marcel Parent (b.1945), Marcel Dionne (b.1951), Guy Damien Lafleur (b.1951), Richard Lionel "Rick" Martin (b.1951), Denis Charles Potvin (b.1953), Jean Ratelle (b.1953), Mike Bossy (b.1957), and Mario Lemieux (b.1965).

40 BIBLIOGRAPHY

Bumsted, J. M. *The Peoples of Canada*. New York: Oxford University Press, 1992.

Hamilton, Janice. *Quebec*. Minneapolis: Lerner Publications, 1996.

LeVert, Suzanne. *Let's Discover Canada: Quebec*. New York: Chelsea House, 1991.

Ouellet, Danielle, and Jean Provencher. *Discover Canada: Quebec*. Toronto: Grolier, 1993.

Sorensen, Lynda. *Canada: Provinces and Territories*. Vero Beach, Fla.: Rourke Book Co., 1995.

Wansborough, M. B. *Great Canadian Lives*. New York: Doubleday, 1986.

Weihs, Jean. *Facts about Canada, Its Provinces and Territories*. New York: H. W. Wilson, 1995.

SASKATCHEWAN

ORIGIN OF PROVINCE NAME: Derived from the Cree Indian word *kisiskatchewanisipi*, which means "swift-flowing river," and was first used to describe the Saskatchewan River.

NICKNAME: Canada's Breadbasket (also: The Wheat Province).

CAPITAL: Regina.

ENTERED CONFEDERATION: 1 September 1905.

MOTTO: *Multis e gentibus vires* (From many peoples strength).

Coat of Arms: In the center, the provincial shield of arms displays a red lion, which symbolizes loyalty to the British Crown, and (over a field of green) three gold wheat sheaves, which symbolize Saskatchewan's agriculture. Above the shield is a crest with a beaver holding a western red lily and carrying a royal crown on its back. Supporting the shield are a lion on the left and a deer on the right; both wear collars made of Prairie Indian beads. Beneath the shield the provincial motto appears on a scroll entwined with western red lilies. The red signifies the fires that once swept the prairies, green represents vegetation, and gold symbolizes ripening grain.

FLAG: Horizontal bars of equal width with green above (for the northern forests) and yellow below (for the southern grain region). The provincial shield of arms appears in the upper quarter on the staff side and a western red lily lies in the half farthest from the staff.

FLORAL EMBLEM: Western red lily (also known as the prairie lily).

TARTAN: Saskatchewan Tartan (gold, brown, green, red, yellow, white, and black).

PROVINCIAL BIRD: Prairie sharp-tailed grouse.

TREE: White birch.

TIME: 6 AM CST = noon GMT; 5 AM MST = noon GMT.

1 LOCATION AND SIZE

Saskatchewan, almost rectangular in shape, is located between the two other prairie provinces, with Manitoba to the east and Alberta to the west. The Northwest Territories are to the north, and the US states of Montana and North Dakota are to the south. Saskatchewan covers some 251,700 square miles (651,900 square kilometers). It is the only province formed entirely of man-made borders.

2 TOPOGRAPHY

The northern part of Saskatchewan lies on the Canadian Shield geologic formation which stretches across much of Canada. As a result, there are numerous lakes (nearly 100,000), rivers, bogs, and rocky outcroppings. About one-eighth of the entire province is covered with water. The southern part of the province is relatively flat prairie, with occasional valleys created by erosion from the glacial era. The south is where most of the population lives. The highest point is at Cypress Hills, 4,566 feet (1,392 meters) above sea level. The province has three major river systems, which all empty into Hudson Bay: North and South Saskatchewan, Assiniboine, and Churchill. Saskatoon, the largest city, is divided by the South Saskatchewan River.

Athabasca Provincial Park has sand dunes 100 feet (30 meters) high and semi-arid vegetation. Nowhere else in the world are dunes found so far north.

3 CLIMATE

The whole province enjoys a hot, dry summer. The town of Estevan in the southeast averages 2,540 hours of sunshine per year, more than any other city in Canada. In Regina, the normal daily temperature ranges from 0°F (-18°C) in January to 66°F (19°C) in July. Normal daily temperatures for Saskatoon are -2°F (-19°C) in January and 66°F (19°C) in July. The recorded high temperature in Saskatchewan of 113°F (45°C) was set on 5 July 1937 at Midale; the record low, -70°F (-56.7°C), was set on 1 February 1893 at Prince Albert.

4 PLANTS AND ANIMALS

Saskatchewan's southern plains were once covered by native prairie grass. Grass fires started by nature would often sweep over the plains. Western wheat grass, snowberry, and silver sage are common to Grasslands National Park, located in the extreme south. To the north, several types of berries and wildflowers, Labrador tea, and feather moss are commonly found under the aspens and black spruce trees of Prince Albert National Park.

Saskatchewan Population Profile

Estimated 1994 population:	1,016,000
Population change, 1981–91:	2.1%
Leading ancestry group:	British
Second leading group:	German/Austrian
Foreign born population:	6%
Population by ethnic group:	
Aboriginal peoples:	75,400
Urban/Rural populations:	
Urban:	623,397 63%
Rural:	365,531 37%
Population density:	4.04 persons per square mile (1.6 per square kilometer)

Population by Age Group

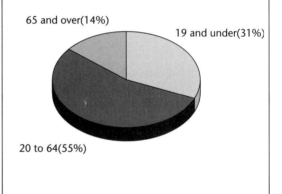

65 and over(14%)

19 and under(31%)

20 to 64(55%)

Top Cities with Populations over 10,000

City	Population	Natl. Rank
Saskatoon (metro area)	210,023	17
Regina (metro area)	191,692	18
Prince Albert	41,259	64
Moose Jaw	35,552	75
North Battleford	18,457	103
Yorkton	18,023	105
Swift Current	14,815	120
Estevan	11,379	132

SASKATCHEWAN

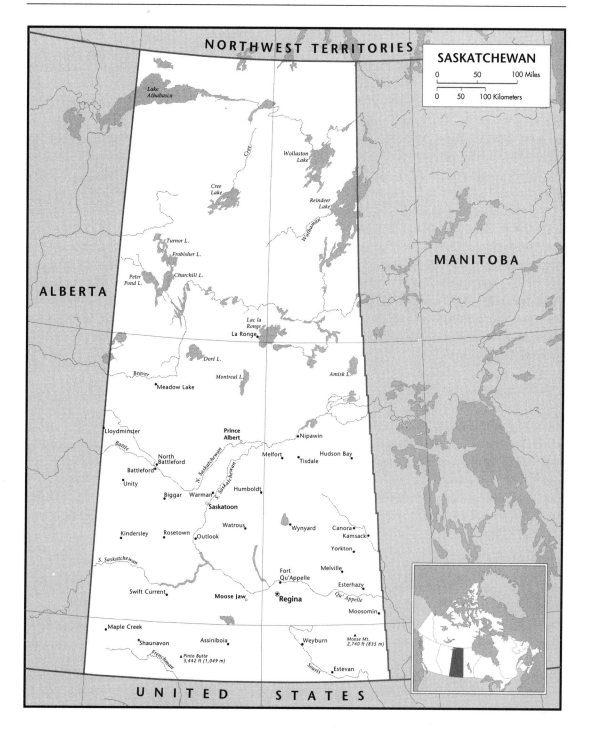

NORTHWEST TERRITORIES

SASKATCHEWAN

0   50   100 Miles

0   50   100 Kilometers

ALBERTA

MANITOBA

Lake Athabasca

Wollaston Lake

Cree Lake

Reindeer Lake

Cree

Waltoman

Turnor L.

Frobisher L.

Peter Pond L.

Churchill L.

Lac la Ronge

La Ronge

Doré L.

Beaver

Montreal L.

Amisk L.

Meadow Lake

Lloydminster

Prince Albert

Nipawin

Battle

North Battleford

Melfort

Hudson Bay

Battleford

Tisdale

N. Saskatchewan

Unity

S. Saskatchewan

Humboldt

Biggar

Warman

Saskatoon

Watrous

Wynyard

Canora

Kindersley

Rosetown

Outlook

Kamsack

Yorkton

S. Saskatchewan

Melville

Fort Qu'Appelle

Esterhazy

Swift Current

Moose Jaw

Regina

Qu'Appelle

Moosomin

Maple Creek

Shaunavon

Assiniboia

Weyburn

Moose Mt. 2,740 ft (835 m)

Frenchman

▲ Pinto Butte 3,442 ft (1,049 m)

Souris

Estevan

UNITED   STATES

The prairie sharp-tailed grouse, one of the province's most common native game birds, is the official bird of Saskatchewan. Other common bird species include the Hungarian partridge, ruffed grouse, and spruce grouse. Bison, eagles, osprey, white pelicans, beaver, elk, moose, and wolves inhabit Prince Albert National Park. Golden eagles, pronghorn antelope, prairie rattlesnakes, sage grouse, prairie falcons, bobcats, and porcupines are found in Grasslands National Park. Endangered and threatened species include ferruginous hawks, short-horned lizards, and burrowing owls. Lake trout, walleye, northern pike, and Arctic grayling are among 68 fish species in the province.

5 ENVIRONMENTAL PROTECTION

Saskatchewan's annual carbon dioxide emissions are the second highest in Canada. Solid waste generation amounts to about 936,700 tons (850,000 metric tons) per year, or 0.94 tons (0.85 metric tons) per person. Saskatchewan has 867 municipal landfills and 12 hazardous waste sites.

6 POPULATION

Saskatchewan's estimated 1994 population of 1,016,000 ranked it sixth out of the 12 Canadian provinces and territories. The population has fallen slightly in recent years, with a 2% decrease from 1986 to 1991. As of 1991, the population was 50.4% female and 49.6% male, with 31.4% of all residents under 20 years of age. About 63% of the population lived in cities in 1991. About one-third of Saskatchewan's total population lived in the province's two largest cities in 1993.

Saskatoon had 187,072 residents, while Regina had 178,764. Other large cities and their 1991 populations include: Prince Albert, 41,259; Moose Jaw, 35,552; North Battleford, 18,457; and Yorkton, 18,023.

7 ETHNIC GROUPS

Saskatchewan is Canada's most multicultural province. It is the only one where the number of people of British or French background is smaller than the number of people from other ethnic groups. Various European ethnic groups are found here, including British, French, German, Ukrainian, Scandinavian, Dutch, Polish, and Russian. In addition to Aboriginals (Native Peoples), many other non-European peoples live in Saskatchewan as well.

8 LANGUAGES

In 1991, 83.8% of all Saskatchewans claimed English as their first language, 2.2% reported French, and 14% reported some other first language.

9 RELIGIONS

Most Saskatchewans are Christian. In 1991, 53.4% of the population, or 528,088 people, was Protestant. Membership in leading Protestant denominations in 1991 included United Church of Canada, 225,476; Lutheran, 83,070; Anglican, 71,203; Pentecostal, 17,801; Baptist, 15,823; and Presbyterian, 11,867. Catholics—32.5% of the population—numbered 321,402, with 300,634 Roman Catholics and 20,767 Ukrainian Catholics. About 2% of Saskatchewans are Eastern Orthodox. Other faiths are also

Photo Credit: Canadian Tourism Commission photo.

Regina is the capital of Saskatchewan. However, the area is also important to wildlife. The airspace between Regina and Saskatoon is one of the busiest corridors for migrating ducks and geese in North America.

represented in smaller numbers, including Buddhists, Hindus, Sikhs, and Jews. About 111,749 Saskatchewans had no religious affiliation in 1991.

10 TRANSPORTATION

During the frontier era, waterways such as the Clearwater and Churchill Rivers became established fur-trade routes, as did the overland Carlton Trail.

At 150,000 miles (250,000 kilometers), Saskatchewan today has more road surface than any other province. As of 1994, there were 481 miles (774 kilometers) of divided four-lane paved highways, 11,654 miles (18,755 kilometers) of two-lane paved roads, and 3,633 miles (5,847 kilo-

meters) of gravel roads. In 1992, registered passenger automobiles numbered 441,042; trucks and power units, 272,177; and motorcycles, buses, and government vehicles, 14,945. Both Regina and Saskatoon have bus systems with more than 110 buses in each fleet.

International airports are located at Regina and Saskatoon. In 1992, Regina Airport handled 579,000 arriving and departing passengers on 6,348 flights, and Saskatoon Airport's 5,351 flights served 570,700 passengers.

11 HISTORY

The first European explorers and trappers to visit Saskatchewan encountered settlements of Aboriginal people. The Chipewyan Indians lived in the north, the nomadic Blackfoot roamed the eastern plains, and the Assiniboine inhabited the west. The territory of the Cree, who were long-time residents of the north, also extended southward to the plains.

The earliest explorer was Henry Kelsey, a Hudson's Bay Company agent. Around 1690 he followed the Saskatchewan River to the southern plains of Saskatchewan. Following the trappers came fur-trading companies and trading posts, which became the foundation of many present-day settlements.

For 200 years, the Hudson's Bay Company owned and administered the vast Northwest Territories. The Canadian government purchased the Territories in 1870, wishing to take advantage of the region's potential for agriculture and settlement. After the Dominion Lands Act of 1872 was passed to encourage homesteaders, the new railway began bringing settlers in to farm these rich lands. In 1905, Saskatchewan separated from the Northwest Territories and entered the Canadian confederation, with Regina as the provincial capital.

Early Years as a Province

During World War I (1914–18), Canada lost more than 68,000 soldiers. Veterans returning to Saskatchewan faced a bleak future of scarce low-paying jobs, while tariffs on imports kept prices for consumer goods high. Saskatchewan farmers, as in the other prairie provinces, had prospered from high wheat prices during World War

I. But with the end of the war, global grain markets collapsed and wheat prices fell 50% by 1920.

During the 1920s, grain prices recovered and Canada experienced a period of rapid growth in industry. Transportation improvements—especially railways and roads—enabled businesses to flourish. Automobiles, telephones, electrical appliances, and other consumer goods became widely available.

Saskatchewan, like the other prairie provinces, was one of the poorest areas of Canada during the Great Depression. In addition to the falling grain prices of the 1920s, droughts and frequent crop failures devastated the economy of the province. Social welfare programs rapidly expanded during the 1930s, with much of the burden placed on the provincial and municipal governments. Provincial income in Saskatchewan decreased 90% during the 1930s, and some two-thirds of the province's population became reliant on welfare.

1940s–1990s

Following World War II (1939–45), consumer spending and immigration to Canada rapidly increased. Urbanization spread quickly by means of the National Housing Act, which made home ownership more easily available. Unemployment insurance and other social welfare programs were also created following the war. In 1945, the Co-operative Commonwealth Federation (CCF) became the first socialist government elected in North America. Its leader, Tommy Douglas, led the fight for public hospitalization and medicare. The recovery of the 1940s and 1950s saw the economy, once made up entirely of agriculture, become more varied. Oil, uranium, potash, coal, and other minerals were developed.

Canada's unity as a confederation has often been widely questioned. Most recently, the popular defeat of both the Meech Lake Accord of 1987 and the Charlottetown Accord of 1992 have failed to solve the issue of Québec's role in Canada. Meanwhile, many western Canadians have come to feel that the federal government treats them as less important than other Canadians. As a result, in many areas of Saskatchewan and other western provinces, voters have recently elected representatives who favor increased power for the provinces and decreased power for the federal government.

12 PROVINCIAL GOVERNMENT

The structure of the provincial government reflects that of the federal government. For example, the provincial premier, as the majority party leader of the legislature, functions much like the Canadian prime minister. Provincial legislators, like their federal counterparts in Parliament, are elected to represent a constitutional jurisdiction and pass legislation. They do so as members of the 66-seat Legislative Assembly. A provincial lieutenant-governor approves laws passed by the legislature, much like the Governor General at the federal level. There is no provincial equivalent, however, to the federal Senate.

13 POLITICAL PARTIES

After Saskatchewan entered the confederation in 1905, political parties catered to the interests of farmers. The Liberal Party gained the majority of seats, eventually holding 91% of them in 1934. Soon, the Co-operative Commonwealth Federation (CCF) became more important, and often held the majority from 1944 to 1971.

The most recent general election was held on 21 October 1991. The parties held the following number of seats in Saskatchewan's Legislative Assembly in 1994: New Democratic Party, 55; Progressive Conservative, 10; and Liberal Party, 1.

PREMIERS OF SASKATCHEWAN

Term	Premier	Party
1905–16	Thomas Walter Scott	Liberal
1916–22	William Melville Martin	Liberal
1922–26	Charles Avery Dunning	Liberal
1926–29	James Garfield Gardiner	Liberal
1929–34	James Milton Anderson	Conservative
1934–35	James Garfield Gardiner	Liberal
1935–44	William John Patterson	Liberal
1944–61	Thomas Clement Douglas	CCF
1961–64	Woodrow Stanley Lloyd	CCF
1964–71	William Ross Thatcher	Liberal
1971–82	Allan Emrys Blakeney	New Democratic
1982–91	Donald Grant Devine	Conservative
1991–	Roy John Romanow	New Democratic

14 LOCAL GOVERNMENT

Saskatchewan's municipalities are classified as the following: rural municipalities, villages, resort villages, towns, and cities, as well as northern towns, northern villages, northern hamlets, and northern settlements. Villages must have at least 100 permanent residents and a tax base of c$200,000, while resort villages do not need permanent residents. Towns must have at least 500 permanent inhabitants. Cities are required to have a minimum population of 5,000. Saskatchewan has 9 cities and 144 towns.

15 JUDICIAL SYSTEM

The Canadian Constitution grants provincial jurisdiction over the administration of justice, and allows each province to organize its own court system and police forces. The federal government has exclusive domain over cases involving trade and commerce, banking, bankruptcy, and criminal law. The Federal Court of Canada has both trial and appellate divisions for federal cases. The 9-judge Supreme Court of Canada is an appellate court that determines the constitutionality of both federal and provincial statutes. The Tax Court of Canada hears appeals of taxpayers against assessments by Revenue Canada.

In 1990, there were 32 homicides in Saskatchewan, for a rate of 3.2 per 100,000 persons. Breaking and entering offenses in 1989 numbered 446 per 100,000 people for businesses and 819 per 100,000 people for residences.

16 MIGRATION

The Métis, people of mixed European and Aboriginal descent, were among the first settlers, many of them having migrated from Manitoba. A major wave of immigration began in 1899 and continued until 1929.

In 1991, Saskatchewan had a net loss of 9,829 residents due to migration between provinces. That year, Alberta was the province of origin for 47% of incoming internal migration and the province of

destination for 52% of outward internal migration. Since the mid-1980s, Saskatchewan has had a net loss from migration.

17 ECONOMY

During the early 20th century, with land available at token prices, agriculture gradually replaced the fur trade. Today, other prominent industries include mining, meat processing, electricity production, and petroleum refining.

18 INCOME

In 1993, average weekly wages amounted to c$472.39 and the average hourly earnings rate was c$12.01. Average family income in the province was c$42,518 in 1989.

19 INDUSTRY

By value of shipments, the leading areas of manufacturing in Saskatchewan include food, c$1.09 billion; electrical and electronic products, c$122.8 million; chemicals and chemical products, c$97.2 million; fabricated metals, c$87.7 million; and forestry products, c$62.8 million. In 1993, the total value of shipments by manufacturers was c$3.8 billion.

20 LABOR

In 1993, the labor force amounted to 479,000, of whom about 7.9% were unemployed. That year, the service sector was the largest area of employment, at 34.5%, followed by agriculture, 17.7%; trade, 15.9%; transportation, communication, and utilities, 7.5%; public administration, 6.8%; manufacturing, 5.7%;

The town of Swift Current is the base for oil exploration in western Saskatchewan and is a regional trade center for livestock and grain.

finance, insurance, and real estate, 5.5%; construction, 3.9%; and forestry, fishing, and mining, 2.5%. There are just over 100,000 union members in Saskatchewan.

21 AGRICULTURE

About one-third of Saskatchewan's area consists of cultivated lands. In 1905, when Saskatchewan entered the Canadian confederation, agriculture was the only industry, and it centered on wheat farming. Today, Saskatchewan supplies 28% of Canada's grain production, and crops include canola, rye, oats, barley, and flaxseeds, as well as wheat. The quantities of principal field crops produced in 1993 were: wheat, 16,999,452 tons (15,426,000 metric tons); barley, 5,441,676 tons (4,938,000 metric tons); canola, 2,548,926 tons (2,313,000 metric tons); oats, 1,275,014 tons (1,157,000 metric tons); flax, 377,986 tons (343,000 metric tons); and rye, 181,830 tons (165,000 metric tons). Crop receipts in 1993 amounted to almost c$3.5 million, with wheat accounting for 46% of the total.

22 DOMESTICATED ANIMALS

Saskatchewan is a major Canadian producer of cattle and hogs. As of 1994, the livestock population included 2,625,000 cattle, 43,000 dairy cows, 908,000 hogs; and 95,000 sheep. The total value of livestock and poultry in 1993 was c$2.14 billion.

23 FISHING

Although commercial fishing is not a large contributor to the provincial economy, sport fishing on Saskatchewan's 94,000 lakes is very popular. Sport fishing is important to many local economies, especially in the northern parts of Saskatchewan. Popular game fish for sport anglers include walleye, perch, trout, Arctic grayling, goldeye, burbot, whitefish, and sturgeon.

24 FORESTRY

About half of Saskatchewan is covered with forest. Northern Saskatchewan's 135,100 square miles (350,000 square kilometers) of forests are the province's most important renewable natural resource, with softwoods the focal point of forestry development. White birch, found primarily in the northern three-fourths of the province and long used by the Plains Indians to make birch bark canoes, is today used for lumber, plywood, veneer, and fuel. The value of primary forestry products in 1993 was c$440 million.

25 MINING

Saskatchewan has nearly two-thirds of the world's recoverable potash reserves and is Canada's leading exporter of potash. In 1993, the total value of nonfuel mineral production was c$1.27 billion, with potash accounting for 63%. Saskatchewan's uranium production accounted for 23% of the world total in 1992, when it was valued at c$381.1 million. Other leading

minerals for the province's mining industry include sodium sulfate, sand and gravel, salt, and gold.

26 ENERGY AND POWER

Saskatchewan has Canada's largest reserves of heavy oil, in addition to light and medium crude deposits. In 1991, crude oil production totaled 16.24 million cubic yards (12.42 million cubic meters) and was valued at c$1.19 billion. Saskatchewan's 14,000 oil wells produce about 12% of Canada's annual oil output. Of Saskatchewan's total exported crude oil, 66% went to the United States. Crude oil from both Saskatchewan and Alberta is transported to market via the Interprovincial Pipe Line (IPL). The IPL originates in Edmonton and passes through Saskatchewan on its way to eastern Canada and the United States.

In 1991, 13.6 billion kilowatt hours of electricity were generated, while consumption within the province totaled 12.4 billion kilowatt hours.

27 COMMERCE

Retail trade in 1993 amounted to c$5.7 billion, 3% of the national total. Leading retail areas by sales in 1993 included supermarkets and grocery stores, c$1.4 billion; motor and recreational vehicle dealers, c$1.2 billion; general merchandise stores, c$739 million; and gasoline service stations, c$486 million.

28 PUBLIC FINANCE

The fiscal year runs from 1 April to 31 March. For fiscal year 1992/93, total revenues were c$5.6 billion; expenditures totaled c$6.3 billion. The largest expenditure areas were health, education, interest on debt, social services, and agriculture and food.

29 TAXATION

As of 1993, the basic personal income tax rate was 50%, with high income surtaxes of 15% and a flat tax rate of 2% on net income. The retail sales tax was 9%. Major consumption taxes were levied on gasoline and tobacco. In 1991, the average family in Saskatchewan had a cash income of c$48,500 and paid c$21,397 in taxes.

Corporate income tax rates in 1993 were as follows: small business rate, 8.5%; general business rate, 17%; and capital tax rate, 0.6–3.25%.

30 HEALTH

In 1993 there were 14,304 live births in Saskatchewan, for a rate of 14 per 1,000 residents. The death rate in 1993 was 8.1 per 1,000 residents, with 8,205 deaths occurring that year. As a result, Saskatchewan had a natural increase of 6,099 people. Therapeutic abortions in Saskatchewan numbered 1,336 in 1990, for a rate of 6.1 per 1,000 females aged 15–44 and a ratio of 8.3 per 100 live births. Reported cases of selected diseases in 1990 included chicken pox, 1,370; gonococcal infections, 903; giardiasis, 649; salmonellosis, 313; and hepatitis type A, 275. There were 14 new AIDS cases reported in 1990; in 1991, the total number of cases was 49.

Saskatchewan had 134 hospitals and health centers in 1993. The Regina General Hospital is the largest health care facility in southern Saskatchewan, with 483 beds. In the late 1980s, the province had 132 general hospitals with 6,948 beds and 3 specialty hospitals with 818 beds.

31 HOUSING

In 1990, the average resale value of a home in Regina was c$71,054. The average rent for a two-bedroom apartment in Regina in 1990 was c$486, while the metropolitan area apartment vacancy rate was 5%; monthly rent in Saskatoon averaged c$438, with a metropolitan area apartment vacancy rate of 7.5%.

32 EDUCATION

In 1990/91, Saskatchewan had 212,278 students enrolled in its elementary and secondary schools. Of the total student enrollment, 198,933 went to public schools, 10,112 to federal schools, 3,199 to private schools, and 34 to schools for the blind and the deaf.

There are two major universities in the province: the University of Saskatchewan in Saskatoon with total enrollment of 23,000 students in 1992/93 and the University of Regina with about 11,000 full- and part-time students in 1992/93. Among the University of Regina's colleges is the Saskatchewan Indian Federated College, the first university-level institution in North America operated by and for Native North Americans. Enrollment in career programs in community colleges in 1990/91 was 3,433.

33 ARTS

The Regina Symphony Orchestra is Canada's oldest symphony orchestra. Regina's Globe Theatre company is the city's oldest theater and performs in the old city hall downtown. Saskatoon also has a symphony orchestra and several theaters. In 1990/91, Saskatchewan's five performing arts companies gave 498 performances before a total attendance of 138,337.

34 LIBRARIES AND MUSEUMS

Regina has the Plains Historical Museum, the Royal Canadian Mounted Police's Centennial Museum, the Saskatchewan Museum of Natural History, and the Saskatchewan Science Centre. Saskatoon is the home of the Western Development Museum, the Ukrainian Museum of Canada, the Ukrainian Museum of Culture, and the Saskatoon Sports Hall of Fame. The Right Honourable John G. Diefenbacker Centre in Saskatoon maintains the collection of papers, letters, and memorabilia of the late prime minister.

35 COMMUNICATIONS

As of 1994, Saskatchewan had 19 AM and 10 FM radio stations, and 12 television stations. The Regina metropolitan area has 9 local AM and FM radio stations (including CBC French) and 4 broadcast television stations; Cable Regina offers 17 other Canadian and American cable stations.

36 PRESS

Daily newspapers include *The Leader-Post* (Regina), *The Star Phoenix* (Saskatoon),

the *Times-Herald* (Moose Jaw), and the *Daily Herald* (Prince Albert).

37 TOURISM, TRAVEL, AND RECREATION

Named after Queen Victoria (Victoria Regina), the capital is the site of Wascana Centre, one of the world's largest urban parks. Regina also has Buffalo Days, a week-long provincial exposition and summer fair. Festivals in Saskatoon include Folkfest (an ethnic heritage event), Winter Festival, and the Northern Saskatchewan International Children's Festival. Authentic powwows at Indian reservations, although not tourist events as such, are a cultural highlight of Saskatchewan in the summer. Tourists spent c$251 million in the province in 1993.

38 SPORTS

Professional sports teams in Saskatchewan include the Saskatoon Blades and the Regina Pats of the Western Major Hockey League. Saskatoon also has the Saskatchewan Storm of the World Basketball League, while Regina is the home of the Saskatchewan Roughriders of the Canadian Football League (CFL). The Roughriders are the oldest professional football team in North America and were the CFL champions in 1966 and 1989. The University of Saskatchewan Huskie football team won the national championship in 1990. Popular recreational sports include baseball, football, soccer, and curling (a game imported from Scotland in which large rounded stones with attached handled are slid down an ice-covered playing area toward a circular target).

A cross country skier in Duck Mountain Provincial Park, east of Kamsack near the Manitoba border.

39 FAMOUS SASKATCHEWANIANS

Almighty Voice (1874–97) was a famous hero/outlaw and martyr who led a Cree Indian band resisting European settlement on the Saskatchewan prairie. T. C. "Tommy" Douglas (b.Scotland, 1904) was a famous political figure who led the Co-operative Commonwealth Federation (CCF) to victory in the 1940s, thus estab-lishing the first socialist government in North America. Gerhard Herzberg (b.Germany, 1904), recipient of the 1971 Nobel Prize in chemistry, was a professor at the University of Saskatchewan from 1935–45.

Noted Saskatchewans in entertainment include emcee and producer Art Linkletter (b.1912), actor Leslie Nielson (b.1926), and singer and songwriter Buffy Sainte-Marie (b.1941). Distinguished Saskatchewan authors include novelists W. O. Mitchell (b.1914), Rudy Wiebe (b.1934), L. R. Wright (b.1939), and short story writer Guy Vanderhaeghe (b.1951).

Hockey legends from Saskatchewan include Eddie Shore (1902–85), Emile Francis (b.1926), Gordon "Gordie" Howe (b.1928), Glenn "Chico" Resch (b.1948), and Bryan Trottier (b.1956).

40 BIBLIOGRAPHY

Bumsted, J. M. *The Peoples of Canada*. New York: Oxford University Press, 1992.

Margoshes, Dave. *Discover Canada: Saskatchewan*. Toronto: Grolier, 1992.

LeVert, Suzanne. *Let's Discover Canada: Saskatchewan*. New York: Chelsea House, 1991.

Richardson, Gillian. *Saskatchewan*. Minneapolis: Lerner Publications, 1995.

Sorensen, Lynda. *Canada: Provinces and Territories*. Vero Beach, Fla.: Rourke Book Co., 1995.

Wansborough, M. B. *Great Canadian Lives*. New York: Doubleday, 1986.

Weihs, Jean. *Facts about Canada, Its Provinces and Territories*. New York: H. W. Wilson, 1995.

YUKON TERRITORY

ORIGIN OF NAME: The name Yukon was first used by the Hudson's Bay Company trader John Bell in 1846. He called it "Yucon," derived from the Loucheux Indian word *Yuchoo,* meaning "the greatest river."

ORGANIZED: 13 June 1898.

CAPITAL: Whitehorse

COAT OF ARMS: The blue and white wavy vertical stripes symbolize the Yukon River, while the twin red peaks represent the mountains and the gold circles stand for the mineral wealth of the territory. The red Cross of St. George honors the early British explorers and traders; the patterned circle centered on the cross represents fur trading. The crest is topped by a black and white malamute dog, which played an important role in the early history and development of the Yukon.

FLAG: Is divided into three panels: green at the mast (symbolizing forests), white in the center (representing snow), and blue at the fly (signifying water). On the white panel (which is 50% wider than the other two panels) the territorial coat of arms appears above a wreath of fireweed.

FLORAL EMBLEM: Fireweed.

TARTAN: Green, dark blue, magenta, yellow, and white on a light blue background.

TERRITORIAL BIRD: Common raven.

TIME: 4 AM PST = noon GMT.

1 LOCATION AND SIZE

The Yukon Territory in Canada's northwest covers 186,660 square miles (483,450 square kilometers). The perimeters of this mountainous territory form a rough triangle bordered on the east by the Northwest Territories, on the south by British Columbia, and on the west by the US state of Alaska. The northern tip of the triangle meets the chilly waters of the Beaufort Sea. Mount Logan, Canada's highest peak (and North America's second-highest) at 19,537 feet (5,951 meters), is located in southwestern Yukon.

2 TOPOGRAPHY

The Yukon can be divided into two broad geographical regions: taiga and tundra.

Taiga is the boreal forest belt (typified by stands of pine, aspen, poplar, and birch trees) that circles the world in the subarctic zone, including most of the Yukon. Tundra is the vast, rocky plain in the arctic regions, where the extreme climate has stunted vegetation. The Yukon River is the fifth-longest in North America.

3 CLIMATE

The Yukon has a subarctic climate. The high altitude of much of the territory and the semiarid climate provide relatively warm summers with temperatures frequently reaching 77°F (25°C) or more during the long summer days. In winter the temperature ranges between 39°F and -58°F (4°C and -50°C) in the south and slightly colder farther north. The warmest recorded temperature in the Yukon was 97°F (36.1°C) on 14 June 1969 at Mayo; the coldest was -81°F (-63°C) on 3 February 1947 at Snag. Above the Arctic Circle (latitude 66 north), the Yukon is known as "the land of the midnight sun" because for three months in summer, sunlight is almost continuous. In winter, however, darkness sets in, and the light of day is not seen for a quarter of the year.

4 PLANTS AND ANIMALS

The Yukon's mountains are home to woodland caribou, lynxes, black bears, and Dall's sheep. Moose, gray wolves, golden eagles, and gyrfalcons also inhabit the Yukon. The short growing season produces an explosion of small wildflowers every year. Edible vegetation includes wild raspberries and strawberries, mossberries, and dewberries.

5 ENVIRONMENTAL PROTECTION

The Yukon has 26 solid waste disposal sites; total solid waste generation annually amounts to 7,714 tons (7,000 metric tons), or 0.25 tons (0.23 metric tons) per person. Releases of nitrogen dioxide and carbon monoxide (gases that cause smog) annually total 18,734 tons (17,000 metric tons), while emissions of sulfur dioxide and nitrogen oxide compounds annually amount to 2,204 tons (2,000 metric tons). About 3.2% of the territorial budget is spent on maintaining environmental and natural resources.

Yukon Territory Population Profile

Estimated 1994 population:		30,000
Population change, 1981–91:		20%
Leading ancestry group:		British
Second leading group:		other European
Urban/Rural populations:		
Urban:	16,335	58.8%
Rural:	11,462	41.2%
Population density:		1 person per 6.2 square miles 1 per 16.1 square kilometers)

Population by Age Group

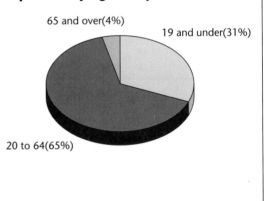

65 and over(4%)

19 and under(31%)

20 to 64(65%)

Top Cities and Towns

City/Town	Population	Natl. Rank
Whitehorse	17,925	106
Faro	1,221	2,133
Dawson City	972	2,522
Watson Lake	912	2,630

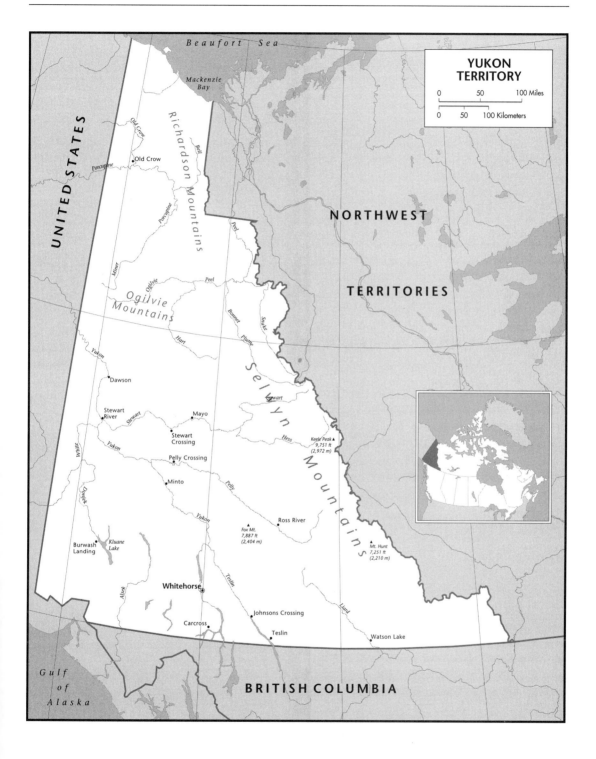

[6] POPULATION

As of 1991, 27,797 people lived in the Yukon; the 1994 estimated population was 30,000. Almost 60% of the population lives in Whitehorse, Yukon's capital city. Major towns include Faro, population 1,221; Dawson City, 972; and Watson Lake, 912.

[7] ETHNIC GROUPS

Some 23% of the population are Aboriginals (Native Peoples). The Yukon's vast interior forests were occupied by the Athapaskans, whose cultural and linguistic traditions go back more than 1,000 years. Today, there are six distinct groups of Athapaskan Indians: Kutchin, Han, Tutchone, Inland Tlingit, Kaska, and Tagish.

[8] LANGUAGES

In 1991, English was reported as the mother tongue of 88.7% of the Yukon's residents, while 3.2% declared French as their first language and 8.1% had other first languages (mostly Athapaskan dialects).

[9] RELIGIONS

In 1991, 43.1% of the population—or about 12,000 people—was Protestant, including 4,100 Anglicans, 2,400 members of the United Church of Canada, 1,000 Baptists, 650 Lutherans, 600 Pentecostals, and 350 Presbyterians. The Yukon also had about 5,600 Catholics. There were less than 100 people each of the following: Eastern Orthodox, Jews, Moslems, Buddhists, Sikhs, and Hindus. About 35.2% of the population—nearly 9,800 people—had no religious affiliation in 1991, the highest such rate in Canada.

[10] TRANSPORTATION

During World War II (1939–45), the United States built the Alaska Highway, creating a new overland transportation route. The Alaska Highway traverses southern Yukon and links Watson Lake with Whitehorse before continuing on to Alaska. In 1979, the Canadian government opened the Dempster Highway, Canada's first all-weather road to cross the Arctic Circle. The paved Klondike Highway links Dawson with Whitehorse and is the primary north-south road. In 1990, the Yukon had 30,909 registered motor vehicles, of which 12,770 were passenger cars; 17,348 were trucks, truck tractors, and buses; and 791 were motorcycles and mopeds.

[11] HISTORY

The first modern European visitors were Russian explorers who traveled along the coast in the 18th century and traded with the area's Indians. Sir John Franklin, an English explorer, anchored off the Yukon's arctic coastline in 1825, and the Hudson's Bay Company moved into the interior in the 1840s.

American traders arrived after the 1867 Russian sale of Alaska to the United States. With the discovery of gold near Dawson City in 1896, the Klondike became one of the most populous regions in northwestern Canada. The sudden increase in population during the Klondike gold rush prompted the federal government to give the Yukon more control over

Photo Credit: Canadian Tourism Commission photo.

Mount Logan, in Kluane National Park in the southwest part of the Yukon Territory, is the second-highest mountain in North America.

its affairs. In 1898, the Yukon Territory was officially established to ensure Canadian jurisdiction; the Yukon Act provided for a commissioner and an elected legislative assembly.

Early 20th Century

During World War I (1914–18), Canada lost more than 68,000 soldiers. Returning veterans faced a bleak future of scarce low-paying jobs, while tariffs on imports kept prices for consumer goods high. During the 1920s, however, Canada experienced a period of rapid growth in industry. Transportation improvements—railways and roads—enabled businesses to flourish. Automobiles, telephones, electrical appli-

ances, and other consumer goods became more widely available.

Just as in the United States, all of Canada suffered during the Great Depression. In addition to the problems with grain prices during the early 1920s, droughts and frequent crop failures devastated the national economy, which still relied heavily on agriculture. Social welfare programs rapidly expanded during the 1930s, with much of the burden placed on the provincial and municipal governments.

1940s–1990s

Following World War II (1939–45), consumer spending and immigration to Can-

Whitehorse is the Yukon Territory's principal urban area. About 60% of the population lives in Whitehorse.

ada rapidly increased. Urbanization spread quickly by means of the National Housing Act, which made home ownership more easily available. Unemployment insurance and other social welfare programs were also created following the war. Under the leadership of Prime Minister Louis St. Laurent, old age pensions were increased in 1951 and a national hospital insurance plan was introduced in 1957.

The 1970s saw the emergence of negotiations over Aboriginal land claims. In 1993, the Council for Yukon Indians, the government of Canada, and the Yukon territorial government signed an Umbrella Final Agreement which set out the terms for final land claim settlements in the Territory. Final land claim agreements were also reached with the Vuntut Gwich'in First Nation, the Champagne and Aishihik First Nation, the Teslin Tlingit Council, and the First Nation of Nacho Nyak Dun. These agreements will help establish definitive land titles and provide such benefits as cash, land, and participation in wildlife and other management boards. In addition to their land claim settlements, the four First Nations also negotiated self-government agreements which give them more control over land use on settlement lands and greater authority in such areas as language, health care, social services, and education.

In 1993, the Canada-Yukon Oil and Gas Accord was signed, which will lead to the transfer of authority and control over onshore oil and gas resources from the federal to the Yukon government. The agreement provides a commitment to negotiate shared management of oil and gas resources in the Beaufort Sea and ensures that the Yukon is a beneficiary of onshore and offshore oil and gas revenues. Other agreements have been signed for transfer of authority and control in forestry, fishery, and transportation.

12 PROVINCIAL GOVERNMENT

In both the Yukon and the Northwest Territories, political power rests with elected representatives. Although a federally-appointed commissioner is technically in charge of the administration, the role of that office has diminished and generally follows the lead of the elected territorial government. A 16-seat assembly serves as the legislative body, operating under the political party system. The territorial government leader is the leader of the majority party of the assembly's elected representatives. An executive council, which operates much like a provincial cabinet, consists of appointees of the commissioner who were recommended by the government leader.

As a territory, the Yukon does not have full provincial status, although it achieved a style of government similar to that of the provinces in 1979.

13 POLITICAL PARTIES

As of 1996, standings in the Yukon Legislative Assembly by political party were as follows: Yukon Party, 7; New Democrat, 6; Independent, 3; and Liberal Party, 1.

Commissioners of Yukon Territory

Term	Commissioner	Title
1897–98	James Morrow Walsh	Commissioner
1898	William Ogilvie	Commissioner
1898	Thomas Fawcett	Commissioner
1898	Gordon Hunter	Commissioner
1898–1901	Edmund Cumming Senkler	Commissioner
1901–02	James Hamilton Ross	Commissioner
1902–03	Zachary Taylor Wood	Commissioner
1903–05	Frederick Tennyson Congdon	Commissioner
1905–07	William Wallace Burns McInnes	Commissioner
1907–12	Alexander Henderson	Commissioner
1907–13	F. X. Gosselin	Commissioner
1912–16	George Black	Commissioner
1913–18	George Patton MacKenzie	Commissioner
1916–18	George Norris Williams	Administrator
1918–25	George Patton MacKenzie	Commissioner
1925–28	Percy Reid	Commissioner
1928–32	George Ian MacLean	Commissioner
1932–36	George Allan Jeckell	Comptroller
1936–47	George Allan Jeckell	Controller
1947–48	John Edward Gibben	Controller
1948–50	John Edward Gibben	Commissioner
1950–51	Andrew Harold Gibson	Commissioner
1952–55	Wilfred George Brown	Commissioner
1955–62	Frederick Howard Collins	Commissioner
1962–66	Gordon Robertson Cameron	Commissioner
1966–76	James Smith	Commissioner
1976–78	Arthur MacDonald Pearson	Commissioner
1978–79	Frank B. Fingland	Commissioner
1979	Ione Jean Christensen	Commissioner
1979–80	Douglas Leslie Dewey Bell	Administrator
1980–86	Douglas Leslie Dewey Bell	Commissioner
1986	John Kenneth McKinnon	Commissioner

Government Leaders of The Yukon Territory

Term	Government Leader	Party
1978–85	Christopher William Pearson	Conservative
1985	Williard Phelps	Conservative
1985–92	Anthony Penikett	New Democratic
1992–	John L. Ostashek	Yukon

14 LOCAL GOVERNMENT

To meet municipal incorporation requirements, a village must have 300–1,000 residents; a town, 500–3,000 inhabitants; and a city, more than 2,500 residents. There is no minimum population requirement to incorporate a hamlet. Whitehorse is the only city; Dawson City, Faro, and Watson Lake are towns; Haines Junction, Mayo, Teslin, and Carmacks are villages.

15 JUDICIAL SYSTEM

The Canadian Constitution grants territorial and provincial jurisdiction over the administration of justice, and allows each territory and province to organize its own court system and police forces. The federal government has exclusive domain over cases involving trade and commerce, banking, bankruptcy, and criminal law. The Federal Court of Canada has both trial and appellate divisions for federal cases. The 9-judge Supreme Court of Canada is an appellate court that determines the constitutionality of both federal and territorial statutes. The Tax Court of Canada hears appeals of taxpayers against assessments by Revenue Canada.

The annual number of homicides varies but usually ranges from one to six. Because of the small population, the Yukon sometimes has the highest homicide rate in Canada. Breaking and entering offenses in 1989 numbered 1,028 per 100,000 people for businesses and 864 per 100,000 people for residences.

16 MIGRATION

The Yukon was the first area in Canada to be settled by people. Anthropologists believe the ancestors of the Amerindians may have inhabited the Yukon 10,000 to 25,000 years ago when they migrated from Asia across a Bering Sea land bridge. American traders arrived after the 1867 Russian sale of Alaska to the United States. With the discovery of gold near Dawson City in 1896, the Klondike became one of the most populous regions in northwestern Canada. The gold rush of 1897 saw more than 30,000 people from the lower parts of Canada migrate to the Yukon and the Northwest Territories within one year. The sudden increase in population during the Klondike gold rush prompted the federal government to give the Yukon more control over its affairs.

In 1991, the Yukon gained a net 489 residents from migration within Canada (2,381 people entered and 1,892 left). Of these migrants, British Columbia was the province of origin for 46% of incoming residents and was the province of destination for 54% of those leaving the territory.

17 ECONOMY

The gold rush of the 1890s quickly transformed the Yukon into a market-oriented economy. Gold is no longer the only natural resource sought. In fact, mining for other metals has become the most important economic activity in the territory. Tourism and hydroelectricity are also important economic sectors.

18 INCOME

In 1992, the average full-time worker in the Yukon Territory earned c$37,287 per year.

19 INDUSTRY

Industry in the Yukon is reliant on the processing of raw materials. Food products, wood, printing and publishing, nonmetallic mineral products, and chemical and chemical products are important manufacturing sectors. In 1990, the value of manufactured shipments for both the Yukon and the Northwest Territories was c$75.4 million.

20 LABOR

At the end of 1995, the Yukon had 15,200 persons in the labor force. The month-to-month unemployment rate in 1995 ranged from 8.3% to 11.1%. In 1994, the industrial aggregate sector accounted for 49.3% of the total employment; construction, 3.0%; goods producing industries, 6.3%; transportation, storage, communications, and other industries, 5.5%; trade, 7.2%; community, business, and personal services, 17.3%; and public administration, 11.4%. Government employment annually averages over 35% of total employment.

21 AGRICULTURE

Agriculture—expensive by North American standards—is a small but expanding industry. Although growth of the agricultural industry is limited by climate and the availability of productive land, new research programs hold promise for the future.

22 DOMESTICATED ANIMALS

The fur trade is important for about 3% of the population, mainly Aboriginal.

23 FISHING

A small fishing industry operates in Dawson City to export salmon. Other commercial fisheries supply local consumers.

Photo Credit: Canadian Tourism Commission photo.

A miner pans for gold near Dawson. During the Klondike gold rush of 1898, Dawson's population swelled to 30,000, making it the biggest city north of San Francisco at the time.

24 FORESTRY

To reduce reliance on the mining, tourism, and governmental sectors, efforts have recently been made to promote the forest industry.

25 MINING

Mining, the Yukon's largest industry, accounts for more than 30% of the economy. The total value of production in 1992 was c$467.9 million, with metals accounting for nearly all of this amount. Production in 1992 included 230,608 tons

(209,263 metric tons) of zinc, 138,768 tons (125,924 metric tons) of lead, 259,860 pounds (117,904 kilograms) of silver, and 8,444 pounds (3,831 kilograms) of gold.

26 ENERGY AND POWER

In 1991, electricity generated totaled 461 million kilowatt hours and consumption within the territory amounted to 409 million kilowatt hours.

27 COMMERCE

Retail sales in 1995 amounted to c$239.2 million. Retail sales in the Yukon follow a trend with higher sales during the summer months and lower sales in the winter. December is an exception, with high retail sales during the Christmas season. The largest retail sectors in 1995 were supermarkets and grocery stores, accounting for c$70.9 million in sales; recreational and motor vehicles, c$30.8 million; and other semi-durable goods, c$12.9 million.

28 PUBLIC FINANCE

The fiscal year extends from 1 April to 31 March. For fiscal year 1992/93, total revenues were c$357.1 million, with about 80% coming from the government of Canada. Expenditures were c$373.4 million. Major expenditure areas were health and social services, education, community transportation services, justice, government services, and renewable resources.

29 TAXATION

In 1992, the basic personal income tax rate for Yukoners was 17.2% on the first c$20,000 of taxable income. The tax rate progressively becomes higher and is 35.5% for c$100,000. In 1993, 13,880 Yukoners filed taxable returns.

30 HEALTH

In 1992 there were 529 live births in the Yukon, for a rate of 17.5 per 1,000 residents. The death rate in 1992 was 3.9 per 1,000 residents (the lowest in Canada), with 117 deaths occurring that year. Therapeutic abortions in the Yukon numbered 142 in 1990, for a rate of 20 per 1,000 females aged 15–44 and a ratio of 25.6 per 100 live births (Canada's highest abortion ratio). Reported cases of selected diseases in 1990 included chicken pox, 147; gonococcal infections, 85; giardiasis, 39; pertussis, 28; and salmonellosis, 11. There were no new AIDS cases reported in 1990; in 1991, the total number of cases was 2. There are three hospitals and health centers in the Yukon.

31 HOUSING

The median monthly rent for an apartment in Whitehorse was c$650 in 1995. That year, the median rent for Watson Lake was c$565, and c$400 for Haines Junction. As of March 1996, Whitehorse had 904 apartments, of which 90 were vacant. The average selling price of a house in Whitehorse was c$148,500 in early 1996.

32 EDUCATION

All 29 elementary and secondary schools in the Yukon are public; enrollment in 1995 was 5,700. Postsecondary community college enrollment in 1990/91 was 176, of which 89 were enrolled in career programs and 87 were in university transfer programs. The only postsecondary institution in the territory is Yukon College, with 15 community campuses across the territory.

33 ARTS

In 1990/91, the Yukon's performing arts company gave 50 performances before a total attendance of 5,000.

34 LIBRARIES AND MUSEUMS

The territorial Department of Education oversees a small system of volunteer and community libraries, with branches in Carcross, Carmacks, Dawson City, Faro, Haines Junction, Mayo, Ross River, Teslin, Watson Lake, and Whitehorse. The Dawson City Museum and the MacBride Museum (located in Whitehorse) are two of the territory's larger historical museums. The Kluane Museum of Natural History (located in Burwash Landing) displays wildlife and native handicrafts.

35 COMMUNICATIONS

As of 1994, the Yukon had 3 radio stations (2 AM, 1 FM).

36 PRESS

The only daily newspaper published in the territory is *The Whitehorse Star.*

37 TOURISM, TRAVEL, AND RECREATION

Tourism, offering a wilderness experience in a unique and relatively unspoiled environment, provides a further base for jobs and services.

38 SPORTS

Local sporting organizations (for such sports as badminton, basketball, track and field, and volleyball) are popular in the territory, as are canoeing and kayaking.

39 FAMOUS YUKONERS

Martha Louise Black (1866–1957) was the Yukon's first, and Canada's second, female Member of Parliament. Popular historian Pierre Berton (b.1920) is a native of Whitehorse.

40 BIBLIOGRAPHY

Bumsted, J. M. *The Peoples of Canada.* New York: Oxford University Press, 1992.

Hancock, Lyn. *Yukon.* Minneapolis: Lerner Publications, 1996.

LeVert, Suzanne. *Let's Discover Canada: Yukon.* New York: Chelsea House, 1992.

Sorensen, Lynda. *Canada: Provinces and Territories.* Vero Beach, Fla.: Rourke Book Co., 1995.

Tempelman-Kluit, Anne. *Discover Canada: Yukon.* Toronto: Grolier, 1994.

Wansborough, M. B. *Great Canadian Lives.* New York: Doubleday, 1986.

Weihs, Jean. *Facts about Canada, Its Provinces and Territories.* New York: H. W. Wilson, 1995.

CANADA

CAPITAL: Ottawa.

FLAG: The national flag, adopted in 1964, consists of a red maple leaf on a white field, flanked by a red vertical field on each end.

ANTHEM: Since 1 July 1980, *O Canada* has been the official anthem.

MONETARY UNIT: The Canadian dollar (c$) is a paper currency of 100 cents. There are coins of 1, 5, 10, 25, and 50 cents and 1 dollar, and notes of 2, 5, 10, 20, 50, 100, and 1,000 Canadian dollars. Silver coins of 5 and 10 dollars, commemorating the Olympics, were issued during 1973–76. c$1 = us$0.7227 (or us$1 = c$1.3837). US currency is usually accepted, especially in major cities and along the border.

WEIGHTS AND MEASURES: The metric system is the legal standard.

HOLIDAYS: New Year's Day, 1 January; Good Friday; Easter Monday; Victoria Day, the Monday preceding 25 May; Canada Day, 1 July; Labor Day, 1st Monday in September; Thanksgiving Day, 2d Monday in October; Remembrance Day, 11 November; Christmas Day, 25 December; Boxing Day, 26 December. Other holidays are observed in some provinces.

TIME: Newfoundland, 8:30 AM = noon GMT; New Brunswick, Nova Scotia, Prince Edward Island, and Quebec, 8 AM = noon GMT; Ontario east of 90° and western Quebec, 7 AM = noon GMT; western Ontario and Manitoba, 6 AM = noon GMT; Alberta and Saskatchewan, 5 AM = noon GMT; British Columbia and Yukon Territory, 4 AM = noon GMT.

1 LOCATION AND SIZE

Canada consists of all of the North American continent north of the United States, except Alaska and the small French islands of St. Pierre and Miquelon. Its total land area of 9,976,140 square kilometers (3,851,808 square miles) makes it slightly larger than China and the United States. The country's total boundary length is 252,684 kilometers (157,602 miles). Canada's capital city, Ottawa, is located in the southeastern part of the country.

2 TOPOGRAPHY

Canada's topography is dominated by the Canadian Shield, an area of Precambrian rocks surrounding the Hudson Bay and covering half the country. East of the Shield is the Maritime area, separated from the rest of Canada by low mountain ranges, and including the island of Newfoundland and Prince Edward Island. South and southeast of the Shield are the Great Lakes–St. Lawrence lowlands, a fertile plain in the triangle bounded by the St. Lawrence River, Lake Ontario, and Georgian Bay.

West of the Shield are the farmlands and ranching areas of the great central plains. Toward the north of this section is a series of rich mining areas, and still farther north is the Mackenzie lowland, traversed (crossed) by many lakes and rivers. The westernmost region of Canada, extending from western Alberta to the Pacific Ocean, includes the Rocky Mountains, a plateau region, the coastal mountain range, and an inner sea passage separating the outer island groups from the fjord-lined (narrow sea inlet) coast. Mt. Logan, the highest peak in Canada, in the St. Elias Range near the Alaska border, is 5,951 meters (19,524 feet) high. The Arctic islands constitute a large group extending north of the Canadian mainland to within 885 kilometers (550 miles) of the North Pole. They vary greatly in size and topography, with mountains, plateaus, fjords, and low coastal plains.

The Nelson-Saskatchewan, Churchill, Severn, and Albany rivers flow into Hudson Bay. The 4,241-kilometers (2,635-miles) Mackenzie River drains an area of almost 2.6 million square kilometers (1 million square miles) into the Arctic Ocean. The Great Lakes drain into the broad St. Lawrence River, which flows into the Gulf of St. Lawrence.

3 CLIMATE

Most of northern Canada has subarctic or arctic climates, with long cold winters lasting 8 to 11 months, short sunny summers, and little precipitation. In contrast, the populated south has a variety of climates.

Cool summers and mild winters prevail along the Pacific coast of British Columbia. Mean temperatures range from about 4°C (39°F) in January to 16°C (61°F) in July, the smallest range in the country. In Ontario and Quebec, especially near the Great Lakes and along the St. Lawrence River, the climate is less severe than in western Canada.

Canada Population Profile

Estimated 1994 population:	29,361,700
Population change, 1981–91:	12.1%
Leading ancestry group:	French
Second leading group:	English
Population by ethnic group	
Multiple backgrounds:	29%
French:	23%
English:	15%
German:	3%
Scottish:	3%
Canadian (self-reported category):	3%
Italian:	3%
Irish:	3%
Chinese:	2%
Ukrainian:	2%
Other single origins:	15%
Aboriginal peoples:	395,000
Métis:	75,000

Population by Age Group

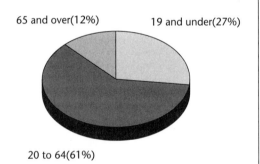

65 and over(12%) 19 and under(27%)

20 to 64(61%)

Top Ten Metropolitan Areas

Metropolitan Area	Population
Toronto	3,893,046
Montréal	3,127,242
Vancouver	1,602,502
Ottawa-Hull	920,857
Edmonton	839,924
Calgary	754,033
Winnipeg	652,354
Québec City	645,550
Hamilton	599,760
St. Catherines-Niagara	364,552

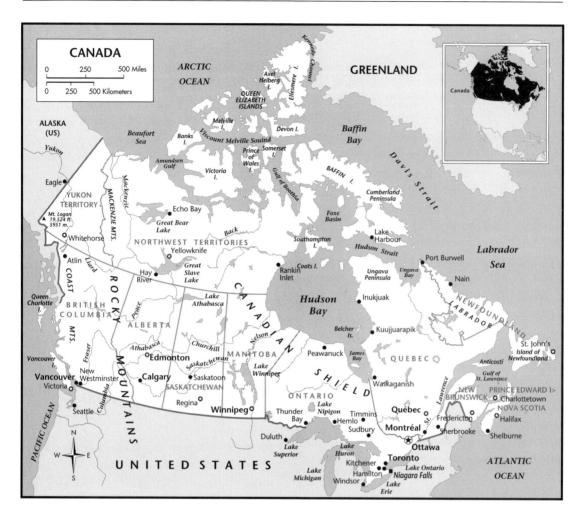

LOCATION: 41°41′ to 83°7′N; 52°37′ to 141°w. **BOUNDARY LENGTHS:** Arctic Ocean coastline, 9,286 kilometers (5,770 miles); Atlantic coastline, including Kennedy Channel, Baffin Bay, Davis Strait, 9,833 kilometers (6,110 miles); US, 6,416 kilometers (3,987 miles); Pacific coastline, 2,543 kilometers (1,580 miles); Alaska, 2,477 kilometers (1,539 miles); Hudson Strait and Hudson Bay shoreline, 7,081 kilometers (4,400 miles). **TERRITORIAL SEA LIMIT:** 12 miles.

The northwest and the prairies are the driest areas. The windward mountain slopes are exceptionally wet; the protected slopes are very dry. Thus, the west coast gets about 150–300 centimeters (60–120 inches) of rain annually; the central prairie area, less than 50 centimeters (20 inches); the flat area east of Winnipeg, 50–100 centimeters (20–40 inches); and the Maritime provinces, 115–150 centimeters (45–60 inches). The annual average number of days of precipitation ranges from 252 along coastal British Columbia, to 100 in the interior of the province.

4 PLANTS AND ANIMALS

A great range of plant and animal life characterizes the vast area of Canada, with its varied geographic and climatic zones. The flora of the Great Lakes–St. Lawrence region include white pine, sugar and red maples, and beech trees. Coniferous trees (evergreens) abound in the Maritime region, and black spruce in the eastern Laurentian zone.

From the prairie grassland to the Arctic tundra there are aspen, bur oak, cottonwood, and other deciduous (those that shed leaves seasonally) trees. Conifers dominate the northern section. Many types of grasses grow on the interior plains. The wet area along the west coast is famous for its tall, hard conifers. In the Rocky Mountain area are alpine fir, Engelmann spruce, and lodgepole pine. The great Arctic region is covered with low-growing grasses, mosses, and bushes.

Animals range from deer, black bear, and opossum in the Great Lakes–St. Lawrence region to moose, caribou, and timber wolf in the northern forests, and grizzly bear, mountain goat, and moose in the Rocky Mountain area. Birds include the robin, wood thrush, woodpecker, northern Pigmy-owl, band-tailed pigeon, snowy owl, ptarmigan, and arctic tern. Walrus, seals, and whales inhabit Canada's coastal waters.

5 ENVIRONMENTAL PROTECTION

Among Canada's most pressing environmental problems in the mid-1980s was acid rain, which poses a threat to natural

Photo credit: Susan D. Rock.

Pristine wilderness in Canada's Pacific Northwest.

resources in about 2.6 million square kilometers (1 million square miles) of eastern Canada. As of 1994, acid rain has affected 150,000 lakes in total throughout Canada. About half the acid rain comes from emissions from Canadian smokestacks, but Canada has blamed United States industry for 75% of Ontario pollution.

Canada's rivers have been polluted by agriculture and industry. As of 1994, 50% of Canada's coastal shellfish areas are closed because of dangerous pollutant levels. Canada ranks 12th in the world for hydrocarbon emissions with a total of 2,486.1 metric tons.

Canada has more than 90 bird sanctuaries and 44 National Wildlife Areas, including reserves in the western Arctic to protect waterfowl nesting grounds. The annual Newfoundland seal hunt, producing seals for pelts and meat, drew the anger of environmentalists, chiefly because of the practice of clubbing baby seals to death (adult seals are shot). In 1987, Canada banned the offshore hunting of baby seals, as well as blueback hooded seals.

In 1987, endangered species in Canada included the wood bison, sea otter, right whale, Acadian whitefish, spotted owl, leatherback turtle, American peregrine falcon, whooping crane, and the southern bald eagle. As of 1991, the brown bear, the gray wolf, and the California Condor were also endangered. Of a total of 197 mammals, 5 are endangered, as are 6 bird species. Out of a total of 3,220 plant species nationwide, 13 are endangered.

6 POPULATION

The total population according to the census of 1991 was 27,296,859. In late 1994, the population was estimated at over 29 million. Of the 1991 population, 13.5 million (51%) were female. A population of 30,425,000 was forecasted for the year 2000.

The average population density in 1991 was three per square kilometers (7.7 per square miles). The population is unevenly distributed, ranging from 0.02 per square kilometers (0.045 per square miles) in the Northwest Territories, to 22.8 per square kilometers (59 per square miles) on Prince Edward Island. Nearly two-thirds of the people live within 160 kilometers (100 miles) of the United States boundary. The population movement has long been from rural to urban areas.

The Toronto metropolitan area had a population of 3,893,046 in 1991; Montreal, 3,127,242. Other large metropolitan areas are Vancouver, 1,602,502; Ottawa-Hull (Ottawa is the federal capital), 920,857; Edmonton, 839,924; Calgary, 754,033; Winnipeg, 652,354; and Quebec City, 645,550.

7 ETHNIC GROUPS

According to the 1991 census, 83.5% of the population was Canadian-born. Persons wholly or partially of British origin (including Irish) made up 44.6% of the total population in 1991; those of total or partial French origin (centered mainly in Quebec, where they constitute 80% of the population), 31.1%. Other European groups included Germans (3.3%), Italians (2.8%), Ukrainians (1.5%), Dutch (1.3%), and Poles (1%). Nearly 28.9% of the total population claimed multiple ethnic origin.

Amerindians numbered 365,375 (1.4%) in 1991 and formed the sixth-largest ethnic group. As of 1992/93 there were 604 Indian bands living on 2,364 reserves. These Indians were classified into 10 major groups by language. There were also 75,150 métis, of mixed European and Indian descent.

Most of the 30,090 Inuit (Eskimos) live in the Northwest Territories, with smaller numbers in northern Quebec and northern Newfoundland (Labrador).

8 LANGUAGES

English and French are the official languages of Canada and have equal status and equal rights and privileges as to their use in all governmental institutions. The federal constitution also gives English and French speakers the right to publicly funded education in their own language at the primary and secondary levels, wherever the number of children justifies it.

The constitution provides for the use of both English and French in the legislature and courts of Quebec, New Brunswick, and Manitoba. Although there are no similar constitutional rights in Ontario and Saskatchewan, these provinces have made English and French the official languages of the courts. In 1984, the Northwest Territories Council adopted an ordinance providing for the use of aboriginal languages and establishing English and French as official languages.

Although Canada is frequently referred to as a bilingual country, in 1991 only 16.3% of the people were able to speak both English and French. In Quebec, 82.3% of the people spoke French as a native language in 1991; in the other provinces, most of the people spoke only English.

Native speakers of Italian numbered 510,980; German, 466,240; Chinese, 498,845; Ukrainian, 187,015; Portuguese, 212,090; and Polish, 189,815. There were 73,870 native speakers of Cree, the most common Indian language; there are at least 58 different Indian languages and dialects.

9 RELIGIONS

In 1990, the principal religious denominations and their memberships in Canada were the Roman Catholic Church, 11,582,350; United Church of Canada, 2,013,258; Anglican Church of Canada, 848,256; Presbyterian Church of Canada, 245,883; Lutherans, 78,566; and Baptists, 201,218. Also represented were Greek Orthodox, Russian Orthodox, Greek Catholic, Mennonite, Pentecostal, and other groups. The estimated Jewish population in 1990 was 310,000.

10 TRANSPORTATION

In spite of the rapid growth of road, air, and pipeline services since 1945, railways are still important because they can supply all-weather transportation in large volume over continental distances. There were 93,544 kilometers (58,134 miles) of railways in 1991. About 90% of the railway facilities are operated by two great continental systems, the government-owned Canadian National Railways (CNR), with 51,745 kilometers (32,153 miles) of tracks, and the privately owned Canadian Pacific Ltd. (CP), with 34,016 kilometers (21,137 miles). CNR and CP also maintain steamships and ferries, nationwide telegraph services, highway transport services, and hotel chains.

Because of difficult winter weather conditions, road maintenance is a continual and expensive task. There are about 884,272 kilometers (549,487 miles) of roads, including 250,023 kilometers (155,364 miles) of paved highway. Canada ranks next to the United States in per capita use of motor transport, with one passenger car for every 2 persons. Motor vehicles in use in 1991 totaled 16,805,096, including 13,061,084 passenger cars, 3,679,804 trucks, and 64,208 buses. Plans to construct a bridge from Prince Edward Island to the mainland were underway in 1992.

Canada makes heavy use of water transport in domestic as well as foreign commerce. The major part of Canada's merchant fleet—480,000 gross registered tons in 1991—consists of tankers. Montreal is Canada's largest port and the world's largest grain port. Other well-equipped ports are Toronto, Hamilton, Port Arthur, and Fort William on the Great Lakes, and Vancouver on the Pacific Coast.

The St. Lawrence Seaway and Power Project, constructed jointly by Canada and the United States provides an 8-meter (27-feet) navigation channel from Montreal to Lake Superior. The Athabasca and Slave rivers and the Mackenzie, into which they flow, provide an inland, seasonal water transportation system from Alberta to the Arctic Ocean. The Yukon River is also navigable.

International air service is provided by government-owned Air Canada and Canadian Airlines. Regional service is provided by some 570 smaller carriers. Canada has 1,400 airports, with 1,155 of them usable. The Lester Pearson airport in Toronto is by far the busiest, with 17,278,000 passengers handled in 1991.

11 HISTORY

The first inhabitants of what is now Canada were the ancient ancestors of the Inuit, who probably entered the region between 15,000 and 10,000 BC. Although most Inuit lived near the coast, some followed the caribou herds to the interior and developed a culture based on hunting and inland fishing.

The first recorded arrival of Europeans was in 1497 by the Italian-born John Cabot, who led an English expedition to the shore of a "new found land" (Newfoundland) and claimed the area in the name of Henry VII. In 1534, the French, under Jacques Cartier, claimed the Gaspé Peninsula and discovered the St. Lawrence River the following year.

By 1604, the first permanent French colony, Port Royal (now Annapolis Royal, Nova Scotia), had been founded. Four years later, Samuel de Champlain established the town of Quebec. With the discovery of the Great Lakes, missionaries and fur traders arrived, and an enormous French territory was established. Between 1608 and 1756, about 10,000 French settlers arrived in Canada. In 1663, New France became a royal province of the French crown.

The movement of exploration, discovery, commercial exploitation, and missionary activity which had begun with the coming of Champlain, was extended by such men as Jacques Marquette, reaching its climax in the last three decades of the 17th century. At that time, French trade and empire stretched north to the shores of Hudson Bay, west to the head of the

Chateau Frontenac.

The Quebec Act of 1774 instituted the separateness of French-speaking Canada that has become a distinctive feature of the country. It also secured the loyalty of the French clergy and aristocracy to the British crown during the American Revolution. Some 40,000 Loyalists from the colonies fled in revolt northward to eastern Canada.

Alexander Mackenzie reached the Arctic Ocean in 1789 and journeyed to the Pacific Ocean in 1793. British mariners secured for Britain a firm hold on what is now British Columbia. The War of 1812, in which United States forces attempting to invade Canada were repulsed by Canadian and British soldiers, did not change either the general situation or the United States-Canadian boundary. In 1846, the United States–Canadian border in the west was resolved at 49°N, and since then, except for minor disputes, the long border has been a line of peace.

The movement for Canadian confederation—political union of the colonies—was spurred in the 1860s by the need for common defense and the desire for a common government to sponsor railroads and other transportation. In 1864 Upper Canada (present-day Ontario) and Lower Canada (Quebec) were united under a common dominion (authority) government.

In 1867, the British North America Act created a larger dominion that was a confederation of Nova Scotia, New Brunswick, and the two provinces of Canada. Since the name Canada was chosen for the entire country, Lower Canada and Upper

Great Lakes, and south to the Gulf of Mexico. Meanwhile, a British enterprise, the Hudson's Bay Company, founded in 1670, began to compete for the fur trade.

The European wars between England and France were paralleled in North America by a series of French and Indian wars. The imperial contest ended after British troops, commanded by James Wolfe, defeated Marquis Louis Joseph de Montcalm on the Plains of Abraham, bringing the fall of Quebec in 1759. The French army surrendered at Montreal in 1760, and the Treaty of Paris in 1763 established British rule over what had been New France.

Canada assumed their present-day names of Quebec and Ontario.

In 1870, the province of Manitoba was established and admitted to the confederation, and the Northwest Territories were transferred to the federal government. British Columbia, on the Pacific shore, joined the confederation in 1871, and Prince Edward Island joined in 1873.

By the turn of the century, immigration to the western provinces had risen swiftly, and the prairie agricultural empire bloomed. Large-scale development of mines and of hydroelectric resources helped spur the growth of industry and urbanization. Alberta and Saskatchewan were made provinces in 1905.

In 1921, Manitoba, Ontario, and Quebec were greatly enlarged to take in all territory west of Hudson Bay and south of 60°N and all territory east of Ungava Bay. In February 1931, Norway formally recognized the Canadian title to the Sverdrup group of Arctic islands (now the Queen Elizabeth Islands). Newfoundland remained apart from the confederation until after World War II; it became Canada's tenth province in March 1949.

More than 600,000 Canadians served with the Allies in World War I, and over 68,000 were killed. The war contributions of Canada and other dominions helped bring about the declaration of equality of the members of the British Commonwealth in the Statute of Westminster of 1931. After the war, the development of air transportation and roads helped weld Canada together, and the nation had sufficient strength to withstand the depression that began in 1929, and the droughts that brought ruin to wheat fields.

Canada was vitally important again in World War II. More than one million Canadians took part in the Allied war effort, and over 32,000 were killed. The nation emerged from the war with enhanced prestige, actively concerned with world affairs and fully committed to the Atlantic alliance.

Domestically, a far-reaching postwar development was the resurgence in the 1960s of French Canadian separatism. Although administrative reforms—including the establishment of French as Quebec's official language in 1974—helped meet the demands of cultural nationalists, separatism continued to be an important force in Canadian politics. In the 1976 provincial elections, the separatist Parti Québécois came to power in Quebec, and its leader, Premier René Lévesque, proposed that Quebec become politically independent from Canada. However, his proposal was defeated, 59.5% to 40.5%, in a 1980 referendum.

Meanwhile, other provinces had their own grievances, especially over oil revenues. The failure of Newfoundland and the federal government to agree on development and revenue sharing stalled the exploitation of the vast Hibernia offshore oil and gas field in the early 1980s.

In the 1980s, Liberal Prime Minister Pierre Elliott Trudeau worked for "patriation" of the constitution (revoking the British North America Act so that Canada could reclaim authority over its own constitution from the United Kingdom). The

Constitution Act, passed in December 1981 and proclaimed by Queen Elizabeth II on 17 April 1982, thus replaced the British North America Act as the basic document of Canadian government. However, Quebec, New Brunswick, and Manitoba failed to ratify it due to inter-provincial tensions and other problems.

Canada joined with the United States and Mexico to negotiate the North American Free Trade Agreement (NAFTA), which was built upon the United States–Canada Free Trade Agreement (FTA). The three nations came to an agreement in August 1992 and signed the text on 17 December 1992. NAFTA, which seeks to create a single common market of 370 million consumers, was implemented in 1994.

12 PROVINCIAL GOVERNMENT

Canada is a federation of ten provinces and two northern territories. In 1982 the British North America Act of 1867—which effectively served, together with a series of subsequent British statutes, as Canada's constitution—was superseded by the Constitution Act (or Canada Act). Its principal innovations are the Charter of Rights and Freedoms and the provision for amendment.

Under the Constitution Act, the British sovereign remains sovereign of Canada and head of state; for the most part, the personal participation of Queen Elizabeth II in the function of the crown for Canada is reserved for such occasions as a royal visit. The queen's personal representative in the federal government is the governor-general, appointed by the crown on the advice of the prime minister of Canada.

The federal Parliament is made up of the House of Commons and the Senate. A new House of Commons, with 295 members as of 1993, is elected at least once every five years. The leader of the party that wins the largest number of seats in a newly elected House of Commons becomes prime minister and is asked to form the government. The governor-in-council (cabinet) is chosen by the prime minister.

The 104 members of the Senate, or upper house, are appointed for life, or until age 75, by the governor-general on the nomination of the prime minister, with equality of representation for regional divisions. In October 1992, Canadian voters declined a constitutional amendment that would have made the Senate an elected body.

13 POLITICAL PARTIES

Throughout most of the 20th century, national unity has been the primary aim of every Canadian government: leaders of both the English-speaking majority and the French-speaking minority have cooperated to develop a united Canada to which differences arising from national origin were subordinate (of an inferior rank). Canadian nationalism has been fueled partially by reaction against being too closely identified with either the United Kingdom or the United States. In the 1970s, this unity was challenged by a growing demand for French Canadian autonomy.

The Liberal Party (LP), which held office from 1935 to 1957 and again (except for part of 1979) from 1968 to 1984, traditionally emphasized trade and cultural relationships with the United States, while its principal rival, the Progressive Conservative Party (PC), which held power from 1957 to 1968, from May to December 1979, stresses Canada's relationships with the United Kingdom. In economic policy, the Liberals generally champion free trade, while the Conservatives favor a degree of government protection.

The New Democratic Party (NDP) is a labor-oriented party formed in 1961 by the merger of The Cooperative Commonwealth Federation (CCF) and the Canadian Labour Congress.

Brian Mulroney became prime minister following a landslide PC victory in the September 1984 elections. In 1993, the PC fell from power, primarily due to one of the worst Canadian recessions in nearly 60 years and the failure of the PC government to implement constitutional reforms.

Brian Mulroney resigned, and was succeeded by Kim Campbell. Liberals soundly defeated the PC in the October 1993 election. The Liberal party named Jean Chrétien as the new prime minister

14 LOCAL GOVERNMENT

Each province is divided into municipalities, the number and structure of which vary from province to province. In Prince Edward Island, Nova Scotia, New Brunswick, Ontario, and Québec the first order of municipalities consists of counties, which are further subdivided into cities, towns, villages, and townships, although there are minor variations. In Newfoundland and the four western provinces there are no counties; municipalities are either rural or urban, the latter being made up of cities, towns, and villages, but again with minor variations. Municipalities are usually administered by an elected council headed by a mayor, overseer, reeve, or warden. Local governments are incorporated by the provinces, and their powers and responsibilities are specifically set forth in provincial laws.

15 JUDICIAL SYSTEM

Civil and criminal courts exist on county, district, and superior levels. The Supreme Court in Ottawa has appeals, civil, and criminal jurisdiction throughout Canada; its chief justice and eight associate justices are appointed by the governor-general. The Federal Court of Canada (formerly the Exchequer Court) hears cases having to do with taxation, claims involving the federal government, copyrights, and admiralty (maritime) law. The death penalty in Canada was abolished in 1976; that decision was upheld in a vote by the House of Commons in June 1987.

16 MIGRATION

Of a total of 252,042 immigrants in 1993, those from Asia numbered 134,532; Europe accounted for 50,050; Africa, 19,033; the Caribbean, 19,028; the United States, 6,565; and South America, 11,327. Emigration is mainly to the United States. In 1990 there were 871,000 Canadian-born people living in the US.

Canada is a major source of asylum for persecuted refugees. At the end of 1992 Canada harbored 568,200 such persons.

Interprovincial migration is generally from east to west. During 1990–91 British Columbia gained 37,620 more people from other provinces than it lost, and Alberta 7,502, while Ontario lost 22,301 more than it gained, as did Saskatchewan (9,941) and Quebec (7,690).

17 ECONOMY

The Canadian economy is the seventh largest among the western industrialized nations. The postwar period has seen a steady shift from the production of goods toward increased emphasis on services. Although no longer the foremost sector of the economy, agriculture is of major importance to the economy. Canada accounts for approximately 20% of the world's wheat trade. Canada is also the world's leading producer of newsprint and ranks among the leaders in other forestry products.

Differences in prosperity among the provinces increased during the 1980s, with the central provinces relatively robust, the western provinces suffering declines in growth because of lower prices for oil and other natural resources, and the Atlantic provinces depressed. By the second quarter of 1990, the economy had begun to decline, affected by a recession and the central bank's monetary policy. Recovery began in the second half of 1991, although the early 1990s were marked by continuing unemployment.

18 INCOME

In 1992, Canada's gross national product (GNP) was $565,787 million at current prices, or $19,970 per person. For the period 1985–92 the average inflation rate was 3.7%, resulting in a real growth rate in GNP of 0.3% per person.

19 INDUSTRY

The leading industrial areas are foods and beverages, transport equipment, petroleum and coal products, paper and paper products, primary metals, chemicals, fabricated metals, electrical products, and wood products. The value of industrial production in 1990 amounted to c$91.3 billion.

Of the total manufacturing output, about half is concentrated in Ontario, which not only is the center of Canadian industry but also has the greatest industrial diversification. Some important industries operate there exclusively. Quebec ranks second in manufacturing production, accounting for more than 25% of the value of Canadian manufactured goods. British Columbia ranks third.

20 LABOR

Employment in 1992 was 12,240,000. There were 13,797,000 in the total civilian labor force in 1992. Of those in civilian employment in 1992, 27.7% were in industry; 3.5% in agriculture; and 73% in services. In 1992, unemployment stood at 11.3%. Payments of c$19.3 billion went to the unemployed in 1992, a record high.

Cold weather and consumer buying habits cause some regular seasonal unemployment, but new techniques and materials are making winter construction work more possible, and both government and many industrial firms plan as much work as possible during the winter months.

At the beginning of 1992, labor organizations active in Canada reported a total membership of 4,089,000. Federal and provincial laws set minimum standards for hours of work, wages, and other conditions of employment. Safety and health regulations and workers' disability compensation have been established by federal, provincial, and municipal legislation.

21 AGRICULTURE

Until the beginning of the 1900s, agriculture was the most common Canadian occupation. Since then, however, the farm population has been shrinking. Even in Saskatchewan, the province with the highest proportion of farmers, farm families account for no more than 25% of the total population. For Canada as a whole, agriculture engaged only 3.4% of the economically active population in 1992.

However, Canada is still one of the major food-exporting countries of the world. Farm production continues to increase, as do the size of holdings, crop quantity, quality and variety, and cash income. Canada generates about $23 billion in cash farm receipts annually.

More than 90% of Canada's cultivated area is in the three prairie provinces of Alberta, Saskatchewan, and Manitoba. The trend is toward fewer and larger farms, increased use of machinery, and more specialization.

The estimated output of principal field crops in 1992 (in 1,000 tons) was wheat, 29,870,000; barley, 10,919,000; corn, 4,531,000; rapeseed, 3,689,000; potatoes, 3,529,000; and oats, 2,823,000.

During 1989–90, Canada was the second largest exporter of wheat through the International Wheat Agreement (after the United States); over 9.9 million tons were exported, mostly to Japan, Pakistan, and Iran.

22 DOMESTICATED ANIMALS

Canada traditionally exports livestock products, producing more than the domestic market can use. Animal production (livestock, dairy products, and eggs) now brings in about half of total farm cash income.

Livestock on farms in 1992 numbered 13,002,000 head of cattle; 10,395,000 pigs and hogs; 914,000 sheep and lambs; and 118,000,000 hens and chickens. In 1992, livestock slaughtered included 3,339,000 head of cattle, and calves, 15,285,000 hogs, and 538,000 sheep. Chicken and turkey production totaled 733,000 tons. Milk production in 1992 was 7.3 million tons; butter production amounted to about 100,000 tons, and cheese production to 291,139 tons. Most dairy products are consumed within Canada. In 1992, 317,060 tons of eggs were produced.

23 FISHING

With a coastline of nearly 29,000 kilometers (18,000 miles) and a lake-and-river system containing more than half the world's fresh water, Canada ranks among the world's major fish producers. In 1991 Canada was the world's third-leading exporter of fresh, chilled, and frozen fish. Exports of dried, salted, and smoked fish in 1991 amounted to $338.5 million, more than any other nation except Norway.

More than one billion pounds of cod, haddock, halibut, pollock, and other fish are caught every year along the Atlantic in deep-sea and shore operations. Vast numbers of lobsters and herring are caught in the Gulf of St. Lawrence and the Bay of Fundy. Salmon, the specialty of the Pacific fisheries, is canned for export and constitutes the most valuable item of Canadian fish production. Also exported are fresh halibut and canned and processed herring. Other important export items are whitefish, lake trout, pickerel, and other freshwater fish caught in the Great Lakes and some of the larger inland lakes. Feed and fertilizer are important by-products.

Export sales in 1991 amounted to $2.17 billion. The United States imported more than $1.45 billion of Canada's fish product exports in 1992.

The government protects and develops the resources of both ocean and inland waters and helps expand the domestic market for fish.

24 FORESTRY

In 1991, forests covered 360 million hectares (890 million acres) or 39% of Canada's total land area. Canada ranks as the third-largest producer of coniferous (evergreens) wood products (after the United States and Russia), and is the leading supplier of softwood products for export.

Chief forest products in eastern Canada are pulp and paper products, especially newsprint, three-fourths of which goes to the United States. In the west, the chief product is sawn timber. In 1991, an estimated 52 million cubic meters (1.8 billion cubic feet) of sawn wood was cut. In addition, 52,040,000 cubic meters of pulp wood, and 8,977,000 tons of newsprint were produced.

25 MINING

Some 52 minerals are currently being commercially produced in Canada. Canada is the world's largest producer of mine zinc and uranium and is among the leaders in silver, nickel, aluminum (from imported bauxite), potash, gold, copper, lead, salt, sulfur, and nitrogen in ammonia. Yet the country has only just begun to fully develop many of its most important mineral resources. Beginning in 1981, large new deposits of gold ore were discovered at Hemlo, Ontario, north of Lake Superior; by 1991, more than 50% of Ontario's gold production came from the three mines in the Helmo district.

Output totals for principal Canadian metals in 1991 (in metric tons) was: iron ore, 35,961,000; copper, 797,603,000; zinc, 1,148,189; uranium, 9,124; nickel, 196,868; molybdenum, 11,333; and lead, 278,141. Gold production was 178,712 kilograms, and silver was 1,338 kilograms.

What are believed to be the world's largest deposits of asbestos are located in the eastern townships of Quebec. Asbestos production in 1991 amounted to 670,000 tons, and was valued at us$240 million. Other nonmetallic mineral production included salt (11,585,000 tons), sand and gravel (200,497,000 tons), peat (762,116 tons), and potash (7,012,000 tons).

26 ENERGY AND POWER

Canada's fossil fuels and hydroelectric resources are abundant. Coal production reached 71.1 million metric tons in 1991.

Output of crude oil in 1992 was 98.2 million tons, at a rate of 2,065,000 barrels per day. Natural gas production rose to 116,600 million cubic meters (4,117 billion cubic feet) in 1992, third in the world after Russia and the United States. In 1992, proved crude oil reserves were estimated at 7.6 billion barrels, and natural gas reserves at more than 95.7 trillion cubic feet. Crude oil pipelines totaled 23,564 kilometers (14,642 miles) in length in 1991.

Canada ranks sixth in the production of electric power in the world and first in the production of hydroelectricity. In 1991, Canada's total net installed capacity reached 104.6 million kilowatts. Total electric power generation in Canada in 1991 was 507,913 million kilowatt hours; 61% of it was hydroelectric, 23% was conventional thermal, and 16% was nuclear. Canada's hydroelectric power totaled 284.1 billion kilowatt hours in 1992, more than any other nation.

27 COMMERCE

Canada's exports are highly diversified; the principal export groups are industrial goods, forestry products, mineral resources (with crude petroleum and natural gas increasingly important), and agricultural commodities.

Imports are heavily concentrated in the industrial sector, including machinery, transport equipment, basic manufactures, and consumer goods. In 1990, exports were at c$120,521 million and imports c$146,057 million.

The United States is by far Canada's leading trade partner. Canada exchanges raw materials such as crude petroleum and processed items such as paper for United States machinery, transportation and communications equipment, and agricultural items, such as citrus fruits.

In 1992, the United States accounted for 77% of Canada's exports and 69% of imports. In 1992, the United States, Canada, and Mexico signed the North American Free Trade Agreement (NAFTA), which was ratified by all three countries the following year.

Besides the United States, Canada traded principally with European Community countries, Japan, and the United Kingdom in 1990.

28 PUBLIC FINANCE

By far the largest item of expenditure of the federal government is for social services, including universal pension plans, old age security, veterans benefits, unemployment insurance, family and youth allowances, and assistance to disabled, handicapped, unemployed, and other needy persons.

Sources of provincial revenue include various licenses, permits, fines, penalties, sales taxes, and royalties, augmented by federal subsidies, health grants, and other payments. Federal grants and surpluses and federal payments to the provinces under the federal-provincial tax-sharing arrangements constitute a major revenue source of the provinces. Corporation and personal income taxes provide a considerable portion of the revenue of Québec. The largest provincial expenditures are for highways, health and social welfare, education, natural resources, and primary industries. Real property taxes account for more than two-thirds of revenue for municipalities and other local authorities. Almost one-third of their expenditures gores to support local schools.

29 TAXATION

The federal government levies direct and indirect taxes, of which the individual and corporation income taxes yield the largest return. Excise taxes (including a general sales tax), excise duties, and customs duties also produce a substantial revenue. Federal inheritance taxes were eliminated as of 1 January 1972. The federal goods and services tax (GST) went into effect on 1 January 1991. It is a 7% value-added tax on most goods and services.

30 HEALTH

Canada adopted a national health insurance scheme in 1971. It is administered regionally, with each province running a public insurance plan and the government contributing about 40% of the cost. Access to health care and cost containment are good, but there are strains on the budget, increased by the demands of an aging population.

Diseases of the heart and arteries account for more than 40% of all deaths, and cancer accounts for just under one-third; the proportion of deaths from causes related to old age is rising. Accidents are the leading cause of death in childhood and among young adult males, and rank high for other population groups. In 1993, life expectancy was estimated at 78 years.

31 HOUSING

There were slightly more than 10 million occupied private dwellings in Canada in 1991. Housing starts were estimated at just over 156,000 during 1991, a 14% drop from 1990 due to the recession. Single homes are the most common type of dwelling, although their relative numbers have gradually fallen in favor of multiple dwellings.

32 EDUCATION

Practically the entire adult population is literate. The age limits of compulsory school attendance are roughly from age 6 to age 15. Primary school lasts for eight years and secondary or high school another three to five years. In 1990, primary schools numbered 12,220. There were 154,698 teachers and 2,371,558 students in primary schools. The same year, secondary schools had 164,125 teachers and 2,292,735 students.

Each province is responsible for its own system of education. While the systems differ in some details, the general plan is the same for all provinces except Quebec, which has two parallel systems: one mainly for Roman Catholics and speakers of French, the other primarily for non-Catholics and speakers of English.

During 1992 there were 69 degree-granting colleges and universities in Canada. In 1991, full-time enrollment in all higher level institutions, colleges and universities was 1,942,814.

Among the oldest Canadian institutions of higher education are the Collège des Jésuites in Quebec City, founded in 1635; the Collège St. Boniface in Manitoba (1827); the University of Ottawa (1848); and St. Joseph's University in New Brunswick (1864). Most university-level instruction is conducted in English. Two private universities on the Scottish model are Dalhousie University in Halifax (1818), and McGill University in Montreal (1821). The first state-supported institution was King's College at York in Upper Canada, which became the University of Toronto, the largest and one of the most distinguished of Canadian institutions.

33 ARTS

The arts and crafts of the Dene Indians and the Inuit may be seen in cooperative workshops in Inuvik in the Northwest Territories; and of the North West Coast Indians, at the reconstructed Indian village Ksan in British Columbia.

One of the world's foremost summer theatrical events is the Shakespeare Festival at Statford, Ontario.

34 LIBRARIES AND MUSEUMS

Municipal public libraries serve the large cities and many small towns and rural areas, and regional units supply library service to scattered population areas. Traveling libraries, operated by provincial governments or university extension departments, also provide mail services for more isolated individuals and communities.

There are close to 2000 museums, art galleries, and related institutions in Canada. The National Arts Center is located in Ottawa, as are Canada's four national museums: the National Gallery of Canada, the Canadian Museum of Civilization, the National Museum of Natural Sciences, and the National Museum of Science and Technology.

35 COMMUNICATIONS

The ten public and private companies in Telecom Canada provide a major share of the nation's telecommunications services, including all long-distance service, and link regional networks across Canada. There were 20,126,490 telephones in Canada in 1991.

The publicly owned Canadian Broadcasting Corporation (CBC) provides the national broadcasting service in Canada. Privately owned local stations form part of the networks and provide alternative pro-

Photo credit: Susan D. Rock.

Canada Place pier in Vancouver.

grams. As of 1991, there were 900 AM broadcasting stations, 800 FM stations, and 2,039 television stations. In the same year there were 27,776,000 radios and 17,252,000 television sets. As of May 1987, radio and television services reached 99% of Canadian homes.

36 PRESS

In 1991 there were 107 daily newspapers. Although some newspapers in Montreal, Quebec, Toronto, Winnipeg, and Vancouver have more than local influence, most circulate only on a regional basis and have a limited number of readers. Rural areas are served by some 1,100 monthly and weekly publications. There are many con-sumer magazines, but only *Maclean's* is truly national.

Canada's leading newspapers (with their 1991 daily circulations) include the following: *Toronto Star* (494,681); *Globe and Mail* (330,000); *Le Journal de Montréal* (281,686); *Toronto Sun* (252,895); *Vancouver Sun* (193,749); and *La Presse* (186,590).

37 TOURISM, TRAVEL AND RECREATION

From the polar ice cap to the mountains, fjords, and rainforests of the west coast, Canada offers a remarkable range of scenic wonders. Among the most spectacular parks are the Kluane National Park in the

Yukon Territory and the Banff (with Lake Louise) and Jasper national parks in the mountains of Alberta. Norse artifacts and reconstructed dwellings can be viewed at the excavation of L'Anse aux Meadows in Newfoundland.

Other attractions include Dinosaur Park in Alberta's Red Deer Badlands; the Cabot Trail in Nova Scotia; and the Laurentians and the Gaspé Peninsula in Quebec. The arts and crafts of the Dene Indians and the Inuit may be seen in cooperative workshops in the Northwest Territories.

Quebec City is the only walled city in North America. Montreal, the second-largest French-speaking city in the world (after Paris), is famous for its fine French cuisine, its vast underground shopping network, and its excellent subway system. Toronto is known for commerce, culture, modern architecture, and an outstanding zoo. One of the world's foremost summer theatrical events is the Shakespeare Festival at Stratford, Ontario.

In 1991, Canada was the world's tenth most popular tourist destination. In that year, 14,988,600 tourists arrived from abroad, 80% of them from the United States and 11% from Europe. Gross receipts from tourism were US$5.5 billion.

38 SPORTS

Fishing and hunting attract many sportsmen to Canada, and ice hockey attracts many sports fans, particularly to the Forum in Montreal. Major league baseball teams play in Montreal and Toronto. In 1992, the Toronto major league baseball team, the Blue Jays, became the first non-American team to both play in and win the World Series. Toronto again won the World Series in 1993.

39 FAMOUS CANADIANS

Political Figures

Because of their exploits in establishing and developing early Canada, then known as New France, a number of eminent Frenchmen are prominent in Canadian history, among them the explorers Jacques Cartier (1491–1557), Samuel de Champlain (1567?–1635), and Jacques Marquette (1637–75).

Artists

Highly regarded Canadian painters include James Edward Hervey MacDonald (1873–1932), Frederick Horsman Varley (1881–1969), and Emily Carr (1871–1945). Two other artists of distinction were James W. G. MacDonald (1897–1960) and Harold Barling Town (b.1924). The portrait photographer Yousuf Karsh (b.Turkish Armenia, 1908) is a long-time Canadian resident.

Musicians

Well-known Canadian musicians include the pianist Glenn Gould (1932–82); the singers Jon Vickers (b.1926) and Maureen Forrester (b.1931); the bandleader Guy Lombardo (1902–77); and, among recent popular singers and songwriters, Gordon Lightfoot (b.1938), Joni Mitchell (b.1943), and Neil Young (b.1945).

Actors

Canadian-born actors who are known for their association with Hollywood include Mary Pickford (Gladys Mary Smith, 1893–1979), Walter Huston (Houghston, 1884–1950), Lorne Greene (1915–87), Raymond Burr (1917–94), William Shatner (b.1931), and Donald Sutherland (b.1935).

Sports

Notable in the world of sports are icehockey stars Maurice ("Rocket") Richard (b.1921), Gordon ("Gordie") Howe (b.1928), Robert Marvin ("Bobby") Hull, Jr. (b.1939), Robert ("Bobby") Orr (b.1948), and Wayne Gretzky (b.1961).

Authors

The *Anne of Green Gables* novels of Lucy Maud Montgomery (1874–1942) have been popular with readers of several generations. Louis Hémon (1880–1913), a French journalist who came to Canada in 1910 and spent only 18 months there, wrote the classic French Canadian novel *Maria Chapdelaine* (1914).

Scientists and Inventors

Among the famous Canadian scientists and inventors are Sir Sanford Fleming (1827–1915), inventor of standard time, and Sir William Osler (1849–1919), the father of psychosomatic medicine. The codiscoverers of insulin, Sir Frederick Grant Banting (1891–1941) and John James Richard Macleod (1876–1935), were awarded the Nobel Prize for medicine in 1923.

40 BIBLIOGRAPHY

Bumsted, J. M. *The Peoples of Canada.* New York: Oxford University Press, 1992.

Canada in Pictures. Minneapolis: Lerner, 1993.

Ingles, Ernest B. *Canada.* Santa Barbara, Calif.: Clio, 1990.

Lee, Douglas B. "Montreal—Heart of French Canada." *National Geographic,* March 1991, 60–85.

Lipset, Seymour Martin. *Continental Divide: The Values and Institutions of the United States and Canada.* New York: Routledge, 1990.

Malcolm, A. H. *The Canadians.* New York: Times Books, 1985.

Nagel, Rob and Anne Commire. "Samuel de Champlain." In *World Leaders, People Who Shaped the World.* Volume III: North and South America. Detroit: U*X*L, 1994.

Shepherd, J. *Canada.* Chicago: Children's Press, 1987.

The Canadian Encyclopedia. 2d ed. Edmonton: Hurtig Publishers, 1988.

Glossary

ABORIGINAL: The first known inhabitants of a country. A species of animals or plants which originated within a given area.

ALPINE: Generally refers to the Alps or other mountains; can also refer to a mountainous zone above the timberline.

AMERINDIAN: A contraction of the two words, American Indian. It describes native peoples of North, South, or Central America.

ANCESTRY: Based on how people refer to themselves, and refers to a person's ethnic origin, descent, heritage, or place of birth of the person or the person's parents or ancestors before their arrival in the United States. The Census Bureau accepted "American" as a unique ethnicity if it was given alone, with an unclear response (such as "mixed" or "adopted"), or with names of particular states.

ANGLICAN: Pertaining to or connected with the Church of England.

ANTHRACITE COAL: Also called hard coal, it is usually 90 to 95 percent carbon, and burns cleanly, almost without a flame.

AQUACULTURE: The culture or "farming" of aquatic plants or other natural produce, as in the raising of catfish in "farms."

AQUEDUCT: A large pipe or channel that carries water over a distance, or a raised structure that supports such a channel or pipe.

AQUIFER: An underground layer of porous rock, sand, or gravel that holds water.

BTU: The amount of heat required to raise one pound of water one degree Fahrenheit.

BUREAUCRACY: A system of government that is characterized by division into bureaus of administration with their own divisional heads. Also refers to the inflexible procedures of such a system that often result in delay.

CAPITAL BUDGET: A financial plan for acquiring and improving buildings or land, paid for by the sale of bonds.

CAPITAL PUNISHMENT: Punishment by death.

CHURCH OF ENGLAND: The national and established church in England. The Church of England claims continuity with the branch of the Catholic Church that existed in England before the Reformation. Under Henry VIII, the spiritual supremacy and jurisdiction of the Pope were abolished, and the sovereign (king or queen) was declared head of the church.

CIVILIAN LABOR FORCE: All persons 16 years of age or older who are not in the armed forces and who are now holding a job, have been temporarily laid off, are waiting to be reassigned to a new position, or are unemployed but actively looking for work.

COMMERCIAL BANK: A bank that offers to businesses and individuals a variety of banking services, including the right of withdrawal by check.

COMMONWEALTH: A commonwealth is a free association of sovereign independent states that has no charter, treaty, or constitution. The association promotes cooperation, consultation, and mutual assistance among members.

COMMONWEALTH OF NATIONS: Voluntary association of the United Kingdom and its present dependencies and associated states, as well as certain former dependencies and their dependent territories. The term was first used officially in 1926 and is embodied in the Statute of Westminster (1931). Within the Commonwealth, whose secretariat (established in 1965) is located in London, England, are numerous subgroups devoted to economic and technical cooperation.

COMPACT: A formal agreement, covenant, or understanding between two or more parties.

CONSOLIDATED BUDGET: A financial plan that includes the general budget, federal funds, and all special funds.

CONSTANT DOLLARS: Money values calculated so as to eliminate the effect of inflation on prices and income.

CONSTITUTION: The written laws and basic rights of citizens of a country or members of an organized group.

CONSTITUTIONAL MONARCHY: A system of government in which the hereditary sovereign (king or queen, usually) rules according to a written constitution.

CONSTITUTIONAL REPUBLIC: A system of government with an elected chief of state and elected representation, with a written constitution containing its governing principles. The United States is a constitutional republic.

CONSUMER GOODS: Items that are bought to satisfy personal needs or wants of individuals.

CONTINENTAL CLIMATE: The climate of a part of the continent; the characteristics and peculiarities of the climate are a result of the land itself and its location.

CONTINENTAL SHELF: A plain extending from the continental coast and varying in width that typically ends in a steep slope to the ocean floor.

CRICKET (SPORT): A game played by two teams with a ball and bat, with two wickets (staked target) being defended by a batsman. Common in the United Kingdom and Commonwealth of Nations countries.

CRIMINAL LAW: The branch of law that deals primarily with crimes and their punishments.

CROWN COLONY: A colony established by a commonwealth over which the monarch has some control, as in colonies established by the United Kingdom's Commonwealth of Nations.

DECIDUOUS SPECIES: Any species that sheds or casts off a part of itself after a definite period of time. More commonly used in reference to plants that shed their leaves on a yearly basis as opposed to those (evergreens) that retain them.

DEMOCRACY: A form of government in which the power lies in the hands of the people, who can govern directly, or can be governed indirectly by representatives elected by its citizens.

DIRECT ELECTION: The process of selecting a representative to the government by balloting of the voting public, in contrast to selection by an elected representative of the people.

DOMINION: A self-governing nation that recognizes the British monarch as chief of state.

DURABLE GOODS: Goods or products which are expected to last and perform for several years, such as cars and washing machines.

DUTY: A tax imposed on imports by the customs authority of a country. Duties are generally based on the value of the goods (*ad valorem* duties), some other factors such as weight or quantity (specific duties), or a combination of value and other factors (compound duties).

EMIGRATION: Moving from one country or region to another for the purpose of residence.

ENDANGERED SPECIES: A type of plant or animal threatened with extinction in all or part of its natural range.

EPISCOPAL: Belonging to or vested in bishops or prelates; characteristic of or pertaining to a bishop or bishops.

FEDERAL: Pertaining to a union of states whose governments are subordinate to a central government.

FISCAL YEAR: A 12-month period for accounting purposes.

FJORD: A deep indentation of the land forming a comparatively narrow arm of the sea with more or less steep slopes or cliffs on each side.

GENERAL BUDGET: A financial plan based on a government's normal revenues and operating expenses, excluding special funds.

GLOBAL GREENHOUSE GAS EMISSIONS: Gases released into the atmosphere that contribute to the greenhouse effect, a condition in which the earth's excess heat cannot escape.

GLOBAL WARMING: Also called the greenhouse effect. The theorized gradual warming of the earth's climate as a result of the burning of fossil fuels, the use of man-made chemicals, deforestation, etc.

GMT *see* Greenwich (Mean) Time.

GNP *see* Gross National Product.

GREENWICH (MEAN) TIME: Mean solar time of the meridian at Greenwich, England, used as the basis for standard time throughout most of the world. The world is divided into 24 time zones, and all are related to the prime, or Greenwich mean, zone.

GROSS DOMESTIC PRODUCT: A measure of the market value of all goods and services produced within the boundaries of a nation, regardless of asset ownership. Unlike gross national product, GDP excludes receipts from that nation's business operations in foreign countries.

GROSS NATIONAL PRODUCT: A measure of the market value of goods and services produced by the labor and property of a nation. Includes receipts from that nation's business operation in foreign countries

GROUNDWATER: Water located below the earth's surface, the source from which wells and springs draw their water.

GROWING SEASON: The period between the last 32°F (0°C) temperature in spring and the first 32°F (0°C) temperature in autumn.

HISPANIC: A person who originates from Spain or from Spanish-speaking countries of South and Central America, Mexico, Puerto Rico, and Cuba.

HOME RULE: The governing of a territory by the citizens who inhabit it.

HUNDREDWEIGHT: A unit of weight that equals 100 pounds in the US and 112 pounds in Britain.

HYDROCARBON: A compound of hydrogen and carbon, often occurring in organic substances or derivatives of organic substances such as coal, petroleum, natural gas, etc.

HYDROCARBON EMISSIONS: Organic compounds containing only carbon and hydrogen, often occurring in petroleum, natural gas, coal, and bitumens, and which contribute to the greenhouse effect.

HYDROELECTRIC POTENTIAL: The potential amount of electricity that can be produced hydroelectrically. Usually used in reference to a given area and how many hydroelectric power plants that area can sustain.

HYDROELECTRIC POWER PLANT: A factory that produces electrical power through the application of waterpower.

IMMIGRATION: The act or process of passing or entering into another country for the purpose of permanent residence.

IMPORTS: Goods purchased from foreign suppliers.

INDIGENOUS: Born or originating in a particular place or country; native to a particular region or area.

INFLATION: The general rise of prices, as measured by a consumer price index. Results in a fall in value of currency.

INPATIENT: A patient who is housed and fed—in addition to being treated—in a hospital.

INSTALLED CAPACITY: The maximum possible output of electric power at any given time.

ISLAM: The religious system of Mohammed, practiced by Moslims and based on a belief in Allah as the supreme being and Mohammed as his prophet. The spelling variations, Muslim and Muhammed, are also used, primarily by Islamic people. Islam also refers to those nations in which it is the primary religion.

ISTHMUS: A narrow strip of land bordered by water and connecting two larger bodies of land, such as two continents, a continent and a peninsula, or two parts of an island.

JUDAISM: The religious system of the Jews, based on the Old Testament as revealed to Moses and characterized by a belief in one God and adherence to the laws of scripture and rabbinic traditions.

JUDEO-CHRISTIAN: The dominant traditional religious makeup of the United States and other countries based on the worship of the Old and New Testaments of the Bible.

MASSIF: A central mountain mass or the dominant part of a range of mountains.

METRIC TON: A unit of weight that equals 1,000 kilograms (2,204.62 pounds).

METROPOLITAN AREA: In most cases, a city and its surrounding suburbs.

MIGRATORY BIRDS: Those birds whose instincts prompt them to move from one place to another at the regularly recurring changes of season.

MIGRATORY WORKERS: Usually agricultural workers who move from place to place for employment depending on the growing and harvesting seasons of various crops.

MONARCHY: Government by a sovereign, such as a king or queen.

MONTANE: Refers to a zone in mountainous areas in which large coniferous trees, in a cool moist setting, are the main features.

MUNICIPALITY: A district such as a city or town having its own incorporated government.

MUSLIM: A frequently used variation of the spelling of Moslem, to describe a follower of the prophet Mohammed (also spelled Muhammed), the founder of the religion of Islam.

NATURAL GAS: A combustible gas formed naturally in the earth and generally obtained by boring a well. The chemical makeup of natural gas is principally methane, hydrogen, ethylene compounds, and nitrogen.

NATURAL HARBOR: A protected portion of a sea or lake along the shore resulting from the natural formations of the land.

NATURALIZE: To confer the rights and privileges of a native-born subject or citizen upon someone who lives in the country by choice.

NATURE PRESERVE: An area where one or more species of plant and/or animal are protected from harm, injury, or destruction.

OFFICIAL LANGUAGE: The language in which the business of a country and its government is conducted.

PER CAPITA: Per person.

PERSONAL INCOME: Refers to the income an individual receives from employment, or to the total incomes that all individuals receive from their employment in a sector of business (such as personal incomes in the retail trade).

PIEDMONT: Refers to the base of mountains.

POUND STERLING: The monetary unit of Great Britain, otherwise known as the pound.

PRIME MERIDIAN: Zero degrees in longitude that runs through Greenwich, England, site of the Royal Observatory. All other longitudes are measured from this point.

PRIME MINISTER: The premier or chief administrative official in certain countries.

PRIVATE SECTOR: The division of an economy in which production of goods and services is privately owned.

PRIVATIZATION: To change from public to private control or ownership.

PROTECTORATE: A state or territory controlled by a stronger state, or the relationship of the stronger country toward the lesser one it protects.

PROVED RESERVES: The quantity of a recoverable mineral resource (such as oil or natural gas) that is still in the ground.

PUBLIC DEBT: The amount owed by a government.

REFUGEE: One who flees to a refuge or shelter or place of safety. One who in times of persecution or political commotion flees to a foreign country for safety.

RELIGIOUS ADHERENTS: The followers of a religious group, including (but not confined to) the full, confirmed, or communicant members of that group.

RETAIL TRADE: The sale of goods directly to the consumer.

SEPARATISM: The policy of dissenters withdrawing from a larger political or religious group.

SERVICE INDUSTRIES: Industries that provide services (e.g., health, legal, automotive repair) for individuals, businesses, and others.

SHIA MUSLIM: Members of one of two great sects of Islam. Shia Muslims believe that Ali and the Imams are the rightful successors of Mohammed (also commonly spelled Muhammed). They also believe that the last recognized Imam will return as a messiah. Also known as Shiites. (*Also see* Sunni Muslim.)

SHIITES *see* Shia Muslim.

SHOAL: A place where the water of a stream, lake, or sea is of little depth. Especially, a sand-bank which shows at low water.

SHORT TON: a unit of weight that equals 2,000 pounds.

SIERRA: A chain of hills or mountains.

SIKH: A member of a politico-religious community of India, founded as a sect around 1500 and based on the principles of monotheism (belief in one god) and human brotherhood.

SOCIAL INSURANCE: A government plan to protect low-income people, such as health and accident insurance, pension plans, etc.

SOCIAL SECURITY: A form of social insurance, including life, disability, and old-age pension for workers. It is paid for by employers, employees, and the government.

SOCIALISM: An economic system in which ownership of land and other property is distributed among the community as a whole, and every member of the community shares in the work and products of the work.

SOCIALIST: A person who advocates socialism.

SOFTWOODS: The coniferous trees, whose wood density as a whole is relatively softer than the wood of those trees referred to as hardwoods.

SUBALPINE: Generally refers to high mountainous areas just beneath the timberline; can also more specifically refer to the lower slopes of the Alps mountains.

SUNNI MUSLIM: Members of one of two major sects of the religion of Islam. Sunni Muslims adhere to strict orthodox traditions, and believe that the four caliphs are the rightful successors to Mohammed, founder of Islam. (Mohammed is commonly spelled Muhammed, especially by Islamic people.) (*Also see* Shia Muslim.)

TARIFF: A tax assessed by a government on goods as they enter (or leave) a country. May be imposed to protect domestic industries from imported goods and/or to generate revenue.

TEMPERATE ZONE: The parts of the earth lying between the tropics and the polar circles. The *northern temperate zone* is the area between the tropic of Cancer and the Arctic Circle. The *southern temperate zone* is the area between the tropic of Capricorn and the Antarctic Circle.

TRIBAL SYSTEM: A social community in which people are organized into groups or clans descended from common ancestors and sharing customs and languages.

TUNDRA: A nearly level treeless area whose climate and vegetation are characteristically arctic due to its northern position; the subsoil is permanently frozen.

VALUE ADDED BY MANUFACTURE: The difference, measured in dollars, between the value of finished goods and the cost of the materials needed to produce them.

WHOLESALE TRADE: The sale of goods, usually in large quantities, for ultimate resale to consumers.

Abbreviations & Acronyms

AD—Anno Domini
AFL–CIO—American Federation of
    Labor–Congress of Industrial Organizations
AM—before noon
AM—amplitude modulation
b.—born
BC—Before Christ
Btu—British thermal unit(s)
bu—bushel(s)
c.—circa (about)
c—Celsius (Centigrade)
c$—Canadian dollar
cm—centimeter(s)
Co.—company
comp.—compiler
Corp.—corporation
CST—Central Standard Time
cu—cubic
cwt—hundredweight(s)
d.—died
e—evening
E—east
ed.—edition, editor
e.g.—exempli gratia (for example)
est.—estimated
EST—Eastern Standard Time
et al.—et alii (and others)
etc.—et cetera (and so on)
F—Fahrenheit
FM—frequency modulation
Ft.—fort
ft—foot, feet
GDP—gross domestic products
gm—gram
GMT—Greenwich Mean Time
GNP—gross national product
GRT—gross registered tons
Hist.—Historic
i.e.—id est (that is)
in—inch(es)

Inc.—incorporated
Jct.—junction
K—kindergarten
kg—kilogram(s)
km—kilometer(s)
km/hr—kilometers per hour
kw—kilowatt(s)
kwh—kilowatt-hour(s)
lb—pound(s)
m—meter(s); morning
m^3—cubic meter(s)
mi—mile(s)
Mon.—monument
mph—miles per hour
MST—Mountain Standard Time
Mt.—mount
Mtn.—mountain
mw—megawatt(s)
N—north
NA—not available
Natl.—National
NATO—North Atlantic Treaty Organization
n.d.—no date
N.F.—National Forest
oz—ounce(s)
PM—after noon
PST—Pacific Standard Time
r.—reigned
Ra.—range
Res.—reservoir, reservation
rev. ed.—revised edition
s—south
S—Sunday
Soc.—Socialist
sq—square
St.—saint
UN—United Nations
US—United States
w—west

INDEX

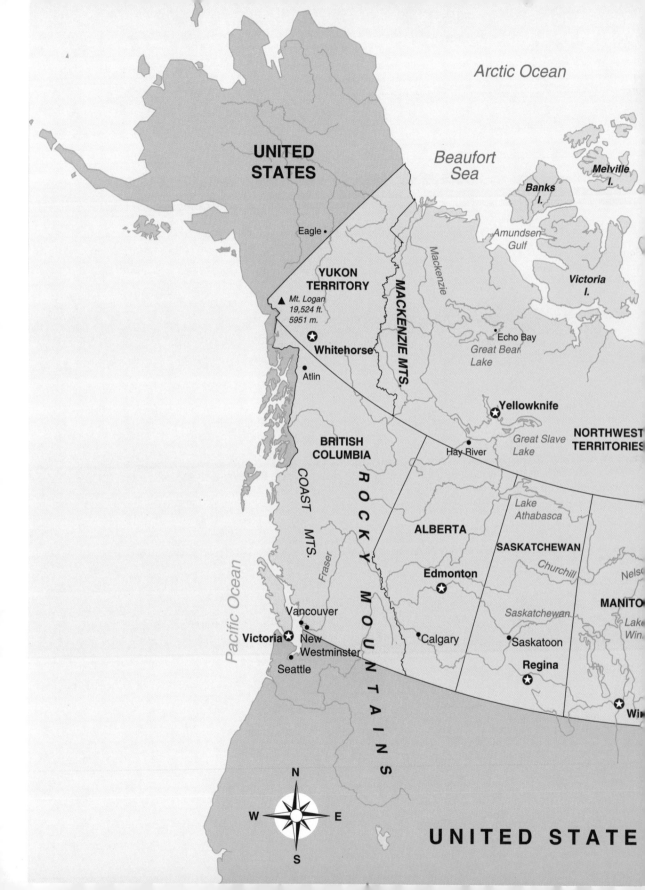

Arctic Ocean

UNITED
STATES

Beaufort
Sea

Banks
I.

Melville
I.

Amundsen
Gulf

Victoria
I.

Eagle

YUKON
TERRITORY

MACKENZIE MTS.

Mackenzie

▲ Mt. Logan
19,524 ft.
5951 m.

Echo Bay
Great Bear
Lake

Whitehorse

Atlin

Yellowknife

BRITISH
COLUMBIA

Hay River

Great Slave
Lake

NORTHWEST
TERRITORIES

COAST

R O C K Y

Lake
Athabasca

MTS.

ALBERTA

SASKATCHEWAN

Churchill

Nels

Fraser

M O U N T A I N S

Edmonton

MANITO

Saskatchewan

Calgary

Saskatoon

Lake
Win

Pacific Ocean

Vancouver

Victoria

New
Westminster

Regina

Wii

Seattle

N

W

E

S

UNITED STATE